Imagine Yourself Well

BETTER HEALTH THROUGH
SELF-HYPNOSIS

Imagine Yourself Well

BETTER HEALTH THROUGH SELF-HYPNOSIS

SEAN F. KELLY, Ph. D.

AND

REID J. KELLY, A. C. S. W.

Foreword by
Max P. Shapiro, Ph. D.

 INSIGHT BOOKS

PLENUM PRESS • NEW YORK AND LONDON

Library of Congress Cataloging-in-Publication Data

On file

This book is not a substitute for medical advice. For such advice, consult a
health care professional.

ISBN 0-306-44942-0

© 1995 Plenum Press, New York
A Division of Plenum Publishing Corporation
233 Spring Street, New York, N.Y. 10013-1578

An Insight Book

10 9 8 7 6 5 4 3 2 1

For Ian and Amy

Foreword

In the current era of health care reform, greater emphasis has been placed on treatments which are relatively brief and focused and involve the active participation of the patient. As a result, interest in the clinical applications of hypnosis has grown tremendously. Much of the literature available on the subject, however, discusses it in remote theoretical terms or presents clinical applications of hypnosis in broad summaries.

Unlike many volumes available on the topic of hypnosis, this book emphasizes the actual use of modern techniques in hypnotherapy. The practical slant of the Kellys' material is a breath of fresh air in a field which can be stifling. The authors have drawn on a rich heritage of case material, and the difficulties presented are the ones seen in the consulting room every day. Rather than theoretical conjecture, the reader gets an extensive picture of the problem solving that is at the heart of good clinical work.

The material in this volume is grounded in psychodynamic principles effectively blended with cognitive and behavioral treatment models. While there are those who continue to debate the superiority of one approach over another, the authors have simply gone about the business of helping people change.

This book is addressed to a variety of different audiences, each with its own level of sophistication and its own reason for reading it.

Clinicians of all degrees of expertise are likely to find value in this material. For those in training, it provides "scripts" of actual treatments. These scripts can both provide models to copy and serve as examples to be analyzed by teachers and students during supervision. Other, more experienced clinicians, while familiar with certain hypnotic techniques, may find here new weapons for the therapeutic armamentarium. The addition of "new arrows in the quiver" is always a welcome event. In other cases, the experienced therapist is likely to find that having read this book will lead to subtle shifts in choice of word or phraseology. Finally, by focusing on the actual monologue of an hypnotic treatment, the practitioner can easily feel his or her way into the situation to assess the potential usefulness of the scripts for treatment practice.

For the person who is considering treatment, this book provides a seedbed to prepare for seeing a professional. The examples of what might occur in hypnotherapy provide insight into the range of interventions possible. This knowledge should, in the first place, yield an informed decision-making process. It should, furthermore, introduce the potential client to what is usual, acceptable therapy, making it easier to distinguish the competent professional from the charlatan.

For the do-it-yourselfer, the book spells out in clear, precise language just how one can use self-hypnosis for healing. Its detailed instructions and options provide an opportunity for the individual to select his or her own best method of self-help.

People interested in learning to use hypnosis to help themselves or others as well as those who are curious about what really happens in hypnosis should be satisfied by this detailed, practical presentation of one highly effective method of enhancing health.

MAX P. SHAPIRO, PH.D.
Instructor in Psychiatry (Psychology)
Harvard Medical School
President, The New England Society of
Clinical Hypnosis

Preface

Hypnosis is becoming increasingly popular as an approach for treating a wide variety of problems. Growing numbers of health care professionals are learning about its applications in their specialties while more and more laypeople wonder about its usefulness.

This book is designed to give the reader access to clinical techniques which can be used to treat a variety of different problems. It does not attempt to teach the history of the field, nor does it explore the powerful theories which are the foundation of clinical practice. Those topics are admirably handled elsewhere.

Instead, this is a handbook which tells explicitly how to go about treating a problem. It is designed primarily for the individual who wishes to learn to use hypnosis for self-help. Such a person would first learn how to enter a trance state. Next, he or she would be taught appropriate exercises to use while hypnotized.

The Contents lists all the various difficulties and disorders for which treatment is described here (though not every complaint for which hypnosis is useful). No one person could suffer from all of the physical and psychological problems that this book teaches one to treat. Instead, it is rather like a cookbook full of recipes for different dishes. The reader is left to select the ones that fit his or her needs.

The book is also designed for the professional health care provider. It gives verbatim strategies for the treatment of many common symptoms and illnesses. It also tries to teach an approach to thinking about treatment that can serve as a spring-board for future development.

Obviously, it does not begin to list every way of using hypnosis, but it does teach one way of using it. We hope it will be a help.

SEAN F. KELLY
REID J. KELLY

Contents

1

Hypnosis in Brief

A human being lives in a world of a curious duality. On the one hand, each of us exists as a physical body made of cells, blood, a nervous system, muscles, and bone. On the other hand, every individual is an intangible soul, with a mind (both conscious and unconscious), intellect, and feelings. The ancient Babylonians dealt with this duality by believing that the mind resided in the liver. Other ancients have placed it in the heart, understanding the brain as a sort of air conditioner, useful only to cool off the blood. Modern science, with much more empirical evidence to support the finding, locates the mind in the brain. Even so, there remains a kind of mystery in just how the neurochemical events inside the cranium result in a sense of being or perceiving oneself as a living person.

Lord Rutherford, the English physicist who proposed the idea that atoms were tiny lumps with relatively vast spaces between them, used to say that he had two desks. One was made of atoms, just as everything in the universe is composed of atoms. The other was made of wood. When he wanted to think about the nature of the universe, he would think about his desk made of atoms. When he wanted to write a letter, he went over to his wooden desk so the paper wouldn't fall into the spaces between the atoms. Of course, he really had only one desk. It's simply too hard to think about intangible atoms and tangible wood all at once. Just so, really there is only one person. It's similarly too hard to think about mental and physical aspects at the same time.

Like a human being or Lord Rutherford's desk, hypnosis exists as both a mental and a physical reality, a psychological as well as a physiological occurrence. Part of what gives hypnosis its aura of mysticism is that it is an approach that works at the connection between mind and body. Something happens by putting one's mind and physical brain into this particular state of consciousness that allows one to shape not only mental events, such as mood, self-confidence, and perception of pain, but also physical ones, such as skin temperature, blood flow, clotting, and blistering.

The magical, mysterious, or somewhat frightening images that the word *hypnosis* can conjure up are best dispelled by learning something about the scientific, medically recognized elements of trance and its treatment possibilities. Hypnosis is not something that works only in dimly lit surroundings with smoke and mirrors. In fact, it works best when the person being hypnotized is an active participant in the venture, one who understands what is going on, and who knows that hypnosis is a state of enhanced concentration, imagination, and attention.

It is evident, if you really think about it, that being conscious is not a single, simple state. A reader absorbed in a thrilling novel, an athlete actively playing a sport, an elderly man vividly remembering a childhood experience, a churchgoer praying, a student learning a new language, a bored child half-watching TV, a factory worker daydreaming about vacation, a composer engrossed in writing music—all of these people are conscious. They are not asleep or knocked out. However, their states of attention are really quite different. For an easy example, consider the way you feel sitting through a boring talk and then compare that with how you feel when something really interesting captures your attention.

People routinely switch from one state of consciousness to another. These natural attentional shifts can occur in reaction to an environment or a situation (e.g., a passenger in a car responds to hours of traveling on a lonely, open highway by feeling "spacey"), by chemical means (e.g., a partygoer gets drunk), or because of a decision to change one's type of awareness (e.g., a student daydreaming in class gives herself a mental shake, chooses to concentrate, and starts paying attention to the teacher).

Hypnosis is one state of consciousness—the particular state of consciousness in which perception is distorted by means of concentration and vivid imagination. Spontaneous hypnotic-like experiences occur naturally and regularly, manifesting themselves in a number of ways. Some people have the capacity to alter their perception of pain. Women were, for instance, having children by "natural childbirth" long before Dr. Lamaze went to school. Religious experiences, visions, and prophecies occur in trancelike states. Both ancient warriors and more modern athletes could picture in their mind's eye a strikingly clear image of an upcoming struggle. With a consequent flow of adrenalin, they were better prepared to strive than if they had stepped onto the battle or playing field needing to warm up. Any student will find a bit of assigned reading quicker and easier to absorb when he can narrowly focus attention on it than when he is more distractable. The tennis player who can learn to imagine the ball being returned slowly, visualizing its spin en route, will be consequently better able to hit it.

The capacity for such spontaneous and naturally occurring hypnotic-like experiences has been cultivated more formally along two different cultural tracks. One can be thought of as following Western tradition, the other Eastern. In the more task-oriented Western tradition, direction is toward the practical. Hypnosis is used to accomplish a job. Thus, whatever a person can potentially do is supposed to become, with hypnosis, possible on a more regular, more efficient, or more effective basis. Hypnosis is, for instance, used to change undesirable habits such as nail-biting and smoking, to treat phobias, and even to cure warts. All of these problems are amenable to other approaches and sometimes spontaneously and naturally self-correct. With hypnosis, however, their successful treatment is often more certain.

Unlike the practical inclination of the West, Eastern tradition leans toward the religious. Developing as meditation, an hypnotic-like state allows one to open oneself up, to become part of a life force, to reach oneness with the universe. Thus, a person learns to relax and become at peace. He or she can then expand outward mentally and feel as close as possible to Nirvana. Setting a koan (an unanswerable question like "What is the sound of one hand clapping?") is designed to distract the conscious mind, making it do something senseless so it won't drag the meditator back into the usual state of consciousness. Repeating a mantra (a word like *om*), or, for that matter, chanting litanies or singing repetitive gospel spirituals, focuses attention away from the usual sources of orientation and draws one out of oneself. Thus, meditation is closely akin to hypnosis, the two differing primarily in relation to their goals.

A Zen master does not "meditate" a practitioner, *force* meditation, or seize control of the practitioner's mind during meditation. Rather the Zen master tells the meditator that if he or she does certain things, the result is a state called *meditation*. Just so, a hypnotist does not perform some bit of sorcery on an unwary subject. Instead, much more like a guide or teacher, the hypnotist shows an individual how to enter a state of concentration, attention, and changed perception that can be put to work toward a goal. However magical that may seem, hypnosis is a psychological event, not an occult one.

Every human being has an innate capacity for hypnosis. Some people are extremely hypnotizable, most are moderately so, and some people have at best a minimal capacity for hypnosis. Each person's capacity to use hypnosis, the *most* that he or she could ever achieve, is an extremely stable trait. Up to that point, however, individuals can, by choice, vary the depth of hypnosis. Sometimes a person might choose to become as hypnotized as possible, just as one might decide to run at top speed. At other times a mild trance would suffice, just as jogging or trotting might be good enough or fast enough for a particular purpose. Finally, while each individual's capacity remains stable and consistent, each of his or her hypnotic experiences is unique, never occurring twice in exactly the same way.

There are two common experiences most people have when hypnotized. The first is relaxation; the second is a sense of watching themselves. Instead of experiencing something as a participant, the feeling is rather that of an observer. Otherwise, hypnotic experiences are uniquely individualistic. Some people can experience what others simply will never be able to. For example, about one person in seven has the capacity to undergo major surgery with no anaesthesia other than hypnosis. Each of the remaining six needs a more usual anaesthesia, but all still differ in their level of pain response. Some of them could use hypnosis to block out completely any pain less than that of major surgery. The rest would find hypnosis helpful in reducing discomfort, though the degree of relief experienced would range from "somewhat better" to "dramatically better."

Some hypnotized people can recall a past event so vividly that it is as if they have really turned back time and are, in part, reliving the event. With hypnosis, other people can remember a happening with such striking clarity that previously forgotten details are retrieved. However, they never have a sense of reliving the event. Some individuals have a moderately to mildly enhanced memory, perhaps with visual imagery, and others find that "hypnotic recall" feels just about the same as simply concentrating on the past.

Because hypnotic responsiveness varies in accordance with different tasks, a person who is able to "relive" a past event is not necessarily able to block out the pain of major surgery, nor is the person who experiences minimal pain relief with hypnosis automatically guaranteed to have only a minimally enhanced memory with it.

Hypnosis is a technique that is useful and has been recognized as such by the major health care organizations. However, just getting into an hypnotic state is not in itself healing. Hypnosis can be thought of as a tool, being in some ways similar to a hypodermic needle. It does not take much skill to push a needle through the skin. Also there is nothing particularly healing about getting a needle stuck into you. It is not the presence of the needle that cures infection or immunizes. It is the proper medicine which is given to the body by means of the needle. Just so, it is not hypnosis per se but rather the healing skills or strategies used in hypnosis that count.

That's what this book is about.

Chapter 2 will teach you how to enter an appropriate state of self-hypnosis. Chapter 3 will teach you how to use hypnosis to become extremely relaxed and to stay that way, because relaxation is beneficial for most types of treatment. The remainder of the book focuses on a series of different problems addressed by hypnosis. To work on your problem, you would first read Chapters 1 through 3, and then you would go to the chapter devoted to your goal. If you wanted to work on two different problems, you would use the exercises of two chapters. In a way, each reader will tailor the book to his or her own needs and style.

The hypnotic techniques presented in the following chapters would also be useful to trained health professionals dealing with patients. They provide models of treatment strategies for those who have already been trained to use hypnosis. However, *this book is not intended to teach an untrained individual to use hypnotic suggestions on others.* A dentist might learn from reading how to relax patients during dental procedures, an oncologist how to help patients' reactions to chemotherapy, and a mental health professional to help patients deal with trauma, phobias, or stress. Reading this book does not make one a dentist, physician, or psychotherapist, however. Further, merely reading about any treatment method does not qualify anyone to practice it. Clinical hypnosis is a powerful technique which requires specialized training, such as that offered by professional societies and teaching hospitals. Reading this book would teach a healthcare professional how an appropriate referral might benefit a patient. It might arouse interest and lead to further training, but it is not a substitute for such training.

Anybody who lacks the proper professional training cannot safely go around hypnotizing others. However, anyone can safely hypnotize himself.

If you needed to remove a splinter from your hand, you would know, by feeling, just how much probing was tolerable. If you were unable to remove the splinter yourself, you would then go to a doctor, not a blacksmith. Just so, anyone who enters a state of self-hypnosis knows what does or does not feel comfortable. Therefore, you will naturally regulate the strength of your trance accordingly. You can relax and be assured that since you are going to use hypnosis for self-help, you will do nothing to hurt or embarrass yourself. If self-help does not work, you would then go to a trained professional, not a stage hypnotist.

The main difference between self-hypnosis and being hypnotized by a professional, or, for that matter, anyone else, is the presence of another person. The state you get into is identical. Being hypnotized sometimes feels a little different from hypnotizing yourself, just as rubbing a soothing balm onto your own arms feels different from having someone else rub it in. The medicinal balm is just as effective. The element of having some company is what is different. Taking a walk in the woods involves the same burning up of calories, the same footsteps, and the same sights whether you are walking alone or with a companion. The important differences have to do with nonwalking elements.

A person seeking to learn about a new subject could purchase a textbook and read it carefully, could take a class, or could hire a tutor for individual lessons. If all were well done, each teaching approach would present the same material, and any one of them could result in the person's knowing the subject. Of course, there would be differences between learning by oneself or learning as part of a group or learning in an intense one-to-one relationship. The difference is not so much in the material as in the setting. So you can learn about hypnosis from this book, from joining an hypnosis group, or by seeing someone individually.

The basic self-hypnosis material presented in this book differs from the suggestions you would garner from a professional in two ways: the level of repetition and the amount of personal tailoring done. If, for example, a hypnotist suggested you feel a soothing sensation, she might repeat the same ideas, with only minor variations in wording, for five, ten, or even thirty minutes. It is not practical to do so in a book. Second, the strategies are presented as they would be to a group instead of to an individual. Since no two individuals are ever exactly alike, it is impossible to tailor-make suggestions when addressing an audience greater than one.

Many of the habits, fears, or ailments discussed in the following chapters are ones that interact with various kinds of difficulties, physical and mental. We will try to clarify when a problem might simply be treated by self-help and when you should go to a health professional to deal with it. For example, hypnosis is very useful in pain control. If your hand were in a fire, though, you would not want to use self-hypnosis to try controlling the pain because what you would really need to do is get your hand out of the fire. If you have a pain in a joint because you may have a broken bone, it would not be good to use hypnosis to try to ignore that pain. Instead you should go to the doctor and have the bone treated. Now, if you go to the doctor, are told that your joint pain is arthritis, and get the appropriate treatment, but pain persists, it would be very fitting and useful to free yourself from this pain with hypnosis.

Hypnosis is not a dramatically different experience from more run-of-the-mill states of mind and has many elements that most people experience spontaneously and frequently. Therefore, if you have *not* had formal training in or experience with clinical hypnosis, you will probably wonder if you were really hypnotized. Now, if you went through an induction exercise, the answer to your question is "Yes, you probably were hypnotized, and the state, entered on your own, was most likely comfortable and not too strong." A more definite "yes" would require the individual attention of an expert to answer. If you have had previous experience with good clinical hypnosis, you should have no trouble recognizing that state again. In any case, the important issue is not "Is this really hypnosis?" but "Will I be helped this way?" Anybody who does not become genuinely hypnotized should still be able to benefit from the hypnotic suggestions, provided he or she concentrates on and vividly imagines the relevant ideas and strategies.

Think of this book as a catalog of potential solutions, like a cookbook. Simply practice the tactics that apply to your particular difficulty. If you look, you will find that the number of treatment suggestions presented for different problem areas varies. Some problems are simpler to treat than others. Furthermore, some hypnotic exercises are bound to be more effective for you than others. For instance, different people have difficulty with different problems of eating. Some snack between meals, some eat when nervous, some are social eaters, and some gorge on the sly. Some chronically eat a little too much, while others go through a feast-or-famine routine. This book comprises a number of hypnotic exercises. No one will find that all are equally useful. Rather, some should strike a chord of "That's my problem exactly," some might seem moderately useful, and some will probably seem irrelevant.

Some of the strategies are ones you will want and need to use again and again. You should practice at least once a day for about twenty minutes (or twice a day for two ten-minute sessions, if that is more convenient). More is fine. Many people have difficulty finding free time to practice. If this applies to you, make time. Twenty minutes out of twenty-four hours is really not very much. Finally, any time you find yourself "dying to eat," wishing to smoke, or ruminating instead of sleeping is a particularly good time to do an hypnotic exercise instead.

When you have found an exercise that you want to use, you might wish to read it into a tape recorder, then play back the tape for yourself. People who use a tape recorder, though, should be careful to make sure that they listen to and concentrate on what they put in the recorder. Too many people have tape recorders that have all sorts of good habits which never reach their owners.

If you like, instead of using a tape recorder, you can try either remembering the relevant ideas and suggestions in a verbatim way or simply recalling the main points of the exercise. These hypnotic strategies and suggestions are not intended to be religious rituals that must be adhered to rigidly, be spoken verbatim, or be performed "just right" to work. Although it is initially necessary to respect and follow the gist of an hypnotic exercise, you can otherwise personalize or reformulate as you will. For instance, you could customize by substituting "focus your eyes on a spot" for "close your eyes," "my mother's spaghetti" for "your favorite food," or "baseball" for "tennis ball." Later, when you have gained sufficient familiarity with the suggestions in the relevant chapters, consider them a starting point. As you are led to other images that help, use them and build on them.

As you read through the following chapters, you will notice

something about the style of the prose in the sections of verbatim instructions. It does not read like a good novel or like anything that is addressed simply to your conscious attention. Instead, it has repetitions of phrases and words and often a slightly soporific cadence. This is not only intentional, it is something you should emulate in your personalized versions of the exercises.

In trying to help yourself (or in teaching a patient to help himself), it's important to understand the whole process of communication. As you go through hypnosis, the strong, healthy, mature part of your mind is addressing some other less healthy part, rather like a loving parent soothing and teaching a child.

You must understand that as you practice this approach you are splitting your consciousness into two parts: healer and patient. As you read and practice the exercises, one part of your own mind, the healer, is working to teach and convince another part, the patient, to change and get better. The best part of you is speaking directly to another part, perhaps a frightened or suffering part. And of course this inner healer will speak with authority as well as compassion. The inner voice will not just speak the message but will deliver it well, repeating key words and phrases so they penetrate beyond the superficial level to make real changes occur.

And now you are ready to begin.

2

Inductions and Enhancers

In order to use hypnosis you obviously must first learn to become hypnotized. Certain mental exercises focus thoughts, remove tension, and result in hypnosis. There are any number of these "induction methods" available to the person who wants to be hypnotized. Two common approaches are presented in this chapter. If you follow these instructions you will find yourself in an hypnotic state, ready to go on to use suggestions.

Read through these instructions, disregarding at first all suggestions to close your eyes. Do, however, keep your eyes focused on the page, and do not let them wander around the room. Once you are familiar with the content of the induction methods, you can use them to get yourself into a state of relaxed concentration.

You might choose to make a tape of whichever induction you like best. You can record yourself either reading the induction exactly as written or, better yet, simply saying the gist of the ideas in your own words. Talk in a calm and natural manner. Just as the soothing effect of a lullaby is due not only to the meaning of the words but also to the crooning sound, so the tone and cadence of your voice are as important in reaching an hypnotic state as the words you say.

If you would rather not use a tape recorder, you can silently reread an induction each time you want to use one. As you read it, let yourself experience the sensations as they are described. If you feel comfortable doing so, you might even simply think of the directions from memory, or, if it works, just feel yourself into the proper state.

Inductions

Relaxation

Settle back in your chair. Sink into it. Let it hold and support you. Feel how strong the chair is and how good it feels to let it bear your weight. (Close your eyes.) Now take a moment to think if there is anything that demands your *immediate* attention. Is there anything so urgent that it cannot wait? If there is, attend to it right away and then come back to this exercise when you are free to do it. If you continue, it means that you know there's nothing else you need to do right now. Any other thoughts that vie for your attention are not useful. You know there's nothing you need to do right now except this. Any other thoughts that compete for your attention are attempts to keep you from working on what you want to change. These distractions are trying to interfere with your purpose, and so you can disregard them without even looking to see what they are.

Now, as you settle into the chair, feeling it holding you (letting your eyes stay comfortably closed), begin to pay attention to your breathing. Nice, slow, regular, and comfortable breathing. Monotonous, even, and regular. Feel how with each breath you exhale, you become a little bit more relaxed, relaxed and comfortable. You know that tension involves your muscles being hard at work. Relaxation is not work. It's the absence of work. With each breath you exhale, you feel your muscles strain a little less, becoming more and more peaceful, comfortable, and relaxed. Think of the tension as a great weight that is being pumped out of you by your powerful lungs. Each slow, regular breath pumps out a little more of the tension. More and more fully relaxed as the tension leaves your body, you settle more and more deeply into the chair.

You find your limbs feel warm, heavy, and limp; totally drained of energy, and lie there, limp and relaxed. The relaxation leaves you feeling limp and motionless, but with a sense of lightness, as though your whole body were becoming incredibly light, though too relaxed to move around more than necessary. Of course you can shift your position and settle in to make yourself even more comfortable, just as you could lazily rub your nose if it were to itch, hold this book and turn pages as necessary, but the sense of peace in your muscles is so strong that you feel no need to move about unnecessarily. Instead, you can just sink right in, settle right in.

You become aware of a sense of relaxation and peace at your very core. Feel how relaxed your backbone is. Let this relaxation spiral out. Relax the muscles of your shoulders and of your hips. Let the relaxation spread out to your knees, to your elbows, and to your neck. Feel the relaxation travel out to your ankles and wrists. Let it spread even further to the joints of your feet and hands, fingers and toes, relaxing your jaw and face.

While you're feeling so comfortably relaxed, so effortlessly settled, imagine the beginnings of a nice floating sensation. Do it however seems best. Perhaps you imagine the chair is on a magic carpet. That's right, a magic carpet that's going to lift you up gently and peacefully and spirit you along with no sense of speed, but just a nice floating feeling. Or perhaps you feel so light you are wafted along by the breeze. Whatever seems best. Let yourself be carried off to a magical place of peace, tranquility, and contentment—a dreamland where you are free to go to work on your problems without the usual cares and concerns of daily living.

But you didn't go to this place today simply to relax. You want to get to this state in order to help yourself. The relaxation is simply the beginning. Now that you have entered the state of hypnosis, you can go on to use it. And now you can use one of the exercises, one which will be useful for you to handle the problem you have decided to work on today. You are going to work on the exercise for as long as you need to or until you are interrupted by something that you choose to pay attention to. At that point, when you are ready to leave this state, you'll simply count backward like this: "Three," take a deep breath, "two," let the breath out, and "one," open your eyes. You will find yourself fully alert, feeling relaxed and refreshed, with no unpleasant after effects. The usual sensations and control will have returned and you will remember everything that went on.

As you become more familiar and comfortable with hypnosis, you may choose simply to open your eyes and bring yourself back to the usual waking state, but at first the counting will help refocus your concentration.

The Whirlpool

Get yourself comfortably seated in a nice and peaceful spot. You needn't have absolute quiet, but you should try to minimize distractions which could make it difficult for you to concentrate on your task. Of course, there will be various background noises, but you should make sure there is nothing that you would listen to with much interest. It's hard to get a situation where you can guarantee you won't be interrupted, but that's all right. If an interruption comes that you choose to attend to, you'll be able to return to the usual state of consciousness quickly and easily. However, it would be good to arrange things to minimize the likelihood of an interruption. Now, as you go through this exercise, if your attention should wander that would be all right. Just keep bringing your attention back, always bringing it back, to paying attention to what is being described.

Imagine a vast body of water. A large body of calm, peaceful water, warm, calm, and clear. As you do, imagine yourself coming upon a whirlpool. That's right, but a nice and gentle one. A whirlpool leading down, drawing down, to an underwater cave. As you float along on the water, able to breath without effort even underwater, you find yourself drawn to the whirlpool. First to the edges, then more and more into it. You know that if you wanted to, you could swim strongly enough to get out of it, that you don't have to go along with it, that you could resist it, but somehow it is easier just to allow yourself to continue to be drawn in further and further, down along the descending sides. Each trip around the whirlpool pulls you a little further down, a little deeper down, a little more down. And as you settle further and further into this whirlpool, allowing yourself to be effortlessly drawn deeper, you find yourself becoming more and more relaxed. The deeper into the whirlpool, the more relaxed; the more relaxed, the deeper in. Feel the muscles of your eyes becoming so relaxed. Feel the relaxation rippling outward, across the muscles of your forehead, cheeks, and jaw. Feel the relaxation as it spreads back across the muscles of your scalp. Let the relaxation spread down through your neck, infusing a relaxing warmth through the muscles of your shoulders. Relax the muscles of your upper arms, of your forearms, hands, and fingers. Feel the relaxation as it washes over your body, like a warm wave, relaxing the muscles of your back, and of the small of your back. Relax the muscles of your chest and of your abdomen. Feel the relaxation spread down through the pelvic area to relax the muscles of your legs, calves, ankles, and feet, so that you've relaxed every muscle in your entire body from the top of your head all the way down to the ends of your toes and the tips of your fingers.

While you're feeling so relaxed, effortlessly allowing yourself to descend gently, peacefully, and comfortably down the whirlpool, you find yourself entering a subterranean world. A place of beauty, peace, and contentment. A place where you can comfortably and safely begin to work on the exercises which can help you change something. You can stay here as long as you need. First, why not take the time to look around. This is your special world. As you imagine it, you create it. Look around and see what it is that you can see. Color and movement as well as shape and form. Is it light or dark? Feel the temperature. Is it warm or cool? Is it moist or dry? Rough or smooth? What can you hear? Is there music or perhaps the sound of birds? Can you hear a gentle breeze? Just see what you can smell. Perhaps a tang of salt air, perhaps the smell of flowers or pine trees. Make this world of yours as vivid as possible by using all your senses.

You can stay in this special world for as long as you need or wish to. Here you can safely work on those exercises which will be most helpful for you to reach your goals. You will find that each time you come back to this special place, it will be easier and easier to get here more and more quickly. As you become familiar with this world, you will learn shortcuts to get here. It may seem that you can get here so easily and quickly with practice that it will make you wonder if you've arrived at the right place. If you recognize your special world, you will know that it indeed is your special state of relaxed concentration and attention.

When you wish to leave your special world behind, you'll be able to do so easily and quickly. You need merely to take a deep breath, hold it momentarily, then let it out and open your eyes. You'll find that the usual sensations and control will have returned. You'll feel relaxed and refreshed, with no unpleasant aftereffects, and you will remember everything that happened very clearly.

Enhancers

Some people find that when they are in the state of relaxed concentration and attention it is helpful to add a second or third exercise to strengthen the state. Any of the following could be used to that purpose. Once you are comfortable with hypnosis, you might wish to expand on one of these enhancers and turn it into the induction exercise itself.

The Stairway

Imagine yourself at the top of a long stairway, a stairway descending into mist and fog. Take a step down . . . and another . . . and another. With each step you take you find yourself sinking further and further into deeper and thicker mist, fog, cloud. With each step that you descend, visibility decreases. It is almost like settling into a world of cotton. Hearing is dulled, touch is dulled. With each step you descend further and further into a world of white where you see nothing but the cloud, hear nothing but a background of white noise, feel nothing but a surrounding, yielding softness, and as your senses are given only this bland, white, featureless environment, your attention turns further and further inward, more and more focused on the internal reality of imagination and imagery.

Numbers

While you are so comfortably relaxed, effortlessly paying attention to the directions you are being given, you begin to count from 1 to 20. With each number you will go even further into a deep, comfortable state of concentration, imagination, and attention: 1– Going down. 2– Further and further into a deep comfortable and relaxed state. 3, 4– More and more, further and further, deeper and deeper. 5– Comfortably down. 6, 7, 8– Drifting down, gently, inexorably down. 9– Into a comfortable state of greater and greater imagination. 10– Halfway there. 11– Sinking down and glad to be going more and more. 12, 13– Further and further, more and more. 14– So much deeper. 15– Deeper into this state of relaxed, intense concentration. 16, 17– Closer and closer, deeper and deeper. 18– Almost there. 19– Nearly arrived at this state of deep concentration, enhanced imagination. 20– Fully relaxed, completely involved.

The Target

While you're so comfortably relaxed with your eyes closed, effortlessly focusing your attention, allow your eyes to open and focus your gaze on a spot on the wall opposite you—not a remarkable or interesting spot, but one on which you choose to focus your attention. If your eyes wander, just bring them back to the target, stare at the target, focus on the target, always bring your gaze back to the target. But as you do, you may find that some interesting things begin to happen. The target may seem to become a little bleary and then very sharp, as it goes in and out of focus. It may seen to move about, left to right, up and down. It may seem to change colors, as you stare at it so intently. It may appear to be faintly outlined, as though by light, or as though it were superimposed on the background rather than being a part of it.

As you continue to stare you notice that your eyes are becoming very heavy, heavy and tired, strained and hot, and you'll find that soon your eyes are going to close of themselves; as they strain to close, it's going to become such an effort to keep them open that you will no longer try, and you will simply allow them to close of themselves. They may be dragged slowly, inexorably down, or it may be that as your eyes blink, one time they will blink closed and not reopen. Your eyes are closing, closing, heavier and heavier and more and more down, as you become more and more relaxed until the eyes close of themselves.

As your eyes have closed and are no longer working to remain open, you find that the sense of relaxation spreads from them and brings your entire body to an even greater sense of relaxation, peace, comfort, and calm.

You have now learned a variety of techniques that will allow you to enter the state of hypnosis. Your purpose is not simply to get into an hypnotic state and relax. Rather, it is important to make use of this state in order to get more fit and healthy. When you want to make use of your capacity for hypnosis, you will enter this state and then go on to practice one or more of the exercises that make up the remainder of this book.

3

The Pleasant Scene

Now that you have learned to become hypnotized you are ready to go on to the next step, using hypnosis. The first application to learn is the pleasant scene.

This very useful exercise serves as the basis of a number of treatment strategies and, much like induction techniques, should be treated as a tool commonly used to get you ready to take the next step.

The pleasant scene provides a way of strengthening the relaxation response which was begun by going through an hypnotic induction. Imagining yourself in a peaceful and protected environment is naturally quite conducive to a strong and powerful sense of relaxation. If you visualize yourself to be in a relaxed place, you will find yourself relaxed. Conversely, if you were to picture yourself in great danger, you would find yourself flooded with adrenalin and ready to deal with the threat.

Concentrating on a peaceful scene keeps the conscious mind from getting into mischief. Consider a person who is under a great deal of pressure at work and needs to learn to relax to decrease stress. Any relaxed muscles resulting from an induction would tense up in response to thoughts about problems at work. While the person is busy focusing all attention on the pleasant scene, however, she cannot think about the problems on the job that create tension.

After entering hypnosis, then, you would continue with the following instructions. This exercise can be used alone or can be followed by more exercises, using this as a place from which to work.

———◆•◆•◆———

As you have settled into this comfortable state of relaxed concentration, imagination, and attention, you take a moment to think about whether there is anything that demands your immediate attention. That's right. Take a minute to see if there's anything that demands to be done right now. If there is anything that cannot wait, then clearly you have to stop what you're doing, come out of hypnosis, and do whatever it is that needs to be done. If that is more important than your using hypnosis right now, then you have no choice but to stop and do it and return to your hypnotic exercise at a later time, when you are free to focus on what you're doing. If you decide, however, that what you should be doing right now is practicing your hypnosis, then everything else is a distraction and is to be treated as such.

If there are any ideas or thoughts that need to be dealt with later, right now you should mentally flag them, so that you will remember and think about them at some later, appropriate time. You're not going to think about them now. Instead you're simply going to mark them mentally so that you will be reminded to think about them at a later, more appropriate time. Now that you've done that, you should be thinking of nothing but this exercise. If any other thoughts come along, you will totally ignore them. You will not even give them the attention necessary to decide whether you will pay attention to them or not. You will not even look to see what the thought is. Whatever it is, it is a distraction. It is a distraction from the important job that you are doing. A distraction from your important work of hypnosis. You will not fight with these thoughts. Instead you will deal with them the way a judo master deals with an attacker. If someone rushes at him, he does not fight the person, but instead throws him past. The master uses the attacker's impetus to deflect him, to toss him aside. If any thoughts try to get your attention, you let them whiz right by you, saying to yourself, "Whatever that thought is, I'll think about it later. Right now, I'm busy."

Now, as you settle in, feeling yourself calm, peaceful, and at ease, you feel yourself comfortably settling into the chair or the mattress or wherever you find yourself seated or lying down. Just sink into it. Let it hold and support you. And as you do, you become aware of a pleasant sensation of lightness. Do it however seems best and safest to you. But you're going to go on an imaginary journey through time and space. Perhaps you're going to feel as though the chair or mattress is like a magic carpet that gently and comfortably lifts you up and carries you on your way. Perhaps you'll find yourself feeling as though you've left your body behind and are free to travel along as a spirit. Perhaps you'll find yourself curling deep inside yourself to find a universe within. Perhaps you'll be able to teleport yourself instantly from one place to the next, as though you were a science-fiction character.

It doesn't matter how you choose to travel, as long as this means of travel is one that feels comfortable to you. But you're going, in your imagination, to travel now through time and space, to a peaceful, comfortable scene. A scene of perfect peace, calm, and tranquility. A place which is all your own. A place where no one can disturb you. A place where no one can hurt you. A place where painful ideas or memories or thoughts cannot even reach. Perhaps you'll find yourself at a place well known to you, a place where you've gone in reality. Perhaps it will be a place that you still go to. Perhaps it is one that no longer exists in reality. Or perhaps you'll go to a place which is like a perfect version of an imperfect place where you've really been. Or perhaps you will find yourself going to a place that could exist only in your imagination. You might travel to a universe of pure color and sound. You might travel among the stars and planets. You might go to an enchanted land.

Perhaps you will find yourself on a mountaintop, surrounded by valleys and ringed by another range of mountains that serve as a fortress. Perhaps you will find yourself in a meadow filled with fresh wild flowers, ringed by beautiful trees. Perhaps you will find yourself on a beach watching the waves rolling in. Wherever you find yourself, that will be fine. You might return to this scene over and over. Or you might find yourself going to different places with different exercises. You may even choose to allow the scene to change before your very eyes as you are in it, magically shifting the shapes, sights, and sounds to suit your fancy.

As you are in this scene, you should work at making it as vivid as possible to all of your senses. You are trying to make this place as real and as vivid as possible to all of your senses.

Suppose, for example, that you have chosen a beautiful beach on a tropical island as your peaceful scene. As you're there on that beach, you look out at the beautiful crystal water, and you watch as the waves come rolling in, one after the next after the next. You watch the waves form, curl, and break. And you watch the foam as it forms upon the waves as they break. As they do, you listen to the sound of each wave and the hiss of the undertow. You look up and you see the lighter blue of a beautiful sky with just one or two small puffy white clouds adding depth to the heavens. You feel the warmth of the sun baking your body, balanced by the coolness of the breeze off the water. You feel a slight bit of mist from the spray of the ocean. You can taste the salt upon your lips or perhaps the aftertaste of some favorite beverage. You hear the songs of the birds and the rustle of the leaves of the palm trees behind you. You feel the coarseness of the sand beneath your feet. You smell the fresh tang of the sea breeze. And you keep on increasing and enhancing the experience with all of your senses—more and more real, more and more complete.

You can stay in this state as long as need be. You can keep yourself occupied, so relaxed and calm, by focusing on making the scene this real. You may choose to do this as a way of keeping your mind calm and at ease while something is going on in your body. You may choose to do this on a regular basis as a way of relaxing yourself and reducing your overall level of stress. In that case, it would be like giving yourself a short but very intense vacation. If you do this, you might want to do it twice a day for twenty minutes at a time. You'll find that as you practice going to this peaceful place, you will be able more and more quickly and easily to reach your destination.

But now that you're in your peaceful place, you may choose

to go on and work on some specific exercise or you may wish just to relax and enjoy yourself. When you are ready to stop, you may do so in either of two ways. You may wish to mark some clear ending as you would with many hypnosis exercises, perhaps by counting backward from 3 and at 1 being fully alert, relaxed, and refreshed. Or depending on the circumstances, you may prefer simply to allow your eyes to come open and to let yourself gradually become more and more alert, but to allow yourself to remain partially in the peaceful place rather like a person who wakes up on a day when there's nothing that needs doing, who is awake but lazing his or her way through the morning in a comfortably drowsy way.

Now you know how to enter the state of hypnosis and how to use it to enter a different world of concentration, relaxation, and imagination. That means you are ready to put your knowledge to practical application. You should now skip ahead to the chapter which addresses your specific problem. You're ready to go to work on it.

4

Anxiety

Anxiety is a common human experience. Everyone has experienced fear at different times and to varying degrees. Sometimes the fear is realistic and specific, while at other times it may consist of a vague dread of the unknown.

At a rudimentary level, anxiety represents the organism arousing itself to be attentive to a possible danger. Thousands of years ago, our evolutionary ancestors lived in a world where dangers and threats were immediate and physical. If a caveman had gone out and tracked down something to eat, another hungry animal, wanting the food, might attack him. To deal with threats of this sort, successfully surviving cavepeople developed a number of helpful physical responses that are still unchanged today. Regulated by the autonomic nervous system, adrenaline can be released into the bloodstream, speeding up the heartbeat, bringing oxygen to all the muscles, moving them to a higher degree of tension to allow quicker response, readying the body either to fight or to flee. Additionally, the blood supply to the skin is held back so there is less bleeding if the skin is cut; the digestive system is turned off and perhaps the bowels emptied to make ready for an encounter. The pupils dilate to maximize vision, and the hair may stand on end to make one look larger and fiercer.

All of these preparations demand enough high energy to get

one very well prepared for a dangerous, immediate physical confrontation. In modern life, however, threats are rarely of this sort. Being ready to attack a wild animal does not make one well prepared for talking with the boss. Being ready to run for one's life does not make one better able to deal with having a test returned. These stresses are neither physical nor immediate, and activation of the autonomic nervous system is not a useful response to them.

In dealing with a frightening situation, then, your first step should be to ascertain if your body's natural fight-or-flight response is in fact the appropriate one for the situation. Is there truly danger, and, if so, what sort and how severe is it? Fear can be a valuable ally if it keeps you from doing something dangerous, such as running along the edge of the roof of a skyscraper. It is not helpful if it prevents you from doing genuinely safe things, such as looking out of a window in an upper floor. The ego, the adult in your mind, must take a look at what is going on while temporarily ignoring your body's fears. It then decides what to do.

When, for example, you are nervous about giving a speech in public, your body responds as though confronted by a physical danger. If, in fact, you were addressing a crazed despot and a wrong word could result in your execution, you might decide that this is a speech that would best not be given. Usually though, you would conclude that your audience was safe and that delivering the speech posed no danger, that indeed you had much to gain by it. With this decision, you would acknowledge that your anxiety, while very present, is not a warning of any real danger.

Instead, such anxiety is much like a child who is frightened by imagined monsters in the dark of night. A parent hearing the cries of a child scared of monsters under the bed would not say to the child, "Oh, my God, monsters! Let's get out of here. Run for your life!" Instead the parent would say, "I know that you're scared, but everything is all right. You're safe. It's OK to relax. You need your sleep. Go back to bed." In just this way, the adult inside you can treat your fright as an irrational dread.

Note that two issues are vital. First, you have to acknowledge the fact that there is an anxiety present. If you say to your-self, "I'm not scared," another part of you is going to be saying with much more conviction, "Like heck you're not. You're very scared." The fear must be acknowledged in order to be managed. One cannot deal with something that does not exist. Second, once the warning of anxiety is acknowledged, one must assess the situation maturely to see whether the anxiety should be acted upon, ignored, or overcome.

If, as another example, you needed to fly to a distant desti-nation, it should make a difference if you were offered a ride on a modern passenger plane where people were happily boarding, where everything seemed to be fine, and where the risk of crash-ing was extremely small, or if you were offered a seat in a ka-makaze plane with dynamite in the nose, no landing gear, and just enough fuel to reach the enemy fleet. In the first case you might decide that the danger could be safely ignored in favor of the speed of reaching the destination. In the second case, "Get me out of here" is the more appropriate response.

Although anxiety may be justified, and although, in very small doses, it may at times be helpful, frequently it is irrational and a hindrance. Excessive anxiety greatly hampers achievement and performance, interferes with the smooth performance of fine motor activity, and is a source of much needless misery. Fortu-nately, it is treatable.

The area of anxiety and its treatment is a huge one that could easily fill many books by itself. Since there are different causes of anxiety, it is also an area where professional help is of-ten needed. Some people who suffer from anxiety or panic disor-ders have a chemical imbalance and respond very well to antide-pressant medication. For others, anxiety can be the tip of an iceberg, the visible symptom of deep underlying psychological problems. A man, for instance, who has been unable to work out issues around separation and assumption of an adult role in life might continue to live with his parents well into middle age. He might have trouble making friends or venturing out into the world for fear of losing his childish relationship with his mother and father. One would expect that any dating would produce anxiety in him. However, the idea that his anxiety over dating could be eliminated without first addressing the underlying fear of what a successful date might produce is naive.

Sometimes anxiety is a manifestation of a problem in the family. For example, a whole family may have very pathological ways of interacting. One of their pathologies might be the unconscious agreement to designate one member of the family as the sick one. The "designated patient" might then be responsible for being chronically anxious and ill at ease in order to allow everyone else in the family to feel that they are OK. Any simple intervention that tries to treat this individual's anxiety is doomed to fail because the problem is not simple anxiety. Rather, it is a complicated pathological family structure.

Hypnosis can be used for symptomatic relief of anxiety. However, if any underlying problem is not also treated, either the anxiety may not yield or another symptom may arise to take its place. In the two hypothetical cases above, the patient not only has an underlying problem but also suffers from acute anxiety. Successful treatment would have to address the anxiety as well as teach the person how to be able to go out and live a life that is not hamstrung by anxiety.

Where anxiety is not so great and where it doesn't indicate a major underlying problem, it can be dealt with in a self-help setting with hypnosis. Since it is impossible to be anxious and relaxed at the same time, relaxation is useful as the first step in combating tension.

Tense and Relax

Anxiety takes place both in the body and in the mind. When one is feeling anxiety, it produces tension in the muscles. Tense muscles, conversely, will produce anxiety. This process or interaction can be broken from either end. Many tranquilizers, such as Valium, work to reduce anxiety by relaxing the muscles. Just as the old question "Am I running because I'm scared, or am I scared because I'm running?" suggests, if the muscles are relaxed they send a message to the brain that all is well, and if the mind is relaxed it sends a similar message to the muscles.

In this exercise you learn to relax your muscles and, consequently, your mind.

As you settle into a state of deep imagination, concentration, and relaxation, you begin to focus on the muscles of your body. Feel how relaxed they are. Focus on how relaxed they are. Your muscles are limp, heavy, effortlessly relaxed. And as your muscles are so relaxed, so deeply, so thoroughly free from tension, lift up your hand. Lift it up to your cheek and touch your cheek. And as you do, you make an association between the physical sensation of touching your cheek and the physical sensation of being so relaxed. This is going to work as a posthypnotic suggestion. Any time you feel your muscles being infiltrated by tension, you know that you can touch your cheek and feel them relax.

With your other hand, the one you didn't use to touch your cheek, make a fist. A tight fist. And as you make a tight fist, you feel the tension spread through the wrist and into your forearm, into your elbow, and into your upper arm. Your arm is tight, tense; the muscles are straining, straining with tension, and as they do, you realize how much hard work is involved in tensing your muscles. And when you've had enough of this, when you've had enough of this tension, just reach up and touch your cheek, and as soon as you do, that touch triggers the relaxation response. You touch your cheek, and your arm relaxes. You touch your cheek, and the tension is drained from it, leaving your arm comfortable, peaceful, and relaxed.

As you reflect on the comparison, you see how much work it takes to keep your muscles tense. Relaxing isn't hard. Relaxation is the easy part. Tension takes a lot of work. Tension uses up a lot of energy. To be relaxed is easy. To be relaxed is to cease straining. You realize how much work has gone into keeping your body tense, and you realize that it's going to be a relief; it's going to be much easier to allow your body to relax, to allow your body to feel good, to be at peace.

You know that whenever your mind is tense, your body becomes tense. And when your body is tense, your mind feels tense. Tense and anxious. It's impossible to feel two completely opposite ways simultaneously. You cannot be tense and relaxed at the same time. And you realize with joy that even though you cannot will a mood change directly, you can make your muscles behave themselves. Just as you can make your hand form a fist, so also can you tell your muscles to relax and slow down. And if your muscles are relaxed and comfortable, your mind will not be tense.

Let's try it some more. Feel tension enter your toes, tightening your toes, tightening those muscles, and then feel that tension spread up, spread through your feet up into your legs. Feel the contractions in the muscles of your hands, in your forearms, upper arms. Feel the tightening in your lower back and feel it spread up through the shoulders up to your neck and the back of your head. It feels almost as if you were expecting a blow and tensing your muscles in expectation of receiving it. Your chest muscles have tightened, making breathing uneven and strained. You feel the sensation of tension, of anxiety, of dread. And you see how unpleasant it is; you feel how unnatural it is; you know what a strain it is.

Now reach up and touch your cheek. Doing so reminds your muscles to relax, and you gratefully feel that sense of relaxation as it washes over your body like a warm wave, soothing and relaxing. And you take a big deep breath and let it out and feel yourself so comfortable and so relaxed, and you realize that this is an experience that you can have any time. That you have the power to keep yourself relaxed.

But now focus for a minute on your breathing—slow, regular, comfortable breathing. As you do, you feel how with each breath you exhale, you breathe out any tension which might be present within you. Any tension that might begin to build up anywhere is exhaled and blown out, leaving your body ever more thoroughly and completely relaxed. Each time you inhale, you become aware of something a little different. And as you inhale, you become aware of the strength of your body. You feel the strength that ripples through your muscles. Your muscles are relaxed but strong. Imagine a lion or lioness relaxed, lying in the sun. Look at that powerful body. The muscles are so strong, power just rippling through the entire body, but also so relaxed, so at ease, so at peace. That big cat is you. You're so relaxed but so strong. You can afford to relax because you realize that you are so powerful, because you are so strong, it's in fact safe for you to be so comfortable, peaceful, and at ease, at rest, at peace. With each breath you inhale, you feel the strength rippling through your body. With each time you exhale, you feel any tension in your body being pumped out, blown out, relaxing you, relaxing you, bringing you peace, comfort, ease.

When you are ready to leave this exercise, simply open your eyes and bring yourself back to the usual waking state.

Heartbeat

Often a person who is feeling anxious becomes very aware of his or her heartbeat. It feels as though the heart is beating too fast and too hard, which is in itself anxiety-producing. So now we're going to work on helping that feeling.

While feeling very relaxed, peaceful, and comfortable, focus all your attention inward to your body and feel your heart beat. It may take a moment, or you may be able to do it very quickly. It doesn't matter which. Just let yourself become aware of your heartbeat. You realize that you can, even though you are very relaxed, even though your heart isn't beating too hard or too fast, you can become aware of it. You can always be aware of your heartbeat if you bother to look. People who are tense frequently become aware of their heart beating not because there is something wrong but simply because their attention is not being directed out into the world around them but instead has been turned inward. People who are frightened of what is going on around them, who are fearful of what is going on outside them frequently retreat inward. Their attention is directed inside, and when they do that, they become aware of their heartbeats. If you should become aware of your heartbeat—noticing how it feels, noticing its rate and strength—you're first of all going to realize that this simply means that you have turned your attention inward. It doesn't mean that there's anything wrong, merely that you're looking inside yourself. Continue to feel your heartbeat;

continue to be aware of your pulse. And as you do, you realize, first of all, that all it is doing is beating.

But that's what it's supposed to be doing. You notice your heart is beating, just as it's supposed to. It would be a problem if it were to stop beating. Of course, if that were to happen, you would know about it instantly. You wouldn't have to keep watch to discover that. It would automatically be brought to your attention immediately. But continue to listen to your heartbeat. As you do, you realize it really is very dull. It just keeps doing the same thing over and over; lub-dub, lub-dub, lub-dub. Two notes repeated endlessly. No matter how long you keep listening, you will hear the same two beats. If you stop listening, they'll continue just the same. If you come back and listen another day, the sound will remain unchanged, beat after beat after beat. It really is quite dull. And you really do have other things to do with your time, with your attention, with your life, other than listening to the same boring sound over and over and over.

So if you find yourself aware of listening to your heartbeat, you're going to be able to remind yourself that this simply means you've turned your attention inward. You can listen for as long as you want, but it soon becomes overwhelmingly boring. When that happens, you are safely free to redirect your attention elsewhere.

Sometimes your heart is beating faster than it needs to. There's nothing really horrible about this, but it's unnecessary. What's happened is that your body has responded as if there were a physical threat to your safety. Your body has become ready to run or to fight. If you are indeed about to run away or get into a physical fight, not a verbal one, this is a very useful response. However, if you're not intending immediate, strong physical action, it's a preparation which is not useful.

Now we're going to tell your body that it's OK for your heartbeat to slow down.

Imagine you are running a race. Imagine you are running in the Olympics. You're running your fastest. You're running as hard as you can. You are pushing yourself in your drive to win this race. Of course your body is working very hard. Your muscles are striving to the utmost. Your muscles need plenty of oxygen to allow them to continue their furious pace. Your heartbeat, of course, has been elevated to bring an adequate supply of oxygen-bearing blood to your muscles. Of course your heart rate is up.

But there it is, just ahead of you: the finish line. You've crossed the finish line, and you raise your arms in victory. You've done it. You've won the gold medal. And you let your body relax. It's done its job. Your breathing patterns change. Your heartbeat changes. As you walk slowly around the track, your muscles tired from the exertion, you feel your heartbeat slow down. The race is over. It's all done. It's right to relax now. It's OK to be at peace and at ease. No more need to strain. Your heartbeat is slowing down, dropping down; the race is over. The race is over, your heartbeat is down, your pulse has slowed, and you feel very good, very relaxed, very much at peace.

As you touch your cheek, you feel how relaxed your muscles are, how peaceful and relaxed. Your breathing is slow and regular, steady and regular. The race is over and your heartbeat is down; your heartbeat is slow. And you realize that this good, healthy, comfortable state is how you can feel all the time. And you realize as well, that your body is best able to deal with the stresses of modern life in this state of relaxation, which allows your brain to do its best rather than in that state of anxiety and tension that you were experiencing.

When you are ready to end this exercise, open your eyes and bring yourself back to the usual waking state.

Music

It is very well known that music has a great deal of power to influence or even control emotion. Consider movies as an easy example. If a beach scene with bathers splashing in the water has a musical score of the Beach Boys' surfing tunes, you would know that everything was pleasant and safe. The greatest danger would be of falling off one's surfboard. If, on the other hand, that same visual scene were accompanied by the music from *Jaws*, you would know that all those swimmers were in grave danger of imminent shark attack.

You can learn to establish a song or piece of music as a background, rather like a score for a movie. It will keep you relaxed, controlling your mood so that fear, which tends to grow on itself once started, does not begin.

———◆•◆•◆———

As you settle deeply and comfortably into the state of hypnosis, you let yourself once again go off to your peaceful scene, your place of calm, sheltered, protected tranquillity. When you've arrived there and are feeling so calm, so totally at peace, you allow yourself to begin to think about a piece of music. It's a very peaceful, relaxed bit of music, one that makes you feel safe and protected, secure from all danger. It's a very good feeling from this bit of music. It will be a piece of music familiar to you, one that expresses these feelings for you. You are not thinking about what someone else would like to hear; you're listening to your own music. Perhaps it's a bit of classical music, perhaps a show tune. Maybe it will be a ballad. It might be as simple as "Rock-a-Bye Baby" or as complex as a symphony.

You just let yourself find what it is that properly accompanies the feelings of peace and relaxation. And when you have found this bit of music, you focus in on imagining it very, very powerfully. And as you do, the music becomes the relaxed, peaceful feeling just as the relaxed, peaceful feeling becomes the music. The music is the relaxation, the relaxation is the music, and the music is there inside you playing on, a steadying, relaxing, and comforting influence.

Now in a moment, you're going to open your eyes, but the music is going to stay with you. You're going to continue to hear this comforting tune playing in your head. Because your personal sound track is such a safe and peaceful one, you are going to know and feel down in the very fiber of your being that all is well, all is safe. As you go along, if you should begin to feel even any precursor of tension or distress, the music will become louder and stronger, reminding you again and again that all is well, all is safe. And as you hear the music, you become relaxed. You feel safe, secure, and at ease and at peace. Now let your eyes come open, and continue to feel so good.

A Trip to the Doctor or the Dentist

A common anxiety-laden event that comes up from time to time is a trip to the doctor or the dentist. Sometimes it's a trip to the doctor for a routine physical, sometimes to the gynecologist for an annual visit, sometimes to the dentist for a checkup and teeth cleaning. At other times a person goes because of a bothersome symptom or because a tooth needs filling. The sense of anxiety or dread which frequently accompanies these occasions makes them at best uncomfortable. For some people, the anxiety is so great that they can't keep the appointment at all and end up neglecting their health.

Although the various sorts of health care visits have different details, many elements are pretty similar from one situation to the next. A dental visit is described in this exercise, but you can adapt the description to the type of appointment you have.

As you have got yourself thoroughly and comfortably relaxed, in a powerful yet comfortable state of hypnosis, you are about to go in your imagination through a complete visit to the dentist. You will be going through all the motions as if you were really there. You are going to experience it as if you, in fact, were visiting the dentist and having necessary work done. Unlike sometimes in the past, however, it is going to be comfortable and free from anxiety, discomfort, or dread. If, as you go along, you find that you are starting to become anxious, you should immediately interrupt this exercise and leave the scene that you were imagining. You should instead go to your comfortable and relaxed, peaceful scene, which you have already discovered. Go there and become totally relaxed. When you are feeling relaxed and comfortable, come back to this exercise, but not at the point where you left it. Instead, rejoin this exercise at an earlier point, a spot that you had previously gone through comfortably. That means that you will be relaxed as you take on something that you know you can comfortably handle because you've already done so. You'll then proceed and probably find that when you reach the spot which had been uncomfortable, you'll be able to proceed through it without anxiety. If you should feel anxious, once again go to your nice scene, become relaxed, then go back to a comfortable point in this exercise, and proceed. You can do it as often as is necessary to allow you to get through any difficult spots without anxiety.

It's important to remember that the point of this exercise is not to learn to tolerate the anxiety and distress that you feel. Instead it is to learn to go through this experience without tension or discomfort.

You've decided that you need to make an appointment to visit the dentist. You're not going to the dentist right this minute. You're not doing anything difficult or uncomfortable. You are just realizing that taking care of your body requires that you bring yourself in to the dentist's office for a checkup. It's not fun, but it wasn't intended to be. In a way, it's rather like taking your car into the shop for a tune-up. You don't think of that as pleasure or fun; rather, it's an irritating sort of thing that you need to do to be certain that your car will be in good condition when you need it. So you reach for the phone and dial the number, focusing on regular, comfortable breathing, keeping your muscles thoroughly relaxed, and remembering that all you are doing right now is making a telephone call to arrange to do something that you have decided is worth doing.

The receptionist answers the phone, and you say who you are and that you would like to make an appointment. You realize that you're safe and secure in your own home, comfortably talking on the phone, keeping your muscles relaxed as you find a mutually satisfactory time. And then, having done so, you hang up. It's done. And you feel very good about yourself and very pleased with your accomplishment. You did what you intended to do. You did what was necessary. You mastered an anxiety.

And now some time has past, and it's the day of your appointment. You're going to focus on staying very much in the present. You don't need to jump ahead to things before they happen. When you're en route, you don't need to imagine yourself in the waiting room, and in the waiting room you don't need to imagine yourself in the dental chair. That can lead to anxiety. Instead, you're going to focus on where you are and what you're doing at any moment.

A strong focus is going to be maintained on the idea that you are choosing to do something that is good for your body. You are able to focus your attention on this notion that this is good for you. When you exercise, for example, it sometimes feels like hard work. Your muscles may feel tired and strained. You may be in part wishing you could stop. But you know that this makes your body healthier. You know that you have decided to do this for your own good, and so you choose to continue to exercise. In the same way, in the back of your mind is an ongoing reminder that you have chosen to take care of your body. And one way you take care of your body is by having the dentist take care of your teeth. You've decided that you are going, and so you don't need to rethink your decision. You have no reason to change your mind, no reason to reconsider, and you realize that thinking about it and questioning your decision merely makes for discomfort. There's nothing to think about; you're just doing it.

As you approach the office, you focus on two things. The first is that your body is very relaxed and is staying relaxed with your slow regular breathing. Each breath you exhale blows out or pumps out any tension that might have accumulated in your body. Second, you focus on what you are doing, which is walking into an office. There's nothing hard or painful or stressful about walking into an office. Your mind does not leap ahead to the future because you are not there yet. When that future occurs, you will have at your disposal techniques to keep that comfortable. It will not be hard, but there's no reason or advantage to thinking about those things before they arrive. So you settle back, go into the waiting room, tell the receptionist your name, and then sit down in the chair. You're glad that you've come a few minutes early because you have work to do.

As you settle in, you realize and focus on the fact that all that really needs to be there is your body. Your mind doesn't even need to be present. You're there to have your teeth checked.

If you had dentures, you could have mailed them in. In a sense, that's what you're doing now. You are the postal worker who is delivering them, but you don't really have to pay much attention to what's going on. That's the dentist's job. Your mind is going to be able to relax and go off to a nice, pleasant scene. In fact, as you sit here in the waiting area, you let yourself enter a nice state of hypnosis. You settle in and let your mind float off to a peaceful scene. That's right. A part of you remains aware of where your body is and what is going on with it, but not much. Mostly you've decided that you're going to drop your body off at the dentist's, have her do whatever needs to be done, and then come back for your body when it's all over. It's going to be rather like dropping your car off at the mechanic's. You don't need to waste your time watching him change the sparkplugs and replace a dirty oil filter. You have better things to do.

So you settle into hypnosis, deeply and comfortably relaxed, with enough awareness so that you will be able to respond when your name is called and do what's necessary, sit where you're supposed to sit, open your mouth and turn your head as instructed, but most of all you will be focusing your attention on something useful. Your attention will be focused on keeping your body relaxed and your mind in a pleasant place.

And now, it's your turn. Your name has been called, so you get up from the chair but keep yourself in this comfortable state. You keep yourself hypnotized. Your eyes are open and you're able to walk normally. And you go into the office and sit down. As soon as you do, you close your eyes and settle back into a state of deep hypnosis and relaxation. You focus on your breathing, slow, regular, and comfortable. You focus even more on keeping your muscles totally limp, totally relaxed.

And as you do so, you become aware that the technician is chattering at you, trying to engage you in an inane conversation to relax you. But you don't need that help to relax. In fact, you're doing quite well on your own. And you have choices here. Some questions will be asked that you really do need to answer. At those times, you will be able to give the appropriate answer in a few words without disturbing the state of relaxation that you are in. In fact, you are always able to talk and to communicate while remaining deeply hypnotized. Questions, then, that need to be answered will, of course, be answered. For other questions or comments, you'll have a choice. You might wish to say, "I'm sorry, but I'm keeping myself deeply relaxed, and so I'd rather not chat." You might wish instead absentmindedly to give vague responses and "um-hum" responses. You realize that at worst the person will think you're not a very good conversationalist. But that doesn't matter. You are not there to make friends. You are not there to dazzle anyone with your wit. You are not there for a heart-to-heart chat. You are there to get work done on your teeth, and you are putting yourself in the best position to do this most comfortably.

As you settle back, you focus your attention on slow, steady, regular breathing and begin to imagine yourself floating off to your pleasant scene. That's right. Visualize it as vividly as you can. Focus with all of your senses on being in this special place. What do you see? Look at the shapes. Look at the colors. Look at the textures. See the movement as things move about in this pleasant environment. Perhaps you feel the warmth of the sun upon your skin, the coolness of a gentle breeze. Listen to the sounds. Perhaps the sounds of birds calling, perhaps the sounds of the breeze rustling the plants, perhaps the gentle strains of distant music just on the edge of your hearing. Smell whatever scents are appropriate. The perfume of flowers, the fresh scent of grass in a meadow, or the salt tang of an ocean. Perhaps you can taste the aftertaste of a favorite beverage as you settle in and relax.

You remember that nerve conduction is speeded up and made to seem more urgent by tensing your muscles. And you know that there are no signals that your body is going to be sending to your brain that really are worth urgent attention. So you know that it is a priority to keep your muscles relaxed, limp, totally without tension, completely at ease and at peace, thoroughly relaxed. Each breath you exhale pumps out any remaining tension. Except to keep it relaxed, there's no need for you to pay a great deal of attention to your body. It can take care of itself. Even more, you have chosen to bring it here to be taken care of. For the next little while, you are going to have a team of health care professionals taking care of your body, protecting it and, if necessary, healing it.

In a distant sort of a way, you become aware of the fact that it's necessary for your mouth to be open, so you let it happen. You retain just enough awareness of what is happening with your body to respond appropriately to any important questions and to cooperate by moving about as is required. Beyond that, however, you are off in your own world.

In a distant sort of a way, there is an awareness of the fact that someone is touching your teeth, doing different things to them. And you realize that this person doesn't need your help. In fact, even if you wanted to help, there is nothing that you could do. As your teeth are being cleaned, for example, there is no assistance that you can provide. The tooth cleaning that you can do by yourself is called brushing and flossing, and you do them at home. What's going on here is different and no real concern of yours. If you tried to help, you would only get in the way. That's right. Leave your body in the hands of the professionals to whom you have already decided to entrust it. You got yourself here, and now you let them do the job you've hired them to do.

As it proceeds, as they look at and poke at different teeth, there's absolutely no need for you to try to anticipate the results. If you think that they are or are not about to find a cavity, it doesn't make any difference. Whether there is a tooth that needs treatment or not is something that is a matter of fact that was true before you got to the dentist's office. If you have a diseased tooth, it was diseased before you arrived. If your tooth is healthy and sound, it arrived that way and will remain so. The dentist will be able to tell soon enough. There's no advantage to anticipating. Instead, you need to settle back and know that you will find out the appropriate result as soon as it's known. Anticipating treatment doesn't make it less likely, less necessary, or even more pleasant. It simply makes your present unpleasant.

And as the dentist looks and pokes and touches your teeth in a way that you are only vaguely conscious of, she says to you, "There's a small cavity in this tooth. We need to fill it before it gets any larger."

You realize that the best thing would be to have this corrective work done to heal your body as soon as possible, so you say, "Let's do it right now."

The dentist says, "Fine," and you realize that your part in this is done. You need to be aware enough to keep your body relaxed and to follow instructions to do things such as open your mouth. But really, all you need to pay attention to is the signal that it's over and you can go home. Until then, you relax and let your mind go back to your pleasant scene while the hired help does the work you have told them to do.

All of your attention is focused on being in your pleasant scene, feeling good, feeling calm, feeling relaxed. Nothing else is important. Everything else is a distraction. If you were to pay attention, you would be aware of a pricking sensation as Novocain is administered. But you realize that this is nothing with which you need to concern yourself. Of course, you are being given Novocain to make the experience more comfortable. But it's not anything that requires your attention or assistance. And then you may become aware, in a distant sort of a way, that the dentist has begun using the hand piece on your tooth. If you should become aware of that, you will think to yourself, "Well, good. It's nice to know that the dentist is doing a good job. Every bit done means a little bit closer to the completion of the work. And when the work is completed, I'll be able to go home and do the rest of the things that I have to do today." As each step proceeds, you're aware of and glad of the sense of progress that you are making. And you keep focusing your attention on feeling completely relaxed.

You feel a great sense of safety. You know that you have entrusted your body to the hands of a competent professional. You know that the dentist knows what to do and is trying to help you. The dentist has your health and well-being in mind and has protected you with Novocain, which will hold away the unpleasant sensations. You know that you are safe.

Now, you know that it is possible that a slight bit of discomfort might come through some nerve that was not completely anesthetized, or perhaps you decided that you would not use any Novocain because you were sure that the discomfort would not be too great. But this does not frighten you. You realize two important things about it. First of all, if it should be too uncomfortable, you need merely signal and let the dentist know. If you say that you are uncomfortable, you will immediately be given something to reduce or even eliminate that discomfort. That means that you know that no matter how bad it becomes, it will not last for long. As soon as you need relief, you will get it. Second, you realize that because it is safe, because you know that any extreme discomfort will be swiftly and efficiently eliminated, you know that any mild discomfort can safely be ignored. Any mild sensation of discomfort is no cause for any alarm. Your body is being healed, not damaged. So you don't need any danger signals. The most you might experience without asking for medication is a mild discomfort, and you realize that that is all it is: just a mild discomfort. There's no need to fear it, no need to be frightened. It's just a mild discomfort. Your decision not to report it says that you don't think it is worth anyone's attention. It is not worth doing something about it. It's a minor irritation that you have chosen to ignore.

You focus on keeping your body relaxed, relaxed and peaceful, and you realize that this is a very short-term event. This is something that will not go on forever, will not even go on for a long time. In fact, it's almost over. You realize, in a distant sort of a way, that the dentist has begun packing the filling material into the prepared area and is now proceeding to sculpt it. Your body stays totally relaxed as you realize that this process is in the last stages, and you are glad to know that the dentist is taking time to do a good job shaping the filling to the shape of your tooth, making sure that it will feel good in your mouth.

And now as you drift along in your pleasant scene, you hear the signal which you have been awaiting. You are done. You leave your pleasant scene and come back to your body and find yourself feeling relaxed, refreshed, and quite happy to have completed this task.

5

Phobias

A phobia is an irrational dread of something. While there are plenty of things that people fear, a fear is a phobia only if it reaches an irrational degree or intensity. It is normal to fear death. However, if a healthy person spends all of his time so terrified by the thought of death that it is impossible to live a normal life, that fear is irrational. It is reasonable to be afraid of falling off the top of a tall building. That is the sort of fear that keeps us from walking over cliffs. However, it is irrational to be so afraid that one cannot comfortably sit by a window in a tall building.

Phobias occur for a number of reasons. Sometimes they represent a conflict between an attraction to and a fear of the same thing. There is a basic wish to experience something mixed with a fear that the wish might come true in a way that would be terrible. People who are afraid to leave their houses, for instance, frequently have a strong, though hardly uncommon, wish to be able to take off and leave responsibilities behind. Such a person might imagine running off to Tahiti or some other exotic locale. However, instead of being able simply to say, in effect, "That would be nice, but I'm not really going to do it," the phobic person is instead immobilized. In order to make sure that this wild urge is not permitted to become fact, the poor person cannot even go down to the K-Mart to run an everyday errand.

Similarly, people with another common phobia, acrophobia, or fear of heights, often have an unconscious wish to fly. As a child, the acrophobe might have fantasized about how nice it would be to be like Peter Pan or Superman, able to float up in the sky or zoom around like a bird. When near the edge of a railing, a part of this now-adult individual might still feel like leaping out and flying away. Of course this person knows that in reality such flight is impossible and accordingly keeps himself firmly inside the railing.

The phobic's overprotective part, however, does not completely trust his common sense. It instead bombards him with a sense of how dangerous it is to be near the edge. It says that he had not only better not lean over the rail, but in fact, he should not even get near the window. Indeed, he had better not even get in sight of an upper floor window, as though such a sight would really overwhelm him with desire to fly and in fact send him running through it.

Sometimes phobias are the result of a bad experience which has been generalized. Sometimes phobias are the tip of the iceberg of a deeper, ongoing psychological conflict. Sometimes a phobia that originally represented a conflict remains as a habit even when the original conflict has been resolved.

The strength of phobic fear seems to have to do with the same kind of imagination that takes place in hypnosis. In hypnosis, one might well imagine going off to a pleasant scene as a way of being better able to deal with an unpleasant reality. A patient undergoing chemotherapy, for example, might imagine being in a more enjoyable situation. Doing so would allow feelings of peace and comfort appropriate to the imagined scene rather than the distressing reality of the chemotherapy. A phobic person, one who is, for instance, terrified on an airplane, is going through a mirror image of this process. While really seated in a safe and comfortable airplane, the phobic is imagining being in a terrifying situation, an unpleasant scene, and emotionally is responding accordingly. This is why the phobic person can often say, "I don't know why I'm so scared. I know perfectly well everything is all right. But I'm scared anyway." He or she has two simultaneous experiences: one known and one felt.

Successful treatment of phobias demands, first of all, that the person understands that what is felt, the fear, is irrational. If you think skydiving is genuinely dangerous, you will not want to learn to be able to do it. It is foolish to try to cure a fear if it is a protection against something you see as realistically dangerous. You would resist learning to endanger yourself. Knowing there is no real reason for fear is a prerequisite for letting go of the phobia.

Phobias that are the result of a bad but not severely traumatic experience, ones that represent only mild internal conflicts, and ones that are now merely habit can often be treated with a self-help approach. Since the same kind of imagination used in the genesis of the phobia takes place in self-hypnosis, imagery-based exercises can be used to cure it. However, phobias that result from a more severe trauma or conflict are best treated in a professional setting, quite possibly with hypnosis as an important part of the treatment. When the phobia represents the tip of the iceberg, the sufferer needs professional help. The treatment must involve dealing with the 90 percent of the iceberg that is submerged as well as, or perhaps before, the visible tip.

The treatments of two common phobias, fear of flying and fear of public speaking, follow. If you have another fear, these exercises can serve as a model upon which to pattern a personal set of suggestions. If your phobia does not yield to this kind of self-help, try working with a professional.

Fear of Flying

A typical person with a fear of flying tends, as indicated above, to have two different experiences when trying to fly. Ms. Jane Doe, for example, might be able to look around on an airplane and see that all is well, that there is nothing to fear. In fact, rather than seeing the plane as a boring bus with wings. Ms. Doe becomes a bit excited about the idea of soaring flight. However, as she begins to imagine that enjoyable idea, an overprotective part of her mind, rather like an overanxious parent, intervenes and points out the obvious reality that she does not know how to fly the airplane. Like a hypervigilant caretaker, part of her starts saying, in effect, "Don't think about enjoying the flight. Don't you realize you could get killed that way?" It says it not in words but by producing vivid, terrifying imaginings of all the possible disasters that would happen if an airplane went out of control.

There are a number of ways to counteract these disastrous imaginings.

Ship the Body

Sometimes people have very little time to prepare for air travel and consequently can't complete the longer, more curative treatment of the "Flight Simulator" (see the next section). The following hypnotic exercise is one which allows enough quick relief to make immediate flight possible.

You wake up and realize today is the day. Later today you are going to be at your designation, right where you want to be. In order to ensure that you will not feel any distress, today is going to be a workday. Because in the past you have had some discomfort when traveling, today you are not going to go along just passively and let things happen as they may. Instead you actively take command, take charge. It's work, but it is work that you are capable of doing. You have decided that it is worth doing this in order to ensure your comfort.

So as soon as you wake up in the morning, you immediately go through an hypnotic exercise and get yourself deeply, comfortably into a state of relaxed concentration, imagination, and attention. And once you are in that state, you let your mind travel ahead through time and space to your destination. You've moved hours ahead through time. You've moved yourself miles away to the place where you are going to be. And when you are there, you are feeling peaceful, comfortable, and relaxed. You work hard at involving all five of your senses, at being there, at making the experience as vivid as possible. You see where you are in fantasy. You see the colors of things. You see motion as things move about. You feel sensations on your skin: warmth, coolness, moisture, dryness, textures. And you smell the air and see if there are any distinctive aromas. You listen to the sounds. Perhaps you taste the aftertaste of a favorite beverage upon your lips. Of course, it's not easy to have all these sensations so vividly simultaneously, but that's all right. You just keep on focusing your attention, making it more and more vivid and real. That is your job for today. At some points during the day, you will be able to immerse yourself totally in this fantasy. At other times, you will have to exist in two different sorts of reality. At these times, you will be able to split your consciousness. You will be able to let yourself be in two places at once. But you will focus on making the imagined scene the more real of the two.

Now, for example, you need to get up and go to the bathroom. That means that while part of your attention is focused on being at your destination, another part does have to pay some moderate attention to the task of going through your morning ablutions. It doesn't really take a lot of complex thought or sharp attention to go to the bathroom, brush your teeth, shower, dry yourself, and put on the clothing you laid out the night before. If anybody wishes to talk with you, you're capable of answering, but you tell them that for the most part you do not wish to chat this morning. Instead you have a job to do. You're busy keeping yourself comfortable and relaxed and at ease. Even as you sit down to your breakfast and go through the motions of eating, your mind is far away. Your mind is already at your destination.

While your attention is focused on staying in fantasy at your destination, keeping it as vivid and real to all of your senses as possible, time has passed. It's time to leave for the airport. But you realize that in a very real way, this does not really concern you. You've long ago decided that this is what you want to do. Your mind is already there, enjoying itself. All that remains to be done is shipping the body so that it catches up with your spirit. It's just a matter of getting your body to the destination. There's no need for a great deal of awareness of the transporting. In a way, your body and your luggage are rather similar. They are going to be put on a carrier which will take them to your destination.

Now you let your body walk itself out the door while your mind remains relaxed and at your destination. Of course there is some awareness of the walking and the getting in the car, but there doesn't need to be much. It's nothing that need concern you. All the decisions—whether to go or not, when to go, where to go—were made a long time ago. They were made by someone you trust. They were made by you. You've made the decisions; you've set yourself in motion. Now you're just carrying out your plan. That's right. In the car, a part of you notes the familiar landmarks as you drive safely to the airport. Or perhaps, if someone else is driving, you've closed your eyes and focused all of your attention on being at your destination.

If you were to choose to drive yourself, you would be able to do so. You would feel as though you were driving on autopilot, letting your body control the car safely to the airport. You're a good enough driver so that you can do so automatically. Or you might choose to be the passenger. Either way is all right. The two important things are delivering your body at each step along the way to your destination and keeping your mind totally relaxed, keeping your body totally relaxed as you imagine yourself at your destination.

And now you've arrived at the airport. You get out of the car, and almost as if in a dream, you walk through the terminal. Your body is walking along and takes note of whatever information needs to be observed. Your eyes look at the departure board to see which gate is yours. You're able to scan the environment and pick out the signs directing you to the appropriate gate. You walk along in a trance with the bulk of your attention focused on being at your destination, happy and relaxed. You become aware of how nice it is to be there at your destination and how happy you are. It makes you feel happy, pleased, contented. Meanwhile, your body continues its trek to the gate.

At the gate, you check in, are assigned your seat number, and are given a boarding pass. They haven't begun boarding yet, so you take a seat, close your eyes, and settle in, bringing yourself back to your destination. Now they're calling your row for boarding. You have your pass in your hand and you wander over to the door; with a slight smile on your lips because you're so happy to be at your destination, you walk without noticing down the corridor and onto the plane.

Now that you're aboard, seated with your seatbelt fastened, comes the easy part.

Your body is safely where you want it to be: aboard the plane which will carry it to your destination. In your mind you are already there. It is merely a matter of allowing your body to catch up with your mind. You close your eyes and allow yourself to go deeper into trance. As you settle there, you go deeper and deeper, becoming more and more relaxed. With each breath, you exhale, you settle in even more, becoming relaxed. Every last bit of your attention is now focused on being at your destination, happy and at peace.

You don't need to pay any attention to what's going on around you. As the flight attendants are talking about such matters as buckling your seat belt or observing the "No Smoking" sign, you settle back realizing that you don't have to pay attention to any of that. Your body is seated, seat belt in place. It can sit there perfectly easily for the duration of the flight. If any of the other passengers should both to look at you, they would be thinking, "There's a cool one. That person has fallen asleep at the gate." You are as relaxed as if you were asleep. In fact, as you focus on relaxing, being at your destination, you might even fall asleep in reality. That will be all right, too. As long as your body is kept comfortable and relaxed, you are fine. If anyone tries to strike up a conversation, if the flight attendant comes by asking if you would like anything, if anyone attempts to disturb your concentration, you have ways of dealing with it. The simplest way is to ignore them totally. Pretend you're asleep. Your body is on this plane to be transported to the destination. Your body is not there to entertain other passengers or to keep the flight attendants happy by answering questions. So someone might think you're not very friendly. At least you're relaxed, calm, and able to be comfortable. Or else you might choose to interrupt your reverie the slightest bit to give some minimal reply. A simple "Yes" or "No" or "I'm trying to rest, please" should suffice.

If you were paying attention to what was going on aboard the airplane, you would be noticing various things happen. The airplane would be leaving the gate, taking off, flying, landing. There would be times that the plane would change its angle, times that the sound would change, times when it would accelerate and slow down. But you don't need to pay any attention to that. All of your attention is focused on being right at your destination, being happy at being there. Just as if you were at your destination waiting for a package to arrive, you would not spend a great deal of time thinking about the package's trip. In the same way, you don't need to think about how your body is being transported.

You stay like this, deeply entranced, deeply relaxed, until in a dim and distant way you become aware of everyone standing up and deplaning. You realize that you've arrived. You are there. The flight is over and you've done it.

It feels very good to have done that. It feels very good to know that you can indeed move your body by air, fly without anxiety, distress, or discomfort.

That knowledge, that knowing that you have this option available to you is now useful as you learn the other way of comfortably traveling by air.

When you are ready to end this exercise, open your eyes and bring yourself back to the usual waking state.

Flight Simulator

This exercise is too long to do at a single sitting. There are suggested stopping points in the text, but you can break it up anywhere along the way according to what's convenient and comfortable. The idea of this exercise is to teach relaxation instead of tension in association with flight, so if you begin to become anxious or at all uncomfortable, you should immediately go back to the peaceful scene. Get nice and relaxed; then, once you're very relaxed, go back to the exercise, but not at the spot where you began to feel tension. Instead, return to a point where you were able to manage quite comfortably, and proceed from there. You are always trying to be comfortable and to proceed in comfort, not tolerating anxiety which might later grow and become overpowering.

Feel yourself comfortably relaxed, getting into a deep comfortable state of relaxed concentration and imagination and attention, and let yourself go off to your peaceful scene. Peaceful, comfortable and relaxed. Visualizing it so vividly, so powerfully, that you're feeling so safe, so totally and completely safe.

You know that pilots learn to fly an airplane by first of all going into a flight simulator. In this flight simulator they are sitting in what appears to be the cockpit of the airplane. Where the windows should be are screens which show films of what one would see if one were looking out the window of the airplane in flight. Around the pilots are all the instruments and controls. The whole room which is the flight simulator is mounted on hydraulic lifts which can tip, turn, and shake the flight simulator as required. When the pilot does something with the controls, it registers on the hydraulic lifts and on the instruments and on the screen as if he had really done that to the airplane. It's really like a very elaborate ride at Disneyland. As you think about it, it seems like kind of fun. The person on such a ride never leaves the ground, never actually has anything happen in reality, but gets to experience what it would be like to be flying an airplane. It would be perfectly safe. If one wanted to, one could practice crash dives and smashing into the ground. Nothing would happen except a possible "game over" appearing on the screen. It's all just a ride, all just a game, all just pretend.

Imagine now that the builders of the flight simulator have enlarged their original machine. The new flight simulator includes not only the cockpit, but also the passenger compartment of a typical airliner. That's right. There's this large compartment, rather like the inside of a bus but with more comfortable seats, and people get in and sit down. Instead of windows there are graphic images that look just like what you would see if you were to look out the window of an airplane. The whole thing is mounted on hydraulics to allow it to move about the way a real airplane would in flight. The designers are very pleased with it because it can perfectly mimic the experience of airplane flight. The only drawback is that when you get off, at the end of the "flight," you are still in your original place. You're not one mile closer to your destination. On the other hand, if you wanted to, you could get up and walk out of the flight simulator at any time you wanted, even if it were "at 40,000 feet somewhere over Ohio."

As you settle back, comfortably relaxed, remember that if at any time you become tense, you will go back to your peaceful scene until you have regained your sense of peace, tranquility, and relaxation. However, you may find that knowing that you are free to return to that relaxed state takes away the need to do so.

(Common break point.)

Now imagine yourself vividly experiencing what it is like to be sitting in your flight simulator airplane while it is on the ground at the gate where you are going. That's right. You are at your destination, the "airplane" is at the gate, and it is time to disembark. You reach down, unbuckle your seat belt, and get in the line of passengers who are heading for the door. You walk by the flight attendant, say, "Thank you for an enjoyable flight," and enter the corridor leading to the terminal.

And you realize that really was not so bad. That really was not so unpleasant.

Now go back to the flight simulator and have the "airplane" ride start a few minutes earlier. The airplane is on the ground at your destination but not quite at the gate. You're taxiing along. As you look out the windows, you can see out ahead. You're aware of the ground passing underneath you. It really is an excellent illusion. And as you're rolling along the ground, you realize the whole point of flying is to get quickly to your destination, and so you're glad to see the airplane moving at a brisk clip along the runway. And now, you've just about reached the terminal. There you are. The plane docks at the terminal. The seat belt sign is extinguished. You unlatch your belt and stand up to join the queue to disembark. You're feeling very good, confident, and relaxed and proud of your ability to have mastered a part of the flight.

(Common break point.)

Now let's try something a little different. Now imagine yourself in the "airplane" in midflight. You've gone to the part of the flight where the takeoff has already occurred and the landing is still in the future. You are relaxed and comfortable, peacefully settled in, relaxed and at ease. The airplane is flying along with you in it. Perhaps clouds are passing by as you look out the window, or perhaps you can see the ground below. You choose the kind of weather and time of day that you would like. And again you realize that the purpose of air travel is to enable one to cover very large distances relatively quickly. You're glad you're in the airplane because you have somewhere you want to be. You want to be there as soon as possible. You don't want to waste time in transit. You want to spend your time at your destination, not traveling. And you're glad that the airplane is traveling so quickly, taking you to your goal, taking you to where you want to be, and you realize as well that this really is a rather boring experience. All you are doing is sitting there. It's rather like riding a bus except it covers the territory more quickly. You're glad it's going faster than a bus, but you realize that the whole procedure really is dull and boring, dull and boring. You're feeling very comfortable and relaxed, letting the airplane do its job to take you to your destination.

Because you're on the flight simulator, you could choose to get off at any time. But you realize that you have no reason to get off. You're trying to get somewhere. If you were driving a long distance down a highway, you wouldn't want to pull over to the side of the road, get out of the car, and have someone else drive the car away, leaving you behind. If you're going somewhere, you're trying to reach a destination. You don't want to be left along the way, so in your flight, of course, you don't want to get out of the plane before your reach your destination. That urge to get out that you may feel is part of a wish that you had arrived at your destination. You wish that you were there so that you could get out of the plane and be where you want to be. But for now, you just continue to fly along, continue to fly along. It's really rather dull, really rather dull.

(Common break point.)

As you fly along, you realize that one thing that sometimes bothers air travelers is turbulence. Turbulence makes the flight feel bumpy. Because airplanes are flying on the air, they respond to bumps in the air just the way a bus would respond to bumps in the road. Think for a moment about driving along in a bus. If you were driving along a smooth, well-repaired highway, the ride would be smooth and calm. If you turned off onto a less well-maintained road or even a gravel road, the ride would become quite bumpy. As the wheels hit bumpy patches, the whole bus would shake. It would be a real nuisance. It would be rather uncomfortable perhaps. But also, you would maintain a sense of proportion. You would not worry, for example, that the bus might fall into a hole in the road and go tumbling to the center of the earth. You would not worry that a bump would knock the bus into the air and have it fly, tumbling for a considerable distance. You would know that all a bumpy road does is to make for a bumpy ride.

Bumpy air is like a bumpy road for an airplane. The bumps may shake the plane and its passengers, but there are no holes in it large enough for an airplane to fall into, any more than a modern road has holes big enough to swallow buses. Why don't you take the opportunity to test how it feels to ride on some bumpy air. You're going along in your flight simulator, cruising along, and it's getting a little boring. It seems like an appropriate time to set the flight simulator on "Bumpy." So, as you continue along, the flight simulator, the "airplane," begins to bump. You're glad that you're seated in a cushioned seat rather than on a wooden bench. There's a kind of comfort that comes from the seat belt, making you feel snug and comfortable. The bumps continue, and you realize they're sort of irritating. They are not dangerous; they can't hurt you; they just mean that you're being bumped around, that your ride is like that of a bus on a side road. There's really nothing to it, just some bumps. In a way, it's a change of pace from the boredom and monotony of the flight. On the other hand, they make it a little difficult to relax or to sip a beverage without its sloshing around. So let's have the flight simulator stop the bumps and go back to a smooth, comfortable flight without bumps.

(Common break point.)

But now you've been flying along for quite a while. The voice of the pilot comes over the intercom saying you've almost reached your destination. It's time to descend and get ready for the landing. And it makes you feel very good because that means that you are there and soon you're going to be at your destination. Soon you're going to be where you want to be. This is why you chose to fly: in order to get there.

You feel the sensation of changed balance as the plane begins to lean forward. You've begun the descent. And as you listen, you hear changes in the sound of the engines. Of course you do. It would be rather amazing if the engines didn't have to change their pitch when changing from the job of traveling long distances to the job of landing. In fact, as you go along and descend, motors are likely to be activated that will change the shape of the wing. Of course that happens. The wing has to be in the optimal shape for a landing. You've begun the descent. It feels very good because it means that soon you're going to be at the terminal; you're going to be on the ground; you will have arrived. Your ears begin to pop. As you're descending, the air pressure increases. It may be a little annoying, but it's harmless, simply a sign that you're descending. Lower and lower, going down, feeling a strong sense of excitement, a sense of excitement that you're almost there. The plane is getting lower, and the lower it gets, the more excited and happy you become, excited and happy that you're getting near your destination. You see the things on the ground becoming larger and larger as they grow closer and closer. As you descend you can see things more and more easily. And you get more of a sensation of speed. And finally, you're almost there, and then it happens as the wheels touch the ground with a little bump. Of course there's a little bump. That's how the plane is supposed to reach the ground. But as soon as you feel it, that little bump says you're no longer traveling; you've arrived. You're on the ground.

As soon as the wheels touch the ground, the engines are going to become very loud indeed. That is because they are being used in reverse. The engines are acting as brakes, slowing you down. Your airplane has been traveling at a tremendous rate of speed and needs to be slowed down. You feel yourself tending to lean forward as the plane is slowed down, and then you feel it slowing down more and more, and you feel very good knowing that you're safe on the ground at your destination and that you're now taxiing along, taxiing along to the terminal gate. You pull up, and the seat belt light goes off. It's time to disembark. You're there.

(Common break point.)

But now you have to practice how you got airborne so that you could land.

Imagine yourself in the simulator. You are at the gate, getting ready to leave. People are bustling around and sitting down, finding their seats, stowing their overhead luggage. You're sitting there relaxed and comfortable. The flight attendants are showing how to use the seat belts and giving instructions before the flight. You are feeling relaxed and calm, with a background sense of "OK, let's get on with it. I want to be at my destination, not here on the ground yacking." Finally you feel the little bump and hear the noise as the plane leaves the gate and begins to taxi along the runway. You're feeling a sense of comfortable anticipation because soon you're going to be on your way. Soon you are going to be at your destination. Even now, as you're slowly taxiing out on the runway, you are en route to your destination. The trouble is that this is a very slow way to get there. You're impatient to be there. You can't wait to pick up the speed. And now the pilot comes on and says that you've almost reached the head of the line of planes and soon you will be going down the runway to take off.

And now you're there. Your plane is at the head of the runway and is at a complete stop. The jets begin to roar as they come up to full strength while the airplane is standing still, held in check by its brakes. And now the brakes are released, and the plane begins to roll, slowly at first, then picking up speed as it goes faster and faster down the runway, more and more quickly, and you feel the pressure as the acceleration pushes you back into your seat. You feel a slight bumpiness as speed magnifies every tiny irregularity in the runway.

And finally you're going so fast that you feel the little bump and lift as the plane becomes airborne, as the wheels leave the ground. You are no longer driving fast; rather, you are flying.

You're flying, but you're at a very low height. You want to get up to cruising altitude as quickly as possible. You want to get up to where the air is thin, to where you can go at top speed. That means that you need to climb quickly, and you feel the tilting as the airplane lifts its nose and climbs up at a steep angle. It's not only tilted back but also begins to lean to the side as the pilot banks and runs to get on the proper course.

And then the plane straightens out and you feel a momentary sense of weightlessness, and the plane is on course. And you hear the motors change pitch. They're no longer at full speed because they're no longer trying to lift the plane into the air. Now you're airborne, and the engines seem quiet by comparison as they push you swiftly through the sky.

And now you've done it. You can feel very pleased, proud, and happy with yourself. You've successfully mastered every stage with the flight simulator. Now it's time to go on to the next step.

(Common break point.)

You have learned to do every part of a trip by plane. So far you've practiced these pieces as separate chunks that have been done out of order. You've successfully done each of these things, and now it's time to put them together. Now it's time to take the flight simulator ride from beginning to end. It's still the flight simulator; there's still no real flying involved, but now you're going to go through it in sequence, from the moment you arrive at the "airport," through the time you board the "plane" and "taxi" down to the "takeoff." You'll go through the flight all the way to the pretend landing and going to the gate. You'll find that it will not be difficult to do this because you've already mastered each part of it. You can repeat these exercises, this time in chronological order.

You've done very well going through the experience of the flight simulator. You now have the ability to imagine yourself traveling as if you were in a flight simulator, in a flight simulator that is so vivid and real that it's impossible to tell from the real thing.

But now we're going to do something a little different. Now you are going to learn another way to fly. In the first exercise you have learned how to let your mind be comfortable while your body was shipped from one place to another. Now in the second exercise you have learned how to be comfortable while going through a realistic imitation of the experiences involved in flight.

But actually, this pretend flight on the flight simulator has been so realistic that in a way you can't tell it from the real thing. The experience of being in the flight simulator is exactly like the experience of being in an airplane, and it is not frightening. You have a way of experiencing all of the events of an airplane flight but none of the fear.

So now let's go on to the final exercise.

Fearless Flying

This is an exercise which allows you to combine the benefits of "shipping the body" with "flight simulator." As is the case with the latter, it is too long to be done at a single sitting and common break points are indicated. Once again, if at any point you should find yourself becoming anxious, immediately interrupt yourself and go to your pleasant scene. From that nice scene, when you have fully relaxed, you can return to an earlier spot in the exercise, one which you have managed easily already. It is also very important that as you go through this exercise, you do not leap ahead. When you are told to imagine thinking about going on vacation, for example, you do not imagine yourself in the airplane already. As you think of each step along the way, be sure to keep yourself right at that moment rather than in some future time.

Imagine yourself just thinking about taking a trip. It might be a vacation to a far-off land; perhaps it is a visit to family or friends who live far away. It's a pleasant trip, one you would like to make. And as you think about it, you realize that the best way to get there is by airplane. The plane will get you there quickly and easily so you can spend your vacation at your destination rather than on the way. As you continue with your preparation, you remember to be particularly careful not to jump ahead to later in the process. Right now all you are doing is thinking about taking a trip and deciding that the best way to travel would be by plane.

You've thought about it and decided that two months from now you are going to take a trip and that you are going to go by air. At this point you don't have to do anything with airplanes; you just need to call the airline or your travel agent and make a reservation. That's right. You get out the phone book, look up the number, and make the phone call. You explain where you would like to go and when. The agent is polite, friendly, and helpful. You discuss fares and options. Together you find the flight which is best for you. You tell the agent that you wish to make a reservation for the flight you have selected.

And you make the reservation. There's nothing frightening. All you've really done is to make a phone call and reserve space on the flight that you want to be on. You thank the agent for her or his help and hang up the phone feeling very good about yourself and your ability to take care of yourself this way. It will be two months before you actually go.

And now you settle into the routine of daily life. By far, the bulk of your attention is focused on the events or circumstances which make up the fabric of your life. When you occasionally think ahead to your trip, your thoughts are of the destination, not the traveling. If you were planning to go to an eagerly anticipated movie, your advance thoughts would be of seeing the movie. They would not be of driving to the theater, finding a parking place, or standing in line for the tickets. Those are nuisances that are done in order to achieve the goal: seeing the movie. So it is with your trip. Your purpose is being there, not getting there.

(Common break point.)

A week passes and the mail comes. As you sort through the stack of envelopes, you find the one you've been awaiting. It contains the tickets to your destination. These are the tickets that will get you where you want to be. You're glad to see them. You spend a minute thinking about how good it will be to be there, then you put them away in a safe place. You have things to do. You go on about your life.

Days pass. It is now six weeks until your trip. You're looking forward to being there, but you can't spend all your time in the future. You go back to the business of living your daily life. Time passes. In a month it will be time to be there. You're looking forward to it, knowing what a good time you will have there. But meanwhile, you have a present in which you live.

More time passes. Three weeks until your trip. Two weeks until your trip. One week to go. Now it makes sense to begin making more active plans. You call the newspaper and tell them to interrupt delivery while you're away. You tell the post office to hold the mail. You talk to a neighbor to say that you're going to be away so please keep an eye on your place. You're going about the details of preparing to be where you want to be next week. Two days pass. It's five days until your trip. You make sure the clothes you wish to take are clean and ready. If necessary, you take them to the cleaners or do the laundry. Two more days pass. Your preparations continue. Another day passes. You're looking forward to being there. As part of your preparation, you get out your suitcases so you will be ready to begin packing.

(Common break point.)

Tomorrow is your trip. You can hardly wait because tomorrow you will be just where you want to be. You do your packing. You decide which clothes you need and want with you there. You pack your suitcase and enjoy the sense of anticipation and excitement that is natural before such an enjoyable visit. You're aware that you are becoming excited at the prospect of being there. This excitement is a normal and natural sensation. Some of the physical manifestations of this excitement are quite similar to those of anxiety, but with the difference that this excitement is about something eagerly anticipated, not something feared and dreaded. If the excitement goes beyond enjoyment, you will be able to rein it in. Or you may choose to stop it without hypnosis by focusing on what it is you are doing at that moment. For example, while you are packing, you might feel yourself getting pleasantly excited because you know that packing is the prelude to being there. If the excitement ceases to be pleasant, you can change it by focusing on the actual act of packing. As you do so, you realize that packing a suitcase is really quite a dull, even boring, exercise. Pick up a piece of clothing, fold it neatly, and put it into a suitcase; then pick up the next piece of clothing and repeat. Actually, there's nothing either frightening or highly pleasurable about this. People who work at laundries folding and putting away the clean clothes do not get combat pay, nor do they pay for the right to do it. It's simply a job. Simply a task. As you prepare for your trip, you have the choice of enjoying the anticipation of being at your destination, or of reducing the tasks to their basic level, carrying something to the car, driving along, parking the car, and so on.

(Common break point.)

Now the day is passed. It's time for bed. Tomorrow you will be at your destination. You realize how glad you will be to be there. And you know that you can comfortably relax because you have your choice of two different ways to be there. There are two different ways of using hypnosis to ensure that you will be able to travel, to ensure that you will get to your goal without discomfort. You can either ship your body to catch up with your mind, which will already be at your destination, or you can travel in the flight simulator. As you settle into bed, you decide that tomorrow you will use the first of these ways. But now you need to get a good night's sleep so you will be well rested for tomorrow.

Now it's the morning. You wake up and say to yourself that today's the day you'll be going to your destination. And you have two ways of getting there. And what's nice about it is that you are in charge of which method you wish to use. You've decided you're going to start by shipping your body. So first thing when you wake up, you start the day with an hypnotic induction. You bring yourself into trance, let yourself be so relaxed and comfortable. Your mind is already at your destination, and you are going to trust those whom you have already chosen to get your body there safely.

Now, you could do this all the way there. You could do this as you practiced when you learned to ship the body.

Or you might get a little bored with that. You might decide

that there are interesting things going on in the world, things that you would like to be involved in and to participate in. If that should happen, you will be able to choose to slip easily into becoming aware of what is going on around you as if it were a flight simulator. If you wish, you can imagine yourself pretending to fly as in fact you travel to your destination. You'll feel completely safe allowing yourself to do this because you will know that should there be even the merest whisper of discomfort, you will be able immediately to shift back to your peaceful scene and ship your body.

Or you may even find as you travel along in the flight simulator that now that you are no longer frightened; this is in fact a rather interesting and enjoyable experience, one in which you would like to participate. If you wish, you can even leave the flight simulator and be in the real airplane, having learned how to be relaxed and comfortable in that environment. They are the same. The choice is yours, and it makes you feel really good to know that you are in control.

When you are ready to end this exercise, open your eyes and bring yourself back to the usual waking state.

Public Speaking

A great many people suffer acute anxiety when they have to perform in public. One of the most common of these so-called performance anxieties is difficulty in public speaking. It ranges from a mild discomfort all the way up to a disabling panic that leaves some people literally unable to speak at all, even though their very livelihoods may depend upon public address.

Fortunately, this is often a very treatable difficulty.

As is the case with many anxieties, people with a fear of public speaking can be roughly divided into two groups. The first group consists of those who really do wish to be able to speak in public, but tension interferes with their performance. This difficulty may arise because people want so much to perform well that they press too hard and so get in their own way. Athletes, for example, may so strongly wish to do well in a pressure situation that instead of simply performing successfully as in practice, they try to do something even better, choke, and end up doing less well.

The other category includes people whose anxieties reflect serious ambivalence about performing. If "I don't want to" is not acceptable as an answer, "I cannot" becomes a useful backup. If a child does not want to do something but is pushed by a demanding parent, an inability to perform may be the only way out. In such cases, learning to control the anxiety associated with performance frequently leads to a struggle that goes something like "You can," "No, I can't," "Yes, you can," "No, I can't." The final result of such an argument can always be summed up as "I'm sorry, I tried my best, but I really can't." This unconstructive process merely adds an extra layer of self-doubt, shame, and guilt to the feelings of inadequacy.

Few people are pure and simple examples of either those who press too hard or those who are ambivalent about performing. Some blending of both characteristics is most common. What becomes important in treatment is the ratio or proportion of one to the other. The more a person fits the former description, the more likely he or she is to improve with a direct approach of hypnotic exercises. In addition, learning to be able to perform in public generally results in such an increase in self-esteem that some of the doubts or conflicts which originally fueled the fear become outmoded, wither, and die.

For those who are more strongly influenced by the second sort of dynamics, a straightforward attempt to make the uncomfortable feelings go away is likely to be less than successful. In fact, one way of assessing the extent to which a person is unambivalently eager to overcome the performance anxiety is to attempt treatment and see how it goes.

If it becomes clear that the symptoms aren't clearing up easily, the best path might well be to stop and reconsider the whole situation. This assessment must begin with the question "Why perform at all?" Frequently the why includes motivations both of one's own and of other people. A person must then ask himself or herself, regardless of what anyone else thinks, "What do I want? Do I truly wish to perform? Or would I really rather not?"

Three possible courses may emerge from this process. First, having been able to examine the complex web of anxiety, a person comes to realize that he or she really does wish to perform. This realization may land the person in the group whose performance anxiety responds well to straightforward treatment. Second, a person may decide that he or she really does not want to perform. With this decision comes the freedom to say, "It's not that I can't, I just don't want to." Since there is then no need to perform, there's no need for anxiety either. Or third, the person might decide that it is important enough to perform so that he or she is unwilling to stop trying even while in part feeling strongly negative about it. In such a case, psychotherapy would be helpful in resolving this conflict.

Practicing Speaking

Although the following techniques are those used for reduction of anxiety in public speaking, they are adaptable to any other sort of performance that involves a rehearsed presentation. An actor could follow these exercises, as could a musician, just substituting "playing an instrument" or "singing" for "speaking." Athletes, such as figure skaters or gymnasts, could use "running through the routine" instead of "talking."

Before beginning, think about a topic which you find interesting, some topic that you know something about and find to be an enjoyable one. In a few moments you are going to begin to think comfortably about saying a few words. If you have to think of what the topic is going to be as well as saying it, that's going to make it a little more difficult. So you are going to help yourself by picking out in advance a topic that you feel comfortable with. Perhaps it will be a hobby of yours; perhaps it will be talking about your job; perhaps it will be chatting about relatives, or sports. You might prefer to talk about something objective, limiting yourself to facts and details, or you might prefer to talk about your opinion, what you think of a subject. Whichever you choose will be fine. Once you've chosen the topic, prepare a brief talk that you might give on this subject. You might find it more comfortable to work out in detail a complete script that you would present verbatim. You may wish to write it down and read it or you might prefer to memorize it, perhaps aided by notes. Or you might prefer to have thoughts and ideas clear in your mind but allow yourself to choose specific words when you are actually talking.

Now settle yourself into a peaceful, comfortable relaxed state of hypnosis, and as you do, imagine yourself going off to your peaceful, comfortable scene. There you are in this place of total serenity and calm. As we go along, ideas will be suggested, and as you think of them, you will be able to stay calm, comfortable, relaxed, and at ease. You know that hypnosis allows you to control your muscles and keep them relaxed. And you know that if you keep your muscles relaxed, you will keep your mind relaxed. If it should start to happen that you go too quickly and start to become anxious, you are not to try to hold on and tolerate or suffer through that tension. The purpose of this exercise is not to teach you to bear discomfort but to learn to become comfortable. If you should become tense or uncomfortable, you should immediately stop the suggestion that you were working on and return to this peaceful, comfortable scene, alone, safe, and secure. When you have recovered your sense of comfort and peace, you should not immediately return to the last part of the exercise you were doing; instead, go back to an earlier part which you have previously mastered. That's right. There's no rush here. You have a whole lifetime to benefit from this change, so go back to a part that you have already easily mastered and go on from there.

While you are all alone, safe and secure in your comfortable protected scene, look around and see that you are alone, that no one is there to overhear you. All alone, safe, no one is listening. Now just say your name out loud. That's right. You know how to do that. You have a voice that works perfectly well. It's made to do things like this. It's natural for it to do such things as speak your name. That's fine. Now, still alone, please begin to give your little talk that you have prepared. You may be doing it verbatim, or you may be speaking extemporaneously, whichever is more comfortable. If it feels more comfortable, you can even switch from one to the other as you go along. That's right. Peaceful and relaxed and saying a few words on a topic of your choosing while you're all alone. And as you finish, you feel very good, very pleased with yourself. You realize that you are quite capable of speaking, quite capable of expressing your thoughts and ideas. There is no problem with your ability to perform the physical act of talking.

Now staying all alone in your comfortable scene, you begin to think about the fact that the actual process of talking is the same whether you are alone or with others. You are not going to test this yet. But you do recognize that what you do, talking, is not directly affected by anyone else.

Let's try something to test that out. You're still alone in your safe and protected place. No one is there to hear you. But imagine what it would be like to pretend that someone is there with you. No one will really be there; no one will really be able to hear. But just imagine what it would be like if someone you like, someone who likes you a great deal, were there with you. You might think of it rather like talking to a photograph of a loved one. The person is not really there, but you are thinking of him or her somewhat. Now, as you remain alone but thinking about someone, once again, while comfortable and relaxed, say your name and give your brief talk. That's right.

You see that talking remained the same when you were all alone whether you were thinking of another person or not. That's excellent.

In fact, that was so good that you might do that same exercise a second time. That's right. All alone in your safe place, thinking about that possibility of someone you like being with you, but all alone and in your solitude peacefully and comfortably delivering your talk. And as you finish, you hear the voice of the friend about whom you were thinking saying to you, "That really was interesting. You did a great job with that talk." And so you realize with a delighted shock of surprise that giving the talk was the same whether your friend was there to hear it or not. You thought you were alone, and so the talk was as easy as if you had been alone. In fact, your friend was there listening. That didn't make the talk any harder. This makes you feel good, calm and relaxed.

Your friend says that he wasn't there for all of it, but he did like what he heard. He'd like you to repeat it, this time with him there listening to the whole thing. You realize that you've already done it, that this is not something new, so you say, "Sure." Although perhaps getting a little bored with this topic, repeat the talk once again. And as you do, you realize quite clearly that talking is something that you do regardless of who is or is not present. You realize that some of your other friends might like to hear what you have to say on this subject.

You probably could invite them over, but instead you decide to take things one step at a time. You and your friend look around and make certain that none of your other friends are nearby. The surprise was pleasant for one time, but you don't need to repeat it. So there you are, just the two of you. But in your mind's eye, you imagine a few select friends there with you forming an audience. Once again, you deliver your talk, this time to one real friend and a few imaginary ones. It goes very well, so well that you decide to take the next step.

That's right. Invite those few friends whom you imagined to be with you to your special relaxed place. Let them sit around and get comfortable, and then when everyone is ready, you get up and make your little speech. Everyone finds it very interesting and has a good time.

It's becoming clearer and clearer to you that speaking is something that you do, not something the audience does. You can speak when you are alone, and you can speak in front of others. In fact the job does not change at all.

Why not invite a few more friends to join you. You might wish to shift the scene to a less private and personal spot to accommodate these extra people. So you go to some comfortable spot and once again deliver your talk. It goes well once again. And you realize that you're capable of giving a good talk over and over and over. It's not luck or an accident. It's something you are quite capable of doing.

Why not let the audience expand a little bit, not so much in numbers, but expand to include not only your friends and loved ones but also people whom you do not know so well, people who are more neutral to you. And you realize this is the same talk, that your task is the same, and so you begin to speak, staying relaxed and comfortable, peaceful and at ease.

And you decide that it's getting a little crowded, and so, for the comfort of the audience, you're going to go to a moderate-sized room with chairs set up in rows and a podium in the front. And there everyone can gather to sit down in comfort and listen to your talk. Of course it goes very well. There's no reason for it to do anything else. Going well is the natural thing for it to do. You realize you could give this talk a million times and it would go well a million times. You understand that if anyone were to attempt to give a talk without adequate preparation, he might have a harder time. If he didn't know the material or didn't know what he was trying to say, he might not give as smooth a delivery. Now of course, people can speak on the spur of the moment or about subjects that they have not fully explored, but it's important that they realize as they talk that their ideas are shaping and being formulated as they speak, and so naturally it feels a little different, less polished, than a formal presentation.

But you know that you can talk about subjects which you have not prepared a talk about. You do it every day. Any time you are thinking, you are going through the process of sorting through your thoughts, organizing your ideas, and thinking of words to express yourself. You know that you can talk, and you have just learned to be able to speak in front of a group. Now, go back to the beginning of this exercise and go through it again. This time will be even easier because instead of giving a prepared talk, you are going to give a few words on whatever happens to be on your mind at that moment. Whatever you are thinking of will be OK. At each appropriate place, just say a few words about whatever comes to mind. When you are ready to end this exercise, open your eyes and bring yourself back to the usual waking state.

Strong and Powerful

There are a number of additional techniques that can be of use. Some people find them helpful by themselves. Many people like to use them in conjunction with the above general exercise. This next exercise is designed to combat feelings of inadequacy or negative judgment.

———◆◆◆———

As you're feeling very relaxed and comfortable, you begin to notice, to pay attention to, your breathing. Your breathing is slow, regular, and comfortable. As you begin to speak, you remember to breathe in a sufficient quantity of air to provide your vocal chords with what they need. And as you do, as you notice your breathing, you realize that whenever you are exhaling your breath, as the breath leaves your body, so does any tension, that as you exhale out the air, you're also pumping the tension out of your body. Even as you speak, as the air leaves your lungs, so the tension leaves your muscles.

But there's something else as well. As you inhale, as you fill your lungs with air, you become aware of a sense of strength rippling through your muscles. Your body is strong and powerful. You are in command. You are in control. Your body is strong and powerful, full of energy, more than able to take on the challenges.

It's a nice blend you feel. You're aware of your strength but relaxed and at ease. You have the power to do whatever needs to be done. But you're relaxed, calm, and comfortable as you deliver your message. That's right. Each time you breathe in, you remember how strong and powerful you are. And with each word you speak, as you exhale the air, you feel your muscles relax.

This strength gives you a sense of size. You feel yourself becoming taller, stronger, more powerful. You feel yourself towering over the audience. You are the most powerful one present. It is you who is speaking. It is you to whom everyone is looking. And you are feeling so strong that you are glad of your role. You're feeling strong and able. You are in charge. You are the boss. But with each word you speak, you let yourself feel the relaxation as the tension drains from your body. You are strong and powerful, but relaxed and at ease, comfortable and at peace, able to do whatever it is you choose to do.

When you are ready to end this exercise, open your eyes and bring yourself back to the usual waking state.

"Remembering" Your Presentation

Instead of worrying about how a speech will turn out, you give yourself a happy ending to "remember." In this way, you go into your presentation feeling successful.

━━━◆●◆━━━

Before you give your talk, you first settle yourself into a deep state of relaxed concentration and imagination and attention, and when you have got yourself deeply into this state, you're going to take a journey in your mind, a journey through time and space. You imagine yourself moving ahead through time to right after your presentation, right after your talk. That's right. You have just completed your talk. It's not in your future. It's in your immediate past. And you look out at the audience and you see that everyone thinks you did a great job. Everyone is very appreciative of the wonderful talk you have just given. And you know that this should be so because you know that it was a good talk. And you know that you presented it well. That's right. You're very happy with the job you did, and your audience is happy, too. They come up to you and say, "Well done." They let you know what a good job you did. Some of them ask questions, the sort of questions that let you know not only that they were paying attention and found you interesting, but also that they respect you. They really care what you think. They really want to know what you have to say about the subject.

And as you bask in the contentment and peace that goes with a job well done, and as you enjoy the appreciation and praise of others, you think back. You think back to a few minutes before. You think back to the moments just before you began to give your talk. And you review in your mind walking up and giving your talk. You're remembering it while basking in the sweet glow of success and the approval of your audience. You are remembering something that you know went well. And as you do, you remember beginning to speak. You remember how clear your voice was. You remember how sharp your ideas were. You remember the good feeling, feeling strong but relaxed as you spoke about this subject. You didn't need to look out at the audience. You knew it was good. You knew your ideas were coming across. You realized that it didn't really matter if others agreed with you or not. It didn't matter whether anyone else approved of you because you knew that this was good and that if they were smart, they agreed with you. If they didn't like what you were saying, that was a reflection on them. But you know that they did. They did appreciate, they did enjoy hearing you. Your words were clear, your message sharp. That's right. And you go all the way through your talk, all the way to the conclusion right up to now, as the audience is coming up afterward, congratulating you on such an excellent job. Well done.

Altered Audience

A great many people are bothered by the thought of their audience. For some, any visible audience is intimidating. For others, it's not the presence of any sort of audience that bothers them, but specific members of the audience. Some people, for example, are glad to see their friends in the audience but would be worried by the presence of a teacher who was grading the talk. Some people do not mind being seen by strangers but do not like to be seen by those who know them. For some people, not only the presence of the audience but also the size of the room is intimidating.

This exercise can be tailored accordingly. The audience can become a faceless blur of nameless people or be filled with friends and well-wishers or stay the same with the exception that the judges' booth remains empty. If the room is bothersome, a familiar one, such as a kitchen, can be used.

———◆◆◆◆———

You know that in order to deliver a successful talk to an audience, your job is merely to do the talking. The audience has to do the listening on their own. Your half of the job remains the same whether the audience is present or not. You have to say the things that you have to say. If you were giving a televised address, for example, your job would be the same if every television in the country were tuned to you or if none were. Your job would be the same whether the television camera were working properly or not. You don't need to see the audience. In fact, as far as you are concerned, the audience doesn't have to be there at all. This technique is not something that everyone can do, but for those who can, it can be extremely useful.

Before you give your presentation, enter a state of deep concentration and hypnosis, and in this state, visualize the place where your audience would be. But instead of a gallery filled with people, you see nothing but empty seats. That's right. Every seat is empty. No one is there. This is great. You are going to present your talk to an empty auditorium. It is going to be as if you were practicing all by yourself with no one with you. You make this image very clear, this image of the empty auditorium. And you hold this image in your mind's eye and suggest to yourself that when you go to give your speech, you will focus on seeing this image, rather than on what your eye would ordinarily see. There is no need for you to look at the reality of the audience. You don't have to do their job. You just need to do your own. You focus on your job of delivering your talk and let your vision be supplanted by your mind's eye, and you see the empty seats and see yourself alone. And in doing so, it becomes exactly as if you are alone with no audience. And you know how easy it is to talk when you are alone.

When you are ready to end this exercise, open your eyes and bring yourself back to the usual waking state.

Variation of Altered Audience

Let yourself settle down, comfortable and relaxed, and think ahead to seeing your audience in front of you. But as you do, take pleasure in the fact that you are going to control what you are going to see. As you look out on your audience, you are going to be struck by two different things. First of all, you are aware of how strong you feel, how good you look. You dominate. You are larger, stronger. You are the speaker. You look bigger, stronger, better than any of them. Of course, that would not be hard to do because as you look at your audience, you realize just how bad they look. It will be fun to see just how bad you make them look. Perhaps they're sitting there in their underwear. It's rather unattractive underwear at that, with fat, fish-belly white skin exposed for all to see, like so many naked emperors. You may notice a certain slack-jawed look of dull incomprehension. There's not much light behind those eyes. They're struggling manfully to keep up with your ideas, but many of them are sitting there scratching their heads like Stan Laurel. Or perhaps they're dressed even more honestly. Perhaps those clowns are in their full makeup and circus gear. You look out over the audience with their painted white faces, round red noses, and odd tufts of frizzy red hair. They may be having a little trouble focusing on your talk because of all the seltzer water and rubber chickens flying among them. Perhaps they have their clown makeup on, but no clothing. And you realize that you may laugh at these people. You may look down on them, you may pity them, but you certainly do not fear them.

When you are ready to end this exercise, open your eyes and bring yourself back to the usual waking state.

Controlling Voice Volume

Sometimes people worry about the way their voice sounds. This is an exercise designed to give you a sense of your own control over your ability to change the volume of your voice to whatever you desire.

As you're deeply relaxed and settled in, visualize in your mind's eye a knob, like the volume control on a radio or stereo. That's right. You see the knob has markings on it from a volume so low as to be inaudible to a very loud volume. But this volume control is not for some mechanical instrument. This controls your voice. In a moment, we're going to test it. In order to do so, you're going to have to make a noise out loud. Because this is just a test, we are going to use not words but a simple sound. Now, without adjusting the volume control, begin to make the sound "oooooo." See how loud that was in your ears. It probably was a low medium volume. It might have been quieter than that or louder though. Whatever it was, you can now tell where the volume was set by your control. Now take that volume and twist it all the way to the left. In a moment you're going to make your "oooooo" sound, and when you do, you re going to see how soft, how almost inaudible it is. Now try it. That's right. "Oooooo." You could hardly hear it, could you?

Now we're going to do a little more playing with it. In a moment, you're going to say "oooooo" once again, and as you do, you're going to begin to twist the volume control to the right to increase the volume. Not to very loud, but to a moderate volume. And then you're going to twist it a little bit back to the left. So you're going to go smoothly up from nearly inaudible to moderate and then back down to fairly quiet. Now try it. "Oooooo." That's excellent. Now we're going to go up to very loud. Starting where you last finished, you're going to go up to a quite high volume, then come back to medium loudness. Now go ahead. "Oooooo."

When you're ready to end this exercise, open your eyes and bring yourself back to the usual waking state.

6

Insomnia

Insomnia plagues a great many victims in one or more of its various forms. Some people are bothered by occasional disturbances in their sleeping patterns while others suffer almost every night. Sleep disorders take many forms. Some people have trouble falling asleep at night but then slumber soundly once they have done so. Others go to sleep easily but wake up in the middle of the night and remain alert for a long time before returning to sleep. Still others awaken early in the morning before getting enough rest. Worst are "white nights" spent without a wink of sleep. Many suffer combinations of these symptoms.

Insomnia can be a product of anxiety, a bad habit, or a symptom of different sorts of problems. Individuals with sleep apnea stop breathing when they fall asleep and so must wake up in order not to suffocate. While insomnia can be a symptom of depression, sometimes people get depressed over their lack of sleep, not the other way around. If there is a question of any illness causing the insomnia, it should of course be worked up by an expert. Frequently, though, insomnia is a problem all by itself. As such it is easily treatable, and you should find that it is not difficult to learn how to get all the rest you need at night.

Not everyone requires eight hours of sleep per night any more than all women are five feet six inches tall. Sleep needs are like most physical traits, varying from one person to the next.

Some people require more than eight hours a night, some require less. Some of those who require less spend a great deal of time and energy worrying that they are not getting "enough" sleep when in fact they are. Women tend to need somewhat more sleep than men, and the amount needed tends to decrease with age, but individual needs are more important than group averages.

Sleep is necessary because it allows two important functions to be carried out, one mental and one physical.

The first task of sleep is to allow dreaming to take place. You do not dream all of the time you are asleep. In fact, dreaming requires only a small fraction of the whole time that you sleep. However this period, known as rapid-eye-movement sleep, or REM sleep, is extremely important. During REM sleep your brain scans the events of the day, which have been recorded in short-term memory during the last twenty-four hours or so, and reviews them. Memories are played back at high speed, and decisions are made about which events are to be put into long-term memory for permanent storage and which can be erased and forgotten. Without dreaming there is no long-term memory. While the day's events are being replayed as if on fast-forward, the mind catches bits and pieces of them and weaves them into a story, the dream.

Sleep is also the time when your body does its house keeping. All day long your muscles are using up energy supplies faster than your bloodstream can replenish them. At the same time, your muscles are producing waste products, mostly lactic acid, faster than your blood can carry them away. This means that as you are active your muscles get further and further behind, using up supplies and building up lactic acid. This process is reversed at night. While you are asleep, your muscles are extremely relaxed. As a result, your blood can supply your muscles with the nutrients they need faster than they are used, so stockpiles are replenished and the muscles are ready to go the next day. In addition, your bloodstream can carry off the built-up lactic acid so that your muscles can start the new day clean and fresh. In a way, you can think of your body as being like an office building. During the day, the office workers, while busy doing their jobs, make a mess of the place. They use up supplies, fill wastebaskets, track mud all over floors, and generally get the building dirty faster than the housekeeping staff can clean it. In the evening, when most of the office workers have left, the cleaners come in. They empty the wastebaskets, replenish the supplies, clean the floors. In the morning, the cycle begins again. So, too, with your body.

Sleep's first job, dreaming, is almost impossible to prevent without resorting to extreme measures. There are drugs which suppress dreaming. In sleep laboratories, experiments are sometimes done in which a subject, sleeping with monitored electroencephalograph leads, is forcefully awakened the instant he or she begins to enter REM sleep. Sometimes people are kept from dreaming in a cruder way. They are forcefully prevented from sleeping. Even then, however, dreams have their way. People who are prevented from dreaming for days at a time will begin to enter dream states while "awake." The brain's need for dreams is so powerful that eventually one has them with or without sleep.

In practical terms, this irrepressibility means that you don't have to worry about getting your dreaming done. You couldn't stop yourself from dreaming. Even if you sleep for only a few minutes a night, your brain will make sure that you get to dream sufficiently. If you sleep for only a few minutes, you will almost immediately enter REM sleep and complete your needed dream work.

That leaves the task of cleaning up your body after the day's work. This housekeeping is an important job, and this is why it takes so long to get your sleeping done. While dreaming takes minutes, cleanup takes hours. However, it's not necessary that your brain's electrical activity be in a state called *sleep* for the process of removing lactic acid to occur. Once dreaming is done, what you really need is a good night's *rest*. What is really essential is that your muscles be extremely relaxed. A person who lies in bed awake and tense all night feels horrible the next morning not because she or he didn't sleep but, more accurately, because her or his muscles were not relaxed enough to allow them to recover from the previous day.

Hypnosis can relax muscles. Hypnosis is not sleep, but some

aspects of it are so like sleep that it was named *hypnosis* after the Greek god of sleep. In these exercises, you're going to learn techniques which ensure either that you will get a good night's sleep or else that you will get a good night's rest through hypnosis.

The Job of Resting

This exercise allows you to gain control over what interferes with getting adequate rest and is the first step in what is often a two-step treatment strategy.

Enter hypnosis. As you settle back, deeply and comfortably relaxed, a sense of peace, calm, and well-being comes over you. This is a sense based upon a feeling of security. You know that you have the capacity to have a good night's rest. Perhaps you'll have a good night's sleep, or perhaps you'll have a good night's hypnosis, but either way you know that you are going to greet the morning relaxed, refreshed, and well rested.

You know that one of the enemies of sleep is anxiety about whether or not you'll be able to do it. Sleep is not something that you can consciously choose to do. As much as you may want it, you can't make yourself do it. And you think about how often you have lain awake tense, nervous, trying to will yourself asleep, afraid that you may fail to do so, afraid that this failure will leave you tired, unable to cope with the next day. In the past this fear has set up a powerful performance anxiety. You have felt so desperate to succeed in falling asleep that it has interfered with your ability to do so. But now you relax because you know that it is all under control.

You know that you have the ability to decide consciously to do something that is under your control, and that if you do this, you will certainly feel rested in the morning. It doesn't matter if your trouble comes when trying to fall asleep, or in the middle of the night if you wake up then, or if you wake up early in the morning. No matter what, you will have the ability to do something which will relax your muscles as much as if you had been asleep. And this knowledge feels so good, so reassuring, so relaxing, that it's almost enough just by itself to let you relax and go to sleep. If that happens, that's fine. Throughout these exercises, you're going to be learning to do things which make it easier to fall asleep and which can substitute for sleep if necessary. If you fall asleep rather than complete the exercise, that will be fine. If you keep doing the exercise rather than fall asleep, that will be fine, too.

As you think about it, you realize that sleep is not a difficult thing to do. Babies don't need to be taught how to fall asleep. Sleeping is one of the very few things that you are born knowing how to do. It's not something tough like walking or talking. Animals know how to sleep, even animals low on the evolutionary scale. You've been afraid that you wouldn't know how to sleep. Sleeping is the easy part. Staying awake is the hard part. With your insomnia, you've learned how to do something that's very difficult. You have learned to overcome your body's natural tendency to sleep. It's hard to stay awake, but you learned how to do it. This is going to be the easy lesson. Learning how to sleep is learning how to do what your body does naturally.

First comes the most important part of all. You have to decide that this is a time for sleep. You have decided that it's time for sleep and that it will remain time to sleep until the time in the morning that you have designated. This important decision means that anything else is a distraction. If there is something that comes to mind that you really must deal with right away, you must get up, get out of bed, and go and do it. If there is some bit of business that really needs to be attended to, that won't wait until morning, then you cannot stay in bed. You have to get up and tend to it. You can't do that lying in bed because you might fall asleep. But you've decided that there's nothing that can't wait. And as you think about that, you realize that everything else has to wait. If you try thinking about some important decision in the middle of the night, you're going to have to think about it in the morning all over again. No one in their right mind would trust a decision made in the middle of a sleepless night, so there's no sense in even thinking about it. There's no sense in thinking about anything. Your job is to be asleep or else to be so restful that it's as if you're asleep. You have no other job at this time. And now that you realize that, you are going to be able to take command, to give yourself the rest you need.

Now that you've made this crucial decision, there are a variety of techniques that you can use to keep you in this relaxed state. Some nights you may wish to use one; some nights you may wish to use another. But regardless, you will get a good night's rest. You just choose the one that seems best to you at that time.

When you get into bed at night, you have a choice of whether to begin your rest right away or to lie awake in bed, perhaps reading or watching TV or talking. While you're choosing to be awake, that is fine. However, as soon as you decide that it is time to begin your rest, you immediately place yourself in an hypnotic trance, getting yourself deeply relaxed and focused. You are not going to let your mind wander where it will. You have a job to do. If you wanted to let yourself just lie there and see if you went to sleep, that would have been OK. However, you've decided that you are going to guarantee your rest, and that means you have a job to do, a job of relaxing.

If you should wake up during the night, you will glance over at the clock and see if it is time for you to get up yet. If it is, then of course you will get up and begin your day, feeling relaxed and refreshed after a good night's rest. If it is not time to get up, however, you will immediately recognize that this is sleep time. If your bladder is full, you can empty it. If you are thirsty, you can get a drink. Otherwise, your job is to return to the resting state either immediately or immediately after your trip to the bathroom. You focus your attention on entering a state of hypnosis and then you go through whatever you like of the following five exercises.

Floating on a Cloud

This exercise strengthens the sense of relaxation and peace begun earlier.

As you've entered this relaxed state of imagination, concentration, and attention called *hypnosis*, you feel yourself comfortably floating along. Do it any way that seems best to you. Perhaps you'd like to imagine yourself on a boat floating along on a smooth, still surface of water. Or perhaps you would like to be lying back on a flying carpet, or perhaps you would like to be floating on a cloud. As you float, you focus all your attention on the sense of peace, of calm, of tranquillity. Your muscles are becoming totally relaxed, totally relaxed. A pleasant, comfortable heaviness overcomes your limbs. Your muscles feel limp . . . warm, heavy, and limp . . . without strength or energy. Of course, as is necessary to remain comfortable, you may occasionally shift your position somewhat, but mostly you remain limp, motionless, too deeply, too thoroughly relaxed even to think about moving.

With each breath you exhale, any tenseness that might be in your body is exhaled as well. You are settled back, peaceful, comfortable, at ease, floating along, drifting along, floating along so nicely, so easily, so peacefully. All of your thoughts are on this sensation of floating, focusing on floating, feeling the floating, feeling alone in the universe, floating along, and as you do, you begin to feel as though you might even be asleep. You begin to lose track of whether you are asleep and dreaming about floating or deeply hypnotized and imagining yourself floating. It's a question to which you don't devote much interest or attention. It's academic. It doesn't really matter. What matters is that you are floating along, so comfortably floating along.

Keeping Your Mind Busy

To prevent your mind from wandering to wakeful thoughts, you give it a task, such as one of those suggested below.

Perhaps you would like to add something to the sense of floating along. There's no need, but if you wish to, you can. Perhaps you find that as you're lying there, so relaxed and at peace, your mind begins to work, begins to think about things that you are worried about or concerned about or happy about. It doesn't really matter what sort of thing. If you are having trouble keeping your mind focused on the floating, then you need to add something. You've already decided that you don't need to think about any of these things, whether good or bad. You've already decided that this is your time for rest. It's just that when you don't think of anything, a mental vacuum is formed. These different thoughts then flow into the vacuum to fill it. You are then left thinking all these thoughts, which may be pleasant or unpleasant but are not relaxing. These thoughts then need to go.

Telling yourself not to think about something doesn't work. If you say to yourself, "Don't think about an elephant," you quickly have in your mind's eye two gray floppy ears, a long flexible trunk, and gleaming ivory tusks. The more you say "Don't think of an elephant," the more you do think of the elephant. If, however, you focus your attention on imagining tropical fish swimming around in a coral reef, focusing all your attention on visualizing those fish, the elephant will be out of your mind.

What you need, then, is some stuffing to fill up the vacuum. You don't want to fill it with anything too interesting because, if it is too interesting, you will pay attention to it and stay awake to see what will happen next. On the other hand, if it is not interesting enough, it will not hold your attention and keep your mind from wandering to exciting subjects.

One thing you might do is to picture in your mind's eye a blackboard. A perfectly black chalkboard with not one trace of white on it. When you have that in your mind's eye, you mentally pick up a piece of chalk and write a perfectly straight 1 and two perfectly shaped zeros. That's right: 100. If the digits are not perfectly formed, they must be erased to a perfectly black chalkboard and redone. When this perfect 100 has been registered, though, you pick up the eraser and erase every trace of it, back to pure blackboard. When it is perfectly black, you again pick up the chalk and make a perfect 9 followed by a second. That's right: 99. Again, if the digits are not made correctly, they have to be redone. If they are perfect, they are erased to a perfectly black background and replaced by 98. You continue in this fashion all the way down to zero if necessary. At zero, you begin the process of counting back up.

If you should fall asleep in the middle of doing this, that will be fine. If you stay awake and go up and down from 100 to zero to 100 to zero for hours, that will be all right, too. You may find as you count down that your concentration wavers and you're not sure, for example, if 94 was your last number or your next number. That's all right, but you do have to start over again at 100. Your task is to stay focused and think of nothing else. If your attention wanders, that's all right, but you have to begin at the beginning as a way of telling yourself that this is your job.

Or perhaps you don't like numbers. That's fine. There's a whole alphabet waiting for you. In fact, there are a number of alphabets. You can do block capitals or small letters the way they're printed by a typewriter. You can do italics. You can do script. You can do the Greek alphabet if you know it. Whichever you choose will be fine.

Or you may wish to focus on your breathing, your slow, regular, peaceful, and comfortable breathing. You may wish to count your breaths. You may wish to count patterns of breathing. Your first breath would be numbered 1. Your next breath would be numbered 1 followed by 2, then 1, then 2, then 3. Each breath is a number; each number is a breath. Then 1, then 2, then 3, then 4. Now time to go back: 1, 2, 3; 1, 2; then 1. You might wish to visualize these numbers as tiles being arranged, making patterns. You might want to imagine a grid of numbers with each breath a block on the graph. Each breath you exhale fills in a square and you work through the patterns of filling in each square. You might like to visualize a checkerboard. Perhaps your breaths will be filling in the black squares. You can choose the patterns you wish, perhaps doing rows or columns or diagonals. It doesn't really matter. You can choose whatever works for you. You may even simply go back to feeling your breathing, how with each breath you sink down a little more, a little deeper, a little further.

Perhaps you visualize yourself descending a spiral staircase into an enveloping but friendly, warm fog. And with each breath, you go deeper and deeper.

Or perhaps you might wish to see colors. You might work at turning the field of vision of your mind's eye, for your real eyes are closed, into a field of perfect blue. That's right. All you can see is pure blue. And then you might change it. You might decide to add yellow until it becomes pure green. If that becomes tire-some, you can subtract the blue and leave pure yellow, and so on through the spectrum. Any of these is fine. They are just provid-ing chaff to give your thoughts a purposeless purpose: to keep them occupied doing something that you can abandon for sleep.

All of these are fine; any of these are fine. It doesn't matter whether you spend the night asleep or deeply hypnotized, using one or all of these techniques. What matters is that you spend the night relaxed so in the morning you will awaken relaxed and re-freshed, ready to meet the new day. If you fall asleep while hyp-notized, that will be fine. When you awaken in the morning at the proper time, you will of course awaken to the usual waking state. If, however, you inadvertently awaken during the night, you will quickly and easily and spontaneously reenter hypnosis to control your ability to meet your need for rest.

7

Study

Hypnosis has proven itself a useful treatment for many people who struggle with studying and test taking. Since tension interferes with preparing for tests and performing as well as possible on them, hypnosis is beneficial because it reduces anxiety. It is also useful as a tool for building appropriate confidence, which allows one to perform at his or her highest level. Further, hypnosis can help to deal with "state-specific learning," the idea that one knows something in certain emotional states but not in others. And finally, hypnosis is useful because it seems to involve the area of the brain involved with memory.

What hypnosis does not do is eliminate the need for study, nor does it make one know how to do things that one never learned before. It is not a substitute for doing the work of learning. It can, however, make one better able to study successfully. It can have an almost magical effect on the performance of someone who does know a subject but does poorly on tests because of nerves.

Many students who are having trouble with a subject get trapped in a common pitfall. Because they are doing poorly, the very thought of the subject makes them anxious. This anxiety is uncomfortable. It makes them want to avoid the source of anxiety. To study the subject is not only to think about it, which is frightening enough, but is also to focus on how much is not known, which is even worse. The problem of not knowing the subject can of course be cured through studying and learning. However, some people find the process of studying or even the thought of studying so stressful that they avoid it. The more they avoid it, the further behind they fall, and the more frightened they become of the subject. For such a person, anxiety interferes with the best way of solving the problem. As the fear drives one away from study, the subject in fact becomes realistically more and more something to worry about.

For some people who in fact know their subject, anxiety can be a major source of interference with proving their knowledge on an exam. Test-taking anxiety, like any performance anxiety, reduces a person's capacity to work to the best of his or her ability. The same sorts of pressures that lead some athletes to choke in crucial situations can make one unable to come up with correct answers that one really does know. Additionally, anxiety can interfere with state-specific knowledge.

State-specific learning is based on the idea that different aspects of oneself are available and in evidence in different situations. For example, a person might be very formal and stiff at work, showing no sign of any warmth or humor. At a party, that same person might be loud, convivial, and funny. Not only would his behavior change from one situation to another, but some important elements of who he was at that moment would be quite different. One of these elements would be certain details of what he knows.

Consider a man visiting a place where he lived years before. Upon his return to that place, he might be flooded with memories that he has not thought of in years. In fact, he might remember things that he had unsuccessfully tried to remember before his arrival. It is as though being there makes him more the person he was in the past. Another example can be seen in the case of a woman seeing a man on the street who looks very familiar but whom she can't really place. Later on, she might go to a local store and naturally greet the clerk whom she knows quite well by name and not realize that the clerk was the someone she had earlier seen in the street. She has knowledge of who that man is, but only in a context.

The same sort of knowledge that's available at some times but not others exists for states of mind as well. A person who has learned a subject while calm and relaxed might in fact truly not know that information when tense. It is not merely a matter of being able to do better when relaxed; rather, unless relaxed, the person literally does not have access to the information. Hypnosis can be very useful in helping a person get to the state of mind in which he or she knows the material.

Finally, hypnosis can be very useful both for studying and for test taking because of its link with memory. It is a widely held belief that much of the key brain activity occurring during hypnosis is near the parietal and temporal lobes, where long-term memory is stored. Hypnosis puts what is being learned into memory very effectively and efficiently. Later, it makes memories accessible, often with great clarity.

The following hypnotic exercises relate both to studying for and taking an important test. If you were having trouble studying or concentrating but were not facing a test, you would simply use the relevant parts of each exercise. If you were facing a test for which you were well prepared but experiencing test-taking anxiety, you would, again, use just what is relevant to you.

The Importance of Confidence

Just as in sports, approaching a task, such as a test, with an "I can't do this" attitude renders poor performance the most likely result. This exercise is designed to associate relaxation and confidence with studying or test taking. The consequent positive attitude should enhance your performance.

Feel yourself settling deeply into hypnosis, and as you do, take some time to focus on your breathing—slow, regular, comfortable, and peaceful breathing. With each breath you exhale, you feel yourself pumping the tension out of your body. Any tension that might be in your body is systematically removed, being pumped out, being pumped out. You feel relaxed, comfortable, and confident.

With each breath you inhale, you become aware of something else. With each breath you inhale, you feel the strength of your body. Your muscles are relaxed, but they are strong and powerful, strong and powerful. Each time you inhale, you feel the strength as it ripples through your body. You feel powerful, capable, competent. Imagine a lion lying out in the sun. See the powerful body so relaxed but so strong. Perhaps see the lion yawn and stretch. See both the relaxation and the magnificent strength there, ready to be used.

You are like that lion: relaxed and strong. You are taking on a task, one that calls for both your strength and your relaxation. In order to do your task, in order to learn your material and take your test, it's important that you do it the right way, important that you go about it in the best way. Just as you would not compete in a track meet dressed in an overcoat and galoshes, so you are not going to prepare for this test in the wrong state of mind.

First of all comes preparing your body. Studying and test taking are very hard work, but they are not physical work. Holding a book in front of you and casting your eyes over it is not hard physical labor. Picking up a pencil and writing answers to a test question does not require massive physical effort. That means that your body is not called upon for great exertion while studying, while taking a test. If your body becomes tense, your muscles are going to be taking up energy that would be better spent on the real task. So the best thing your body can do is to get out of your way. The best thing your body can do is to be totally relaxed. Let your muscles be so relaxed in order to let your mind go about its job. The physical demands of studying and test taking are minimal. Let your body do only that minimal amount of work. Let your body get out of the way and let you achieve your best. Just as an athlete can best compete by having her mind get out of the way of her body, letting her body do what it has trained to do, here the mirror image is true. Your body has to get out of the way of your mind and let your mind do what it was trained to do.

And your mind is very well trained. Your mind is strong and powerful. The physical strength of the lion is a metaphor for the strength of your mind. You have the strength, the power, the ability to do it.

To put that strength to use, you have to know how to take advantage of it. You have to know how to use it. A most important part of using it involves developing your confidence in yourself. You're going to be learning ways to do this, but the most important basic idea is that there is no advantage to self-doubt during studying or test taking.

When you are organizing yourself before beginning a course of study, it is necessary and even vital to assess what you know and what you do not know, what you need to study and how long you should allow. As you go along in your studies and preparation for a test, of course you must occasionally monitor your progress and make the appropriate decisions about your learning program. You do not want to have a sense of false confidence. You do not want to sabotage yourself by telling yourself you don't need to bother studying when in fact you do. You want to learn not false confidence, but real confidence.

And so, when you are preparing the best way you know how, when you are doing what you think is the right amount of preparation, when you are doing the things which should lead to success, all of your thoughts are going to be ones of total success. If you are doing what you need to do, there is no advantage in preparing for failure. There is no advantage to anticipating a poor result. In many of these exercises you will learn techniques to strengthen this confidence in your ability to achieve. As you do them, you constantly keep in mind that they can be done wholeheartedly and without reference to possible failure. Thinking about failure, if you are doing all you should to prepare, has no advantage at all. Anticipating failure will not make it any less painful if it occurs, and it does make it much more likely that it will occur.

You have thought about and decided what you need to do to prepare. If you have done your preparations, there is no advantage to interrupting your study with questions of whether or not you're doing enough. That's a question to be addressed at a time you have set aside to monitor your progress. While you are studying, such thoughts merely keep you from doing the job of studying. While you are taking a test, there is nothing to be gained by questioning your readiness or doubting your ability. Your preparation and ability are what they are at the time of the test. Your job is to use them to their greatest potential. Throughout these exercises, then, you are going to hold onto the idea that it is not only safe but is in fact your best move to keep yourself feeling strong and confident, ready to meet the challenge, ready to succeed.

When you are ready to end this exercise, open your eyes and bring yourself back to the usual waking state.

Studying

This is a very straightforward exercise designed to teach you to study successfully.

◆◆◆

As you settle back into the state of hypnosis, feeling yourself comfortable, peaceful, and relaxed, you think about the fact that you have a subject to learn. It's tempting to avoid it, tempting not to think about it, but you know that in that course of inaction lies disaster. You know that the test will come whether you have prepared or not.

So, the first thing you need to do is to relax. Anxiety may make you feel as though you are paying attention to the matter, but it does nothing to help you. And your goal is not to show that you have suffered and so deserve pity; rather, it is success, great and complete success.

You are not going to make the mistake of rushing headlong into unstructured study. There are many mistakes you can make if you do that. If you say you need limitless studying, then no matter how much you do, it will feel as though you have not done enough. You need to decide on a reasonable study plan that takes into account the realities of how much you need to learn, of how important this is to you, of what other things you need to do, of what resources of time and energy you have available.

You not only have to decide realistically what your study schedule will be in terms of time, but you also have to decide what to study. If the test is on the whole book, it wouldn't do to go to that exam having memorized the first chapter of the text and not having even glanced at the rest. So what you need to do is plan: how much time there is until the test, how much of that time you can devote to this studying, how much of that study time is best devoted to each particular part.

Once you have done this, once you have charted out a realistic and reasonable plan of study, you are ready to go on.

Now it is time to study. You have planned this time in advance; you have decided that until now it was OK to be doing other things, and that later on it will be OK to stop doing this. But right now, it is time to study.

You want to get the most you possibly can out of this studying, so you start by getting yourself ready. You go to a quiet place, free from distractions. You get yourself organized with the materials you need close at hand. You settle yourself down. You are physically ready to begin.

Now you get yourself mentally ready. You know that the quality of your study time is as important as the quantity. So you take the time to close your eyes and put yourself into a mild hypnotic trance. That's right. Settle in, peaceful and comfortable, into a mild state of hypnosis. Focus particularly on the sense of relaxation because you don't want your body to tense up and interfere with your study.

Now, remaining in that mild state of hypnosis, which allows you both to keep your body relaxed and to keep your attention focused, you allow your eyes to come open, and you begin to study. You begin to read your book, take notes, review notes, whatever tasks your study requires. You are able to do them. You find yourself focused, paying attention to the task at hand. You do not think about anything other than the job of studying. You're focused; your body is relaxed. Any extraneous thoughts you brush away, thinking, "I'll think about that later. Right now I'm busy." Page after page, you steadily progress, keeping in mind that right now you don't have to study everything. You don't have to learn everything; you merely have to do what's on your schedule for today. You're doing your studying one page at a time, not focusing on anything but the matter at hand.

And you feel your mind soaking the information up like a sponge. What you learn is clear and sharp. It's going to be remembered well. You know that your study plan includes a daily follow-up of what you studied the day before, reviewing the previous day's learning. As you do this review, you are struck by how well you are retaining what you learned, how little effort it takes to solidify the ground covered in the previous lesson. You feel yourself aware of the steady progress that you are making. Now's not the time to think about the overall plan. Now is the time to be learning bit by bit. And you are pleased to see, to feel, how effectively you are learning, how much the things that you learn are becoming part of your knowledge base.

You continue with your study, focusing hard, studying all-out, studying the hardest you can, putting complete concentration into it. But now, you see how the time has flown. It's over now. It's time for you to stop. And just as it's important to begin, so also it's important to end. There's a lot to be learned over time. You're not going to learn it all in one session. Now it's time to stop and do something else. Next time you study, it will help you to begin by knowing that you will also end. You know that you have accomplished the chunk that you had set out to do in this session, and now you can leave this studying behind, knowing you'll be back. When you are ready to end this exercise, bring yourself back to the usual waking state.

The Mountain

This is an exercise designed to help when you're discouraged and feeling that there's too much to learn.

As you settle into trance, comfortably and peacefully relaxed, picture yourself on a slope. Picture yourself climbing up a mountain. There you are, looking ahead to the peak. It's not an impossible climb. There are no barriers to prevent you from reaching the top, but it seems as if it's such a long way away. It feels as though you have so far to climb. That's the way your studying has felt lately. It has seemed that there's so much to learn, more than you can possibly manage. It seems that there's so much ahead of you, so much to be done.

But as you stop and think about it, you take a moment to look around. You take the time to look down the mountain, to look back to your starting point. As you do, you're astonished to realize that the base of the mountain is so far away that you can not begin to see it clearly. You realize that you've been climbing this mountain for a lifetime. You realize that the amount of knowledge you've gained, the amount of mountain you've already climbed, is tremendous. This climb to the peak from where you are is not climbing a whole mountain. It's simply the final ascent. It may look far away, it may look as if there's a lot of mountain left to cover, but you realize that what this really represents is the last, final push.

It's taken a great deal of effort to get here. It's taken a great deal of time and energy and effort to get to this spot. But you've done it. You've managed to reach this spot, and all you have left to do is the final ascent.

It's the same with your study. Sometimes it feels as if you have so much to learn, so much to study. But when you think about it, you realize that as you study for this test, as you study for this exam, your task would be impossible were it not for the fact that you begin studying already knowing most of what you have to know in order to succeed. You know how to read. You know how to write. You have a tremendous fund of general information.

Even in this subject, as you sit down to study, you are not starting out from point zero. You had to know a tremendous amount simply to begin this course of study. And you had to know a lot to be at the point where you could begin to study.

It feels as if there's a lot left to learn. It is a lot. But it's something that you can do because you're building on the strong foundation that you have laid over the years. You're building on the mountain of knowledge that you have built over time.

When you're ready to end this exercise, open your eyes and bring yourself back to the usual waking state.

They're on Your Side

A common problem for people taking tests is the feeling of antagonism toward the people who make and grade their exams. Some test takers feel that the test is designed to fail them. As a result, they go into the test in an adversarial spirit. They feel attacked, defensive, and tense. Tension, however, does not contribute to successful test taking.

Settle back, deeply relaxed and comfortable, settling into a peaceful and relaxed state, comfortable and at ease. You're feeling safe, safe and secure. You have the good feeling that comes from being among friends. You know you can relax. They mean you no harm. They'll do you no ill. It's safe.

Feeling so safe, you realize you are with some people. You're with the people who made up the test. And you realize that they like you. You realize that they're on your side. They want you to pass. They're hoping you'll pass. They want you to do well. When you take the test, they'll be cheering for you.

It's almost a shock to realize that their wish is for you to do well. If you do badly, it reflects badly upon them. Your failure is also their failure.

This test is designed to sort out people who know the subject from those who don't. You know the subject. So this test is designed to show that you know the subject. The purpose of this test, the goal of this test, is for you to pass. This test is designed to sort out you from those other people who don't know the material.

The people who didn't study, the people who didn't learn, the people who didn't prepare—those are the ones that the test maker is trying to differentiate from you. If you get a score like theirs, the test maker will have failed. You've done your work. You're prepared. The test maker wants you to do well. This test is designed for you to do well.

That doesn't mean you are going to get every question right. That doesn't mean that it will be an easy test. If it were too easy, the testers couldn't tell who hasn't done the work. Just as if it were too hard, they couldn't tell who has done it. Some mistakes are OK. They know that even someone as well prepared as you won't get everything right. But they've built this test, they've designed this test so that you'll get enough right.

They want you to pass. They want you to do well. They want you to succeed. They want you to be one of them.

When you're ready to end this exercise, open your eyes and bring yourself back to the usual waking state.

Getting Your Results

This exercise can be done either just before studying or whenever you are thinking about the test as a way to control any worrying. It can also be done during the test, almost treating the test-taking situation as a memory. It should be helpful for enhancing confidence and motivation.

As you settle deeply and comfortably into hypnosis, you imagine yourself in a wonderful, peaceful place. You're on vacation. All the work is behind you. You're off on a wonderful vacation, relaxing and enjoying yourself. There's no pressure, no demands. You're relaxed and at peace. There's nothing you need to do.

And as you're sitting there, relaxed and content, a smile comes over your face. You just thought about that day when you got the results of your test back. You remember getting those results, and a smile comes across your face. In fact, you have the letter in your pocket. Reach into your pocket and pull out that letter. Savor and enjoy the memory as you reread the letter. That's right. It says how pleased they are to inform you that you did so well. You did very well indeed. You're very proud, pleased, and happy with your results. You scored very, very well. You did excellently. And you hold on and savor that memory, that feeling of success that accompanied this notification.

When you're ready to end this exercise, open your eyes and bring yourself back to the usual waking state.

Taking the Test

This exercise, which you should start doing early in your preparations for an exam, allows you to practice taking the test in a comfortable way. Because the end result of your studying will be taking the test in a relaxed manner, the process of studying should also feel comfortable.

━━━━●◆●━━━━

As you settle back, comfortable and relaxed, imagine yourself moving through time and space, all the while staying very, very comfortable, peaceful, calm, and relaxed. There is no advantage in tension. The best thing your body can do is to remain relaxed. If you should feel any tension entering your body, stop and take a deep breath, and as you exhale, you blow out all the tension. Take the time to relax your body and to let your mind go about its task.

That's right. You're moving forward into the future. It's the evening before the test. If your preparations are not complete, they are nearly so. When you set up your study plan, you knew when you expected to be done studying. Perhaps you have a little more to do tonight. If so, you're approaching it with the realization that now, the night before the test, is not when you are going to do all of your learning. The bulk of your learning has been done over a long period of time. Tonight the most you'll be doing is a final bit of polishing, straightening out a few details in your mind, reminding yourself of things you've already studied and learned. It's the last step up to the top of the mountain. Tonight any study really involves looking back over the territory you've already climbed, reviewing material already learned.

If there is anything you need to do tonight, you do it and get it out of the way. Then your studying is done. Or perhaps your study schedule has been set up to be done already. In either case, sometime this evening you get to the point where you're finished. You're ready for the test.

Now you need to relax. Now you need to do something enjoyable. Now you need to free your mind from the test. Perhaps you'll get together with a friend. Perhaps you'll go to a movie. Perhaps you'll watch TV or rent a video. You might go out and get some exercise. You might curl up with a good book. Whatever you wish to do is fine as long as it is relaxing.

You've put in a lot of work studying and preparing. Now it's important that you give yourself the message that you are ready. Now you have to give yourself the message that you are not scrambling in desperation like someone who ran out of time to study. You are telling yourself that you are prepared, that you don't need that final ten seconds. You're telling yourself that you are confident and prepared. You can afford to relax because you are ready.

As you relax, you don't even think about the test. You're ready, so there's nothing else to think about. If a thought of the test should come along, you say to yourself, "I'll deal with that tomorrow when it's time. I'll answer questions when the test comes. Right now I'm relaxing. I've done my work. I'm ready."

And now it's time for sleep. You go to sleep at a good hour, knowing that your job for tonight is rest, is sleep. You don't need to study. You don't need to think about the test. What is on the test is on the test. What's in your brain is in your brain. Tomorrow your task is to get what's in your brain onto the answer sheet. The best way you can prepare for this, the most you can do, is to relax your body.

You know that your studying has resulted in your knowing a great deal. You're going into that test knowing things. You've studied, you've learned, you've learned what you need to know. When you have been studying, you have been concentrating while in a relaxed state. That means that when you are relaxed and concentrating, you know the things that you have studied. You have access to the things that you have learned.

You know that when a person is scared, he or she is concentrating only on the fear. You know that a person who is concentrating on fear cannot concentrate on what he or she knows. You know that a person who is tense and frightened does not have full access to things that he or she learned when relaxed and concentrating.

And so you know that in order to have access to all the things you've studied while relaxed and concentrating, you need to take the test in a state of relaxed concentration. That gives you the best access to the things you've learned.

If, during the test, you should become momentarily anxious, it would be easy for you to fall into the whirlpool of anxiety that produces an inability to think, which in itself produces more anxiety, and so forth, ultimately resulting in poor performance.

So you're not going to fall into that trap. You won't make that mistake. You remember that your top priority is to stay relaxed. You know that as long as you stay relaxed, you give yourself your greatest ability to gain access to all that you've learned.

And this relaxation starts now as you fall asleep. Your attention and your focus is on relaxation. And so you fall asleep.

And now it's morning. Time to get up. Today is your test, so that means that today is a day that you need to stay relaxed. Relaxation and access to the knowledge that you have go hand in hand. The more you're relaxed and concentrating, the more you know. So you start the morning by going through an hypnotic exercise, getting yourself relaxed, comfortable, and calm, with a powerful undercurrent of confidence. There is no advantage in self-doubt. Staying calm and comfortable, you let a corner of your mind stay in this state of relaxed concentration, imagination, and attention which is hypnosis to help you maintain control over your body and over your mind.

If your study plan has called for it, you can do a review before the test. You're doing this not to learn new material, but rather to freshen up and go over what you already know. When you do, you don't treat it as a test; you're not seeing how well you do. This isn't the test. It doesn't matter if your brief review is all perfect answers or all wrong answers. The test that counts is later. All you're doing right now is something like stretching exercises before an athletic event. Teams aren't scored on how they do in warm-ups. They only keep score once the game has begun.

This is your warm-up. Or perhaps your study plan involves no review this morning. If that's what you decided, then you should stick to that.

Now you go on about your day, doing the things you need to do, focusing on what you are doing at any given time. The only thinking you need to do about the test is what you will do effortlessly. All you need to do is to remember when it is and to get yourself there for it. All other preparation is already done. Your learning is completed. All you need to do is make sure that you allow yourself to perform as well as you can. That means getting to the test in a state of relaxation and concentration.

Now it's time for the test. See where you are. Look around at the classroom. Make yourself very comfortable with this place. See what is there to see. Look at the desks and the chairs. Pay attention to the lighting. See who else is there taking the test with you. See who is giving the test. Focus on all the details of the reality around you.

And focus also on your mood. You are comfortable. You are relaxed and confident. You know that you are ready for this test. You know that there is no help in self-doubt. You approach this test with a sense bordering on the arrogant. You are ready for this test. You are as prepared as you can be. And you take a moment to imagine having received the letter telling you how well you've done. You go through the exercise of seeing yourself having received word of your excellent results on this test. And there's a moment of feeling almost confused about whether this test is something you're about to take that will result in that excellent score or if you've already got the excellent score, and this is merely remembering the test. But the excellent result is a foregone conclusion in your mind. All you need do is stay focused and put in the mental effort to transform your hours of study into a wonderful outcome.

They're about to distribute the tests. But before they get to you, you take a moment to think about how little any particular detail or any one question means. In the course of a long test, a person who is earning an excellent score will not be certain of a number of answers. In effect, a person getting an excellent score will be asked a number of things that he or she doesn't know.

Otherwise, the test was too easy. A test that is a challenge to someone who is excellently prepared will of course ask some things that that person won't know.

The questions that you won't know might be scattered through the test. They might fall into some clumps or clusters. They might all come at the end. They might all come at the beginning. You know that the test doesn't demand that you know the answer to every question. When you begin to take the test, you might or might not know the answer to the first question. It doesn't matter. You might not know the first question, and you might not know the second. You might not have a clue about the third, and not a shadow of a guess for the fourth. This matters not at all. Of course there will be questions you don't know. You will be able to tell yourself, "Good. I'm getting all the hard ones out of the way at the beginning. That means more of the rest will be easy," because you know that what is important is not any single question, but the test as a whole. And the person who made up this test knows that as well. This test was designed for a person like you. This test was designed to pick out people who did the work, people who studied. This test was designed to pick out you. And so, if you don't know any particular answer, or any particular stretch of answers, it's all right. It's the test as a whole that's going to show how much you know. If you hit a question or a run of questions for which you're sure of the answer, you're going to feel, "Of course. Naturally this happens." That's what this test is for: to demonstrate that you know your stuff.

And now the test is here before you. You begin to work. You realize that in your brain you have the answers to enough of the questions to do very well. All you need to do now is to transfer that information from your brain to the answer sheet. In order to do that, you focus on staying very concentrated, relaxed, and doing the necessary work. And as you're taking this test, it is rather like being hypnotized. You focus your attention. It doesn't matter what else is going on. It doesn't matter what other people are doing. It doesn't matter what you are going to be doing after the test is over. All of your attention is narrowly focused on your task.

Time is a special area. You stay aware of time insofar as you have to marshal its use. You neither want to spend so long on a few questions that you don't have time to complete the test, nor do you want to work so quickly that you're done with time to spare but have done a sloppy job. You want to work efficiently, giving about the right amount of time to each part. Beyond that, time does not matter. It doesn't matter what time of day it is. It doesn't matter how long you've been sitting there. You're not doing anything else but taking the test. Your world, your universe, is right here in this test. It won't always be that way. You're not going to spend your whole life on this test, but while you are taking the test, there is nothing else you need to do. You work for as long as it takes. If you become tired, that's all right. Perhaps your body has become a little tense, and that signals to you that you should relax it. Take a deep breath and blow out the tension. If you're becoming hungry or thirsty, you pay it no mind. The test will be over long before you die of hunger or thirst. You've worked so hard to prepare; this is your chance. Now you can show all that you know. And you are eager to take advantage of all the opportunity that you are given.

And now it's coming to the end. You're given the warning that time is almost up, and with a confident sense of achievement, you make the final marks, check over the last bits, and as time is called, you confidently hand in your answers.

Feeling very good, reflecting on how well you did, you happily leave, chatting with the people around you, free to express your confidence in your management of the test. And you feel yourself moving forward in time to the moment of getting your grade, knowing that it will indeed be as good as you deserve. When you are ready to end this exercise, open your eyes and bring yourself back to the usual waking state.

8

Memory

When a person wishes to retrieve a memory of some life experience, when a witness to a crime needs to remember a pertinent license plate number, or when a person must recall where he or she hid some valuables, hypnosis is often the tool that first comes to mind. While trance can indeed be a helpful aid to memory, there remain a number of common misconceptions about hypnosis and memory. People who claim that hypnosis enables them to "remember" such things as the experience of being born or a "previous lifetime" make it seem as though hypnosis were some sort of psychological time machine.

The basis of much of this idea is really a mistaken notion about the nature of memory. Earlier scientific research led people to believe that the brain was rather like some ultimate recording device that took in data from all the senses and made a permanent record of all of it. The eyes, then, would be like movie cameras, photographing everything that they saw. The ears would serve as the microphones to tape recorders, capturing and preserving all sounds, whether attended to or not.

With this model, it becomes natural to assume that one need only find a way of getting into these recorded memory banks and of tapping the appropriate storage area to retrieve a true memory. To remember a specific event, one need merely find where that memory is filed and play it back. In the playback, one can look at details that were not noticed the first time.

Memory, however, does not work that way.

Much of the information that is available to our senses is filtered out before it ever reaches the brain. Even though a person is in a certain place at the time, not every detail will be remembered because not all the available information gets to the brain in the first place. If something does reach the brain, it is not necessarily treated as a priceless nugget of information to be stored away forever. Instead, many bits of data are treated like a newspaper. Attention is paid to it, but then it is discarded and thrown away. Only a tiny fraction of the information that a person perceives is actually put into long-term memory. Everything else is gone.

And even the remaining long-term memory is not a pure, unbiased, objective repository of fact. Instead, it is like history, constantly changing and evolving. As society changes, yesterday's villains become today's heroes and vice versa. The understanding of events changes as viewpoints change. Facts themselves are not immune. The fisherman's catch grows larger with each passing year, and it is not necessarily a question of him lying. His memory is changing.

Since memory itself is not a perfect, objective record of the past, hypnosis cannot possibly be a way of getting perfect, objective memories to the surface. There are no such things. Furthermore, if something was not stored in long-term memory, there is no way of retrieving it. None. It is gone.

When a person tries to remember an experience, whether with hypnosis or not, he or she is likely to use a mixture of fact and fiction. While some realistic details about the actual event are remembered, other instances of similar sorts of events might be remembered and used to fill in the blanks. So, for example, if you were trying to remember who was in class with you on a certain day in the past, you would probably begin by trying to remember who the usual attending students were. In doing so, you might well remember as present the students who usually attended class even though some were in fact absent on that particular day. Memory is, moreover, "completed" by imagination.

Your brain simply guesses about what might fill in the remaining gaps. By the time you get done "remembering" the class attendance or experience of class that day, your memory is a collage of genuine recollections about things that actually occurred, memories of happenings that did take place but not at that precise time or not in exactly that way, and other bits of information that are pure fabrication. Even then the process is not complete. Just as changing the tone of voice can change some words from one meaning to another, so the basic memory image can be shifted, changed, and distorted in subtle ways that can make a world of difference.

Controlled experiments with memory have found that hypnosis increases the amount that people remember. However, the increase includes both accurate and inaccurate memories. For example, a person is shown a table covered with various objects. The table is covered and he is asked to list what he saw. Next he is hypnotized and asked to recall what he saw. He will "remember" more things under hypnosis than he did at first, but the extra items will include some that were there and some that were not. However, he will "remember" all of them with full conviction.

The use of hypnosis generally means that you will remember more than you would if unhypnotized, but some of what you remember will be pure fabrication. You will, unfortunately, have no way of knowing which memories are accurate and which are not. They will all seem equally true. In fact, you would remember an hypnotically distorted version of an event much more clearly than you would recall an accurate, unhypnotically altered account of the same occurrence. When you tried to remember the event, you would be retrieving not the original memory, but the way you thought about it during hypnosis. You would remember the hypnotic imagining, not the initial event.

Hypnosis is not some sort of truth serum, as popular belief would have it. It is a myth that hypnotized people remember the truth and have to speak it willy-nilly. Given motivation, a hypnotized person is just as capable of lying as anyone and probably would be, in fact, a more effective liar than his or her unhypnotized counterpart.

Because it can distort memory, hypnosis should never be used to recall past events that might be the source of testimony in a court case, whether criminal or civil, without first discussing the matter with an attorney. Although hypnotically aided memory may be useful to generate other fields of inquiry on a case, a person whose memory has been enhanced by hypnosis is not, in general, eligible to testify as a witness. Using hypnosis to regain memory tampers with memory in such a way that it is hard to know what the reality is.

While understanding the limitations of all memory, it's worth thinking about reasons why an event or experience might be forgotten in the first place. As stated previously, anything not noticed when an event occurred or not deemed important enough to be put into long-term memory is gone. It can't be remembered. It was not kept. People with certain types of brain damage are unable to transfer experience into long-term memory and so can never learn anything new, can never remember what happened more than twenty minutes ago. Only those events that happened before the brain damage or in the immediate past can be recalled. A person who receives a blow to the head may not be able to remember events leading up to the injury because that blow wiped the slate of recent memory. Those memories do not exist in the brain, and nothing can retrieve them.

Some experiences are not remembered just because there is no reason why they would stand out as memorable. For example, unless it was something special, you might have trouble immediately recalling what you had for dinner two weeks ago. Some things are forgotten because attention was split when they occurred. When you do two things at once, talking and putting down a pencil, for instance, you may forget where you put the pencil. Finally, forgetfulness can be motivated. People commonly forget their dental appointments. It's not that they don't, at least in part, want to go. If they didn't want to go, they wouldn't have made the appointment in the first place. There is, however, another part that wishes they didn't have to go. That part might "solve things," as it were, by hiding the memory of the appointment. People often deal with traumatic or horrible events in their past by forgetting them. It is as though if something can't be remembered, it didn't really happen. When a trauma occurs, a part of a person's mind decides that it is too painful to live with. The memory of the experience is then buried away, out of conscious awareness. It is said to be "repressed." The memory is not simply misplaced. It is also not a "suppressed" memory, something that a person consciously tries to forget. When something is suppressed, the conscious mind knows about it, and just wishes that it didn't. Repression, on the other hand, buries not only the memory but also the instructions to bury it.

Repressed memories are in some way present in the brain and so are retrievable given certain conditions. Now, if a memory was repressed, it was because some part of the mind, an unconscious part, decided that it needed to be buried. As long as there remains a more powerful part of the mind saying, "This is too painful to remember," the memory is most likely not going to come back easily no matter how strongly someone is told to remember it, no matter if hypnosis is used. As people mature, however, as they become stronger and can view a painful past from a safer perspective, they can begin to remember previously repressed memories. This kind of change may happen in the ordinary course of a lifetime or in a therapeutic setting.

Learning to change, to come to grips with the past, to become strong enough to face one's history without repression, is the business of psychotherapy. In a successful course of therapy people can begin to understand themselves in ways that strengthen them enough to be able to remember more of their past and then use these memories to understand themselves even better. Two factors are at work controlling the speed at which past events are remembered in therapy. First of all, a skilled therapist is sensitive to pacing and doesn't rush a patient faster than is wise. Second, a patient will not usually go any faster than he or she is ready to go. So even when a therapist thinks you're ready to remember something, if enough groundwork hasn't been done, you probably won't.

Hypnosis can be an extremely effective adjunct to therapy in helping to retrieve a buried painful past. Using hypnosis to recover repressed memories is, however, something that should never be attempted except in a context of work with a trained professional. Trying to knock out repressions which are still needed could be disastrous. The following techniques are for use in retrieving the simply forgotten past.

Age Regression

This technique is similar to what is used in therapy to recover repressed memories, but it differs in that it aims to retrieve painless, not traumatic, experiences. For people who are curious to see how age regression works, it can provide an interesting window to view either pleasant or neutral memories, rather like looking through an old photo album. For purposes of demonstration, a nice day in fourth grade is used. If fourth grade was not a good year for you, substitute third or fifth grade or some other time. You can change the scene as you wish.

———◆•◆•◆——

As you settle back into hypnosis, you take the time to feel yourself getting very, very deeply involved in the state of hypnosis. Very much focused on this peaceful and comfortable state. As you do, you decide that it would be nice to begin learning to explore your past by using hypnosis. In a few moments, you're going to begin to think about a very pleasant day when you were a child. You're going to begin to think about it so vividly that it's going to feel as though you really are right back there. The thinking about it will be so vivid that it may seem as though it were real. Of course, a part of you will always know exactly where you are and when it is. It may seem rather like a movie playing out before your mind's eye, a movie in which you become so involved that you feel the feelings and experience the experiences more vividly than you would by simply remembering.

Begin to think back to a pleasant day when you were in the fourth grade. And as you begin to think about that day, you're going to begin to feel as though you're moving through time and space all the way back to a pleasant day when you were in the fourth grade. You needn't struggle. In fact you shouldn't try to force the memory; instead, you just settle back and let it come. You settle back and let yourself feel as though you are going back through time and space, and it will be interesting to see just what the memory is. It will be interesting to watch and see what comes from your memory. In your mind, in a moment, you're going to begin to count from one to five, and as you count, you're going to feel yourself moving back in time, back to a very nice day in the fourth grade. You may choose to visualize in your mind's eye a calendar. And as you do, you imagine it flipping backward to earlier and earlier pages, and as you watch the pages flip, you feel yourself at that same pace moving back through time to a much earlier date. Or you may wish just to feel yourself traveling through time and space, becoming younger and smaller. Do it whichever way seems best to you.

But now you begin to count: "One." You are going back, back into the past. It is no longer the current year, nor last year, nor five years ago, but much, much earlier. "Two." You are moving along through time and space, back into the past, into your past. You are going back to a very nice day when you were in the fourth grade. "Three." Deeper and deeper, faster and faster, back into your past. You are thinking about a nice day, and now you're beginning actually to move into it. "Four." Almost there. Soon you're going to be back in the fourth grade on a very nice day. "Five." There you are. Back in the fourth grade on a very nice day.

Where are you? How old are you? What are you doing? Who is with you? What are you wearing? Who is your teacher?

That's excellent. You can stay in the past, at this happy time, for as long as you wish. But then, when you are ready, it will be time to come back, back into the present. The journey back is quicker. You're no longer a small child back in the fourth grade; instead, it is the current date, and you are an adult of your real age, comfortably and deeply hypnotized. But you see how you can use your ability for self-hypnosis to travel back through time and space to recall most vividly appropriate pleasant events from your past. When you are ready to end this exercise, open your eyes and bring yourself back to the usual waking state.

Mood Tracing

People often have feelings in the present that are related to events in the past. Sometimes, for example, a person has a stronger emotional reaction than is warranted by actual circumstances. Sometimes people find themselves experiencing physical events that don't really make sense in the present. One person might, for example, feel some part of his or her body tensing up, another a certain kind of tiredness, a third a physical discomfort.

This technique is used to trace feelings back to earlier times that produced similar feelings. If a physical sensation is to be traced, the sensation and accompanying emotion would be paired and then, with them treated as a unit, traced back. For an example, déjà vu in an enjoyable situation is used below.

●◆●◆●

You wish to understand what precedent was stirred up when you felt that sense of déjà vu. And in order to trace it, you're settling deeply and comfortably into a state of hypnosis, and as you become so deeply hypnotized, you let your mind go back to where you were when you had the sense of déjà vu. You let yourself go back and begin by orienting yourself, seeing where you are, what you're doing. But you do that only in order to remind yourself of exactly how you felt at that time. Not the déjà vu, but as clearly as possible, remember how you felt. It was a pleasant sort of experience, so you focus in on exactly the kind of pleasantness that it was.

All of your effort is focused on not only remembering, but in fact reliving the pleasant feeling that you were experiencing. Let yourself feel it once again. At first, you may be getting just an approximation of how you felt. But as you focus on that mood, on that feeling, it becomes more and more sharp, more and more precisely tuned. And as you get that specific feeling, you nurture it and make it stronger and stronger so it becomes the focus of your awareness. All of your awareness is focused in on that emotion, and as it grows strong enough, you're suddenly going to find yourself pulled back through time and space and find yourself once again remembering or even reexperiencing another, earlier time when you felt the same way. It's as though these two different times are connected by an emotional wire, and as you get in touch with that emotion, you can suddenly be conducted through the wire, back to the earlier experience.

When you are ready to end this exercise, open your eyes and bring yourself back to the usual waking state.

Going Back to Just Before

Because memories are organized and stored by mood, this technique, like the previous method, uses emotion to recall what was forgotten. While the first two memory exercises are useful for exploring a time in the past without necessarily knowing what time it was, this exercise is one designed for remembering a specific focused event. Rather than attacking the memory block head on, go back to before the block, and then move without impedance to the specific event. Remembering where silver was hidden is used as an example.

As you settle back, deeply and comfortably relaxed, you're going to get yourself ready to move back through time and space to the past. Not the distant past, but your past. Your recent past. You're going to go back to a time two months ago, to just before you went on vacation, to just before you hid the silver.

Now be careful not to try to remember where you hid the silver. You've already tried, and you have not remembered, so there's no need to waste your time doing that again. Instead, you're going to do something different. So you just focus on the instructions and let happen what ever you find happening.

Think back, back into your past, back to shortly before your vacation two months ago. And you think back to when you were making your preparations. And as you think about it, you feel yourself moving back, moving through time and space all the way back to that time, and it becomes more and more real and alive, more and more as if you really are right back there. And as you focus on being back there, you find yourself aware of how you were feeling that day, what your mood was. And as you do, you focus not so much on what you were doing; instead, you focus on how you were feeling. Focus on your feelings. On your mood. Were you happy? Excited? Worried? Just what did you feel? You don't need to put a name on it. It's more important that you allow yourself to feel precisely what you were feeling, to experience what you were feeling, and you know that what you're experiencing is much more vivid and real than a specific name of an emotion.

There you are, back there getting ready, and as you focus on how you were feeling, you allow yourself to proceed. You started with a memory that is clear and sharp. And now you proceed. What did you do next? Allow that memory to come. You don't have to try to force it. Forcing doesn't work. Instead, you allow yourself to relive it. You allow yourself just to have the memory. And as you just have it, you see what happened next. And then you see what came after that and after that. And doing so, you are able simply to let yourself discover where it was you put the silver, because as soon as you get to the point where the next thing you did was to hide the silver, you will see where it is. When you are ready to end this exercise, open your eyes and bring yourself back to the usual waking state.

9

Sports

As Yogi Berra said, "Fifty percent of [baseball] is ninety percent mental."

He was right. Athletes perform not only with their bodies but with their minds. In the late moments of a basketball game, for example, the opposition frequently calls time-out before a free throw. They hope that the player who is going to the line will spend the time-out thinking about the task and, in so doing, become tense enough to hinder successful completion of the free throw. Some athletes perform wonderfully well in practice but become less able to perform in an actual game. Some "choke" in clutch situations or in big, important competitions. It is not that these athletes suffer an abrupt decrease in physical ability. They do not suddenly lose strength or hand–eye coordination or agility. Instead, their mental approach to the game has become a hindrance rather than a help.

It is not because these athletes wish to do less well. In fact, it is typically the opposite, that they are trying too hard. A football coach one time went up to a player on the bench and asked if he could do a better job of guarding the other team's star receiver than the starter could. "I'll try, Coach" said the player. "Don't bother getting off the bench," said the coach. "The boy who's in there is trying. I'm looking for someone who can do it." Often it is the very trying to do well that impairs a person's performance.

Athletes who do well in big situations are those who can treat the game precisely as if it were a practice with nothing unusual at stake. Both this "business as usual" stance and the tense awkwardness associated with trying too hard are best explained by the nature of the brain's control over the body.

The two major areas of the brain controlling physical activity are the cerebrum and the cerebellum. The cerebrum, a highly evolved, developmentally advanced part of the brain, is where we think. It's a very good part for imagining an activity. The cerebellum is a more primitive, animal-like part of the brain. As such, it is very useful for smooth, physical activity.

When people want to learn a physical skill, they first use the cerebrum to think about what they want to do. Having decided what movements are required, they begin to go through the motions, trying out the new activity. Their first efforts are typically jerky and awkward. As they practice, the cerebellum learns just what set of motions is necessary. The cerebellum both smooths out the jerkiness in the motions and learns to perform extremely complicated physical tasks with great dexterity. This process is commonly known as "getting it into the muscles" or "muscle learning."

When athletes go to routine practice sessions, their bodies respond to the direction of the cerebellum. When a good player performs in a game situation, he or she allows the cerebellum to maintain control over physical activity. The players who choke, on the other hand, go out and start thinking about making the shot or hitting the ball. As soon as they are thinking about it, they are using their cerebrums. That part of the brain is much better than the cerebellum for thinking, but it is much less good at carrying out learned physical responses. You know, for instance, that if you are going to shoot a basketball, you do not say to yourself, "I am going to launch this ball at four miles per hour, at a sixty-two degree angle from a spot six feet eight inches above the ground." Instead you look at the basket and say to yourself you want the ball to go through it. You imagine it happening, and your body carries out your wish.

Imagination and expectation have a role in every performance, be it playing a musical instrument, walking across a room, putting on clothing, speaking, or competing in sports. When the football defense calls time-out, deliberately forcing the opposition to wait before trying a field goal, not only do they hope the kicker will shift his mind set from "doing" to "thinking," but they also hope he will start to worry about missing. If the kicker is worrying about missing, he is giving himself a mental image of muffing the kick, an inadvertent mental instruction to miss. If he is thinking about kicking the ball wide to the left, he is in effect planning to do just that.

An aphorism in basketball is "You can't teach height." No amount of coaching will make a short person tall. Likewise, the techniques in this chapter will not turn an untalented amateur into an Olympic or professional athlete. These hypnotic exercises are no substitute for putting in the time and effort to practice, nor do they obliterate motivations that might keep a person from doing his or her best. Sometimes a powerful self-destructive streak leads an individual to perform poorly. Sometimes a person is very conflicted about aggression or about competing with a specific opponent. Resolving such counterproductive motivations often needs professional intervention.

What the self-hypnosis in this chapter can do is allow you to practice and perform to the limits of your physical ability with your mind as an ally rather than extra baggage.

For the sake of giving clear examples, a specific sport, often tennis, is used in each exercise. Of course you can alter the instructions by substituting whatever sport you wish.

Visualization

One technique that is routinely practiced by top athletes is to visualize good performance of an upcoming event. When Olympic bobsledders or skiers, for example, prepare for a race, you can see them close their eyes and begin to sway as they imagine themselves racing through the course. The above-mentioned field-goal kicker will help himself immensely by intentionally visualizing himself successfully kicking the field goal through the upright rather than imagining missing it. Controlled studies with basketball teams have shown players to increase their free-throw-shooting percentages significantly simply by spending some time every day with their eyes closed, vividly imagining themselves shooting and sinking 100 consecutive free throws.

Like these athletes, when you think about making a movement, when you visualize it, there is a certain tendency for your body to make that movement, even if only on a microscopic scale. This tendency is enhanced under hypnosis. While the motion may not be visible, it is as though the nerve pathways and muscles necessary for performing an action are tried out. In hypnosis, if you imagine yourself making certain motions, the initial imagining, the shaping of the fantasy, will take place in your cerebrum. However, as you continue this imagining, it will go through the cerebellum where actions are smoothed out. The muscles will, in a tiny way, practice making the motions necessary to perform the imagined feat. Because hypnosis enhances the link between mind and body, you will, in effect, be practicing doing what you are visualizing.

When you feel pressured to think about doing well in an event or contest, this hypnotic exercise can give you something useful to do with your mind. You can put your mind into a productive state of attention and concentration, readying yourself to operate at peak efficiency, without interference from your cerebrum. When you are focusing your imagination on what you want to have happen, when you imagine successfully performing, you are laying out a blueprint for your body to follow.

Settling in comfortably and peacefully, you get yourself into a deep state of relaxed concentration and imagination and attention. And once you have done that, you visualize yourself there on the tennis court. As you do this, it is important that you remember that you are not simply going to recall the way you have felt in tennis games in the past. If you want to remember the way you felt when you have played your best and won, that will be fine. You are not going to remember times that you have played poorly. Those are behind you. There's no need to practice failure. That's not something you want to learn how to do on a regular basis. Your goal is to learn to play your best. First of all, you're going to work on your serve. You're going to do it piece by piece, a bit at a time. You're not facing an opponent yet; you're just serving the ball.

You're not going to try, in a way that interferes, to aim the ball. Instead you're going to hit the ball and know that when you hit the ball correctly, it's going to go where it's supposed to go. When you serve, you are in control, so you get to establish whatever ritual is best for you to prepare yourself. If you wish to bounce the ball, do it exactly the same number of times with each practice. Decide if you're going to hold two balls in your hand for the first serve or if you're going to put the second in your pocket. Always do it exactly the same way. The more variance you can control, the more consistent your serve will be. Think about your breathing. You might, for example, choose to take a big deep breath and exhale right before your toss. You might like to take your breath in as you make the toss and exhale as you hit the ball. You might choose to exhale quietly, or you might choose to make a sound. Figure out what is best for you, and then always do it the same way.

Now you're ready. You look over, see the court into which you are going to hit the ball, and pick out the spot that you intend to hit. That court and that spot are not going to move, so you don't need to keep your eyes there. You've looked over and seen where you want the ball to go. Now you focus your attention on the ball and your racket. Begin whatever sequence of bounces or breaths you are using. Now imagine yourself tossing the ball perfectly, and feel yourself striking the ball exactly as you are supposed to do. The ball goes flying and hits exactly where you wanted it to hit. Now repeat it. Go through your ritual. Toss the ball. Strike it perfectly, and see it hit the target. Now do this ninety-eight more times without a miss. If you imagine yourself tossing incorrectly, you aren't focusing. That's not what you want to learn to do. Start your string of 100 over again. If you don't hit the ball correctly, if it doesn't go where you intended it to go, your concentration wasn't good enough. You were practicing the wrong thing. Start over. Hit a hundred perfect serves in a row.

Once your serve has been practiced, it's time to work on your forehand. Where should your feet be? Where should your weight be? How should it shift from back foot to front foot? How should your racket face be held? What's the direction of your swing?

To get these elements correct, we are going to begin by doing something that cannot be done in reality. You are going to play in slow motion. The ball is hit to your forehand side. It is coming very slowly. You feel yourself moving into position, setting yourself up for a perfect forehand return. You position yourself. You watch the ball as it so slowly comes toward you. You can see the rotation. You get yourself in position and, in slow motion, bring your racket through the ball, shifting your weight properly as you do so. Perfect shot. And now again. And again.

Next we're going to do it at a little bit faster speed—still slow motion, but not quite so slow. Position yourself, and hit the ball. See another perfect shot. Practice this over and over, slowly increasing the speed until you are playing at normal speed. Hit 100 perfect forehands at regular speed.

Now, over succeeding exercises you're going to do the same thing with your backhand, volley, half-volley, and net game. You are not yet playing an integrated game with these exercises. You are just mastering each shot. As a result, whenever you need to hit the ball, whatever the type of shot, your body will be prepared; your muscles will know what to do in order to execute that command.

When you are ready to end this exercise, open your eyes and bring yourself back to the usual waking state.

The Zone

"In the zone" is the phrase used by Arthur Ashe to describe the way he felt when he was playing his finest tennis. He was in the zone when he upset Jimmy Connors to win Wimbledon. The zone is a state of mind that the best players are consistently able to achieve and involves something very much akin to self-hypnosis.

You can use this exercise both as a rehearsal for a match and as a means of focusing your efforts during an actual match. For the latter, you enter a state of eyes-open hypnosis before you begin to play.

Feel yourself settled and relaxed in this good state of self-hypnosis. As you do, your attention becomes more and more narrow, more and more focused. Your concentration is becoming absolute. You are on the court about to play a game. You are about to play a great game, a wonderful game, a complete game. Your thoughts are totally focused on the playing of this game. There is nothing else on your mind. This is the only thing you are here to do.

It doesn't matter whether there are spectators or not. They are irrelevant. They have no bearing on your play. All that matters is what's happening on the court. It's just you and your opponent. And that opponent is not, for the time being, a person you care about. Your opponent is faceless. You may know something about your opponent which may effect your strategy, and you stay very aware of such things. Beyond that, however, it doesn't matter who the opponent is. Your opponent is simply the opponent. It doesn't matter who is favored. It doesn't matter what has happened in other matches. It doesn't even matter what has happened during other points. This is your opponent. You are going to play your very best to beat your adversary. You are not interested in how your opponent feels about the match, in how your opponent feels about winning or losing. You are focused on yourself. You want to win. Even more than win, you want to do your very best. If your opponent, for example, should be a very weak player, you are interested not in playing poorly but in winning. You want to play your best. If it should turn out that your opponent is either a superior player or lucky, that is a matter beyond your control. What you can control, what is important, is that you play your very best to give yourself your best chance of winning the best way you can.

You've been practicing each individual action. You've been practicing each stroke. Your body now knows how to do everything that it needs to do. You don't have to think about the actions your body must perform in order to do any of them. They have become as instinctive as changing your grip.

You focus in, aware of nothing but the court, the ball, your opponent, and the game. You realize that you are seeing things with a preternatural clarity. You know what is going on. You can see things. You feel as though everything else is happening in slow motion, but you are able to move around at your usual speed. You hit the ball, and when you do, you see it moving as though in slow motion. Your opponent appears to be moving very slowly to reach it. When the ball is hit back, you feel you have all the time in the world to react. You see the ball coming slowly. You can pick up the spin. You have plenty of time to get into position, to choose your target, where you want the ball to go, and then watch the ball come right onto the strings of your racket. As it hits, you can almost see the compression taking place as the ball leaves your strings unerringly toward its destination. You go through the entire match hitting the ball well, making point after point. Occasionally a shot may not go in. That doesn't matter. It's forgotten immediately. You waste no time mourning a lost point. A lost point is gone forever, but the next point can be yours, and you intend to take it. And you don't dwell on successful points either. The past is always gone, and your attention is on the present and the immediate future.

And you go all the way through the match, right to the very end, and when you have hit that last winner, your opponent comes up to the net, crosses over, and, extending a hand, says "Great game. I've never seen you play so well." And now that the game is over, your opponent is no longer faceless, no longer the opponent, no longer the enemy. Now you are two people who have shared an experience, so you have something in common. You can be friends now, until your next match.

When you are ready, end this exercise.

Aggression

Some people have trouble in competitive sports because they inhibit their aggressive tendencies. For many, to try to beat an opponent feels like trying to hurt her or him. It feels angry and aggressive. In the real world of good sportsmanship, though, opponents are not only allowed but in fact are encouraged to do their best to defeat the other. It must be so in order to have the best possible game. The finest games are had when people let themselves try their hardest to beat the other, knowing that after the match will come the time for sharing and friendship. This exercise is designed to help the competitor feel as well as know this.

As you settle into this state of intense concentration and imagination, you put yourself on the court once again. Across the court is your opponent, your enemy. Not just your enemy, but the enemy of all that is good and decent. You are going to do everything you can within the rules to defeat your opponent. You not only may, you must.

As you begin to warm up for the game, you recognize that a distinctly cartoonish element has entered the scene. It's almost like a tennis match in ToonTown. It's your serve. You're going to serve a real bomb. So rather than a tennis ball, you take an old-fashioned bomb, one of those old-fashioned black balls of gunpowder with a sizzling wick sticking out of it. "Take this, creepo," you shout as you deliver your first ace of the day. Bam! Blew him away. Next you hit a rocket. A real rocket. The explosion is earth-shattering after the rocket has successfully chased your opponent all over the court, homing in with deadly accuracy.

It's back to tennis balls now. And you hit each one with unbelievable force as you do everything in your power to destroy this enemy. When the ball hits on the baseline, instead of bouncing up it buries itself and plows a furrow beyond the end line. He gets a little bit too close to one shot. It passes straight through him, punching out a neat, clean circle. On and on you go, but in a controlled frenzy. You know that to swing wildly is to swing badly, is to miss the point.

In fact, you realize that you're not playing with bombs and rockets. You're playing with tennis balls, and the best way to win, the best way to defeat this enemy, is not with unchained violence, but rather with deadly, accurate force. Hitting the ball just as you have practiced, placing your shots with surgical precision, mixed with all the power that you can muster.

"You win, you win. I surrender," shouts your enemy. And as soon as the game is over, you recognize that this is no longer your enemy. You are two friends sharing in a healthy competition. The kind of competition that is the most fun, when you both play your very hardest. The real way to be a friend on the court is to be enemies for the duration of the match.

When you are ready to end this exercise, bring yourself back to the usual waking state.

Winner's Circle

Most of the time we think of hypnosis as something done in a very relaxed state. It is possible, however, to use hypnosis while engaged in a physically demanding task. Racing, be it running, swimming, biking, skiing, or rowing, calls for extreme physical exertion, but your racing performance can be enhanced by focusing on the image of a powerful machine while you operate at top speed. This example will use running, but it could be anything. This can be practiced while sitting in a relaxed state but is most useful if done while in fact running, whether in a race or in practice.

━━◆◆◆◆━━

As you're running, your body is going at the pace you have set for yourself. With each stride that you make, with each pounding footstep, with each swing of the arms, with each exhalation, you feel yourself entering the mesmerizing state of deep hypnosis. As you do, you find yourself experiencing the peculiar duality familiar to many top runners. You feel yourself detaching from your body. You know that your body is there and that your body is working very hard. Your body is going along at a very good pace. Your body is charging along the course. Your legs are eating up the track, stride after stride, stride after stride. But you feel yourself becoming remote and far away from your body. This is a real advantage to you. It is really very hard work for your body to put in such a top effort. If you were there with your body, you might notice just how hard your muscles were working, what a strain is on them. Your muscles might feel like quitting. They might feel like saying, "I can't go on at this pace." Your lungs might be saying that they are burning up, that they can't stand it anymore.

Fortunately, you're not there to hear these complaints. Your mind is off in the winner's circle, having relaxed and taken your victory lap already. Your mind is enjoying the fruits of victory. Your mind thinks that it was worth it for your body to go through the hardships, to put in the tremendous effort that it did. In fact your body agrees. Your body realizes that when your mind was not there to take pity on it, it was then forced to do even more than it thought it could, that your mind's being absent meant that no one could say to your muscles, "You poor dears. You've done enough. You can slack off." Instead, your muscles kept on going.

In fact, as your mind leaves your body far behind, a curious thing happens. As your muscles are left there without a mind to keep them human, a transformation takes place. Your legs are no longer legs. They are now steel pistons, pumping up and down. They are machinery, incapable of feeling. Instead, they're mighty pistons, pumping up and down, mechanically churning out stride after stride after stride. Your arms are no longer arms, no longer flesh and blood, but powerful springs, swinging back and forth to provide counterbalance to those mighty pistons. Your lungs are no longer lungs but mighty bellows, sucking in oxygen to stoke the raging furnace which powers this mighty machine. Your heart is an engine, a furious engine pumping energy to those mighty pistons, driving them up and down across the miles, all the way to the winner's circle.

When you are ready to end this exercise or when the race is in reality completed, bring yourself back to the usual waking state.

Man-Eating Tiger

This exercise can be very useful both in providing some motivation to keep pressing during a boring practice or in providing a bit of extra adrenaline during a race. Like the previous exercise, it is most useful if done while in reality running, though imaginal rehearsal is also useful. You can vary the exercise by replacing the tiger behind you with someone in front of you. Perhaps a ravishing nymph or exciting satyr is running ahead of you, inviting you to a wild party. Perhaps someone is running along with a ten-carat diamond or a large sum of money saying it is yours if you can catch him. Or perhaps some pipsqueak of a thief is running away with your wallet. Just use whichever image works best for you.

———◆•◆•◆———

As you run along, directing your mind to reenter the hypnotic state, you use your imagination to help to motivate yourself. As you run, you become aware of something behind you, something chasing you. It's not another runner. It's not human. It's an animal. A very large animal, and it's chasing you. A huge ravenous, man-eating tiger is closing in on your heels. You are no longer racing to win a medal. You're no longer racing for an abstraction like a time on a stopwatch. You are not racing for bragging rights, nor to avoid your coach's disapproval. You are racing for your life. You are racing to avoid being tiger food. And you discover that you have speed beyond anything you've ever dreamed.

Your feet are flying. Your feet feel light. You feel as though you're Hermes, wearing winged sandals. You're so light on the ground you may not even be leaving a footprint. Your feet are flying almost before they touch the ground. You feel yourself flying along. Flying along, but that tiger's never far away. If you should begin to get complacent, if you should begin to think it's OK to slack off, you'll feel the hot carnivorous breath on the backs of your legs and find the energy again to stay one step ahead of those terrible jaws.

When you are ready to end this exercise, simply bring yourself back to the usual waking state.

10

Habits

People are creatures of habit. Imagine how difficult it would be if every trivial decision in a day had to be made by conscious thought. The amount of time and energy it would take to decide "Do I brush my top teeth before my bottom ones? Starting at the left or right side? Which comes first—the molars or the incisors? How many brush strokes per tooth? Will I brush with sideways or up-and-down strokes?" and so on would almost guarantee everyone would arrive at work late and exhausted each day.

People learn to deal with this potentially unmanageable process by developing habits. Habits are routine ways of handling routine decisions. Almost everyone, for example, always puts the same shoe on first. If you pay attention the next time you put on your shoes, you will learn which foot you do first.

Habits are very useful because they simplify decision making and allow a great many actions to be taken care of by a lower level of the brain. Whether brushing your teeth, putting on your shoes, or doing any of a million daily activities, your conscious mind is relieved of the responsibility of treating each decision anew. When you burn your hand, you don't have to think about whether or not to pull your hand away from the heat. You do it without reference to conscious thought. You do it by reflex. Just so, habits allow us to handle much of life without having to waste time thinking about it.

While many habits are constructive or at least neutral, allowing us to proceed through routine matters on automatic pilot, some other habits are not so benign. People who eat too much and exercise too little, abuse drugs, or routinely keep themselves under a great deal of stress have habits that are destructive and problematically complex. Breaking them is certainly possible but can be difficult since to do so involves changing a whole lifestyle.

Often easier to break are habits which are relatively small and self-contained, and that serve as a kind of ritualized way of discharging tension. The hypnotic exercises in this chapter are designed for such habits. These include nail biting, hair pulling, chewing on a lip, and picking at oneself, as well as tapping one's fingers, jiggling a leg, chewing on a pencil, or playing with one's hair.

These sorts of habits might or might not be a real problem. In general, it is a problem if you wish to control your behavior and are unable to do so. If, for example, you bite your fingernails so much that they're not only painful but bleeding, that is a problem. If you bite them so that they're a little bit sore, that's less of a problem. If you occasionally worry at a corner of a nail, that might be no problem at all.

Sometimes these kinds of habits are problems not because of any direct physical injury, but because they may affect self-esteem or social response. For example, a woman might dislike biting her nails because it makes her hands look ugly. A man might report that his wife finds it very irritating when he curls his hair around a finger while he's thinking. Some people dislike tapping their fingers because it lets other people know that they are nervous.

The hardest part of breaking a habit is deciding that you really want to break it. Many people are wont to echo St. Augustine. As a young man he lived in a wild and libertine style and prayed "Dear God, please make me reform my life, but not yet." With nail biters it's often "I really have to stop biting my nails, but first I've got to get this last corner." Likewise, "I know I shouldn't be doing this," or "I really don't want to be doing this," while continuing the activity are common statements.

This contradictory behavior occurs because personality is

not simple, unitary, or necessarily cohesive. It is normal for a person to have different parts of himself or herself, and the presence of these different aspects does not indicate a multiple personality. Some of us talk about "the child" in everyone, others about how "the devil made them" do something. All people have different aspects of themselves, and each part may want something different. A man might suck his thumb, for example, because this gives him a sense of warmth, comfort, and security. He enjoys the childish satisfaction it gives him. He might want to break his habit so that he will seem more grown-up. He wants to get rid of the behavior, yet he also wants to feel warm, comforted, and secure.

Pretending such conflicting desires don't exist tends to make breaking the habit subject to sabotage by the strong component that very much wants to hold onto the old behavior. If the ambivalence cannot be completely resolved, recognizing it at least allows an individual to make a mature decision about his or her habit.

An enormous degree of difficulty encountered in trying to change a habit or a severe amount of distress produced by breaking it indicates the habit might be a manifestation of a more complex problem. In such a case, professional attention can be helpful.

Easiest to change are the habits which are just ways of behaving that have no particular energy driving them. Sometimes, years of experience with a set behavior can so condition a person that his or her muscles tend to keep doing the habit even though there is now no real motivation behind it. It's as if the part of the brain that is used to handling an activity becomes loath to give up control. For an experiment, try reversing the order in which you put on your shoes. You probably don't have any strong reason why you would prefer one foot over the other. The sequence you originally chose was essentially random, but once you have got into one pattern, you may find that it takes a bit of work to change. Your habit seems to have a life of its own.

By far the hardest and most important part of breaking a habit is the decision to do it, really do it. To "try" to break a habit is to think about it, experiment with it, and play with it rather than *do* it. A person who is "trying to stop" biting his nails is still allowing himself do it sometimes. Even worse, he is repetitively putting himself in a position where he has to decide over and over again whether or not to bite his nails. The process of making a decision is much more difficult than living up to a decision. A person who has decided to do something only needs to put the decision into effect. A person who is thinking about it is having to weigh all the factors on both sides and try to come up with a decision about what to do. If each time you think about biting your nails you have to decide whether to do it this time or not do it this time, your task is much more difficult than it is for a person who either is going to bite his nails or else knows that he is never going to bite them again.

Once the decision has been made, once you have truly committed yourself to a new way of behaving, the following kinds of exercises tend to be useful for a number of reasons. First of all, hypnosis, in that it promotes relaxation, can be an effective substitute for a habit which exists as a means of discharging tension. Hypnosis is also a good way of learning new behavior. Just as an athlete can practice hitting a ball under hypnosis, so also a lawyer can practice addressing a jury without cracking her knuckles. Finally, since habits often occur without conscious intent or, in fact, outside the realm of conscious thought, the kind of focused attention found in hypnosis can be a useful way of increasing conscious awareness of the habit. The exercises won't make you decide to change your habit, but they should make it easier to do so once you've reached a decision.

Remember that although each exercise targets one specific behavior, most are applicable to a number of habits. You can substitute your habit for the one mentioned.

Caring for Yourself

People who have a self-destructive habit frequently experience it as benign. The perception of the behavior as harmless leads to forgetting the motivation to change. In fact, the effort of breaking the habit seems hard, while giving way to it seems easy and good. This exercise focuses on the motivation to care for yourself by changing your habit.

━━◆◆◆◆━━

As you settle back, comfortable and relaxed, you think about how good it feels, how relaxed your body is, and you think about how much you want to take care of yourself. You know you do a great many things to take care of yourself. You want good things for yourself. You want to help yourself. You want to keep yourself strong and healthy.

But there's something that you've been doing: something that isn't helpful, something that isn't good. You thought it was good, but it's not. For a long time now, for years, you've been hurting yourself. You've been biting your nails.

You thought that it was harmless. You thought it was simply discharging tension. You thought it made you feel good. It did, but you didn't weigh the price. It discharged tension. It made you feel a little bit good, but you did it at the cost of hurting your body. You were looking with tunnel vision. You thought it was calming and relaxing, without noticing how much it hurt you.

But now you know. You've been hurting yourself. Your habit isn't so harmless. Instead it's been hurting your body, causing your body pain, causing it distress. And now that you know, you have resolved that you are going to take care of your body. Even though you're used to biting your nails, even though it's familiar, you now know that you're not going to do it any more. The decision has been made. You have chosen to stop it. You have chosen to get control. You have chosen to take care of your body. And that choice makes you feel very good. That makes you feel happy about yourself, happy and committed. You have decided to care for yourself, and that means realizing that your former habit is one that's not good for you. Your former habit hurts you. Your former habit is unacceptable. If you should find yourself tempted to do it, you're going to remember that even though a part of you would like to do it, you will not because you have decided that the part of you that wants to do it is a minority and does not have your best interests at heart. And even though it wants to, you are going to say "no" to it, just as a loving parent says "no" to a child who wants something which really isn't good for him or her.

When you are ready to end this exercise, count backward from 3. At 1, open your eyes, find yourself relaxed, refreshed, and fully alert.

Touch Your Cheek

Habits almost always contain an element of tension reduction. This exercise involves a posthypnotic suggestion. Touching your cheek will relax you even when you're not hypnotized. If you would rather substitute some other movement for touching your cheek, you can. For instance, you might touch your thumb and finger together.

As you are so relaxed and comfortable, you're going to give yourself a suggestion that is going to help you to control the urge to bite your nails. Focus on how relaxed you feel, how comfortable and at peace you feel, how thoroughly relaxed and at ease you are. You're feeling completely at peace, completely without tension. As you stay so relaxed, allow your hand to come up toward your cheek, and just before it gets there, take a big deep breath, and as your hand touches your cheek, let the breath out and feel your muscles so relaxed. You needn't keep your hand up there, though you can if you wish. But what you've done is to establish an association, an association between touching your cheek and feeling so relaxed. This association between touching your cheek and being so relaxed is going to be so powerful that it will work not only during hypnosis, but also as a posthypnotic suggestion. Practice it in hypnosis, touching your cheek and feeling so relaxed, and as you do, you'll find that even when not hypnotized, when you reach up and touch your cheek, it will powerfully remind you how to let your muscles relax. The physical trigger of the touch will produce the physical effect of the relaxation. And when your body is relaxed, so also will your mind be relaxed.

Now, in the past, you used to have a habit of biting your

nails. That's a habit that you now have given up. When you used to do it, sometimes it served as a way of relaxing you, of breaking tension. But now you have a new way. If you find yourself feeling tense or anxious and you want to do something physical to relax your muscles, to relax your mind, you'll be able to reach up and touch your cheek. As you do, you'll find yourself becoming very, very relaxed, even more relaxed than when you bit your nails.

A special thing that you'll be able to do to combat the urge is this. If you find yourself bringing your hand up toward your mouth, instead of struggling and fighting, trying to keep your hand down as the part of you that wants to bite your nails tries to lift your hand, instead of trying to push that hand down and having a fight within yourself, you're going to act like a matador. The bull fighter does not try to stop the bull. Instead he sends the bull going past him. If your hand is moving up toward your mouth, you're going merely to deflect the direction away from your lips and onto your cheek. That's right. The motion to bite your nails is turned into touching your cheek and feeling so relaxed, comfortable, and peaceful. You've got all of the advantage of relaxation without hurting yourself, without hurting your fingers.

When you are ready to end this exercise, open your eyes and bring yourself back to the usual waking state.

Warning. Discretion Advised. *The following is one of four highly unpleasant hypnotic exercises in this book. You may prefer to skip them unread. That would be fine. However, some people do very hurtful, repulsive, and grotesque things to themselves. They engage in behaviors that can be extremely self-destructive. One way they do so is by masking the harsh reality of what they are really doing. These exercises are designed to force them to recognize a painful truth in order to change.*

The Torturer

This exercise is an extremely repugnant way of forcing you to notice just how self-destructive a habit can be. Always follow it with a less harsh exercise rather than end hypnosis on such an unpleasant note. If you stop after this one, you might just teach yourself to avoid hypnosis altogether.

Settle back; get yourself comfortable and relaxed. You know that sometimes in the past you've bitten your nails so much that it hurt. It's as though a part of you wanted to hurt yourself. Now you're going to allow yourself to experience something transiently unpleasant in order to change that in the future.

Imagine yourself in a small, dark room. You're bound to a chair. Your legs are tied. A rope holds your body. One hand is tied to the arm of the chair, the other is being held in a powerful grip. There are people in the room with you. One of the them is holding your hand. All of them are paying attention to you. And you realize who they are. You are in the hands of the Gestapo. And they are not friendly, loving hands. They want to hurt you. They want to torture you. They want to cause you pain. They don't like you.

And the leader decides they're going to torture you in a classic way. They're going to tear off your fingernails, one at a time. And you watch with horror as the leader picks up a pair of pliers and begins to get a grip on your first nail. And your horror increases as he puts aside the pliers and decides to do it even more primitively. He puts the end of your finger in his mouth, gets a firm grip on your nail and pulls, tearing off a chunk of nail, ripping it off, right down to the quick. He takes the bleeding fingertip, looks at it, and says, "There's a little corner left." And he grabs that in his teeth and rips away the last remaining bit.

You're sick with horror as you watch him take the next finger and look it over. You realize this person does not love you. This person is hurting you. And you realize that nothing you have done deserves this type of torture. Nothing about you deserves this sort of treatment. He shouldn't be doing this to you. But as you look up and see him bringing the next finger to his mouth, to your shock you discover the worst horror of all. He has your face. And you feel a sick shock of recognition in the pit of your stomach. He is you. You have been hurting yourself. You have been torturing yourself. You have been ripping off your own fingernails.

And you realize you don't deserve this. You shouldn't treat yourself this way. That even if you sometimes get down on yourself, even if you sometimes don't like yourself very well, you still don't deserve this type of torture. And you realize that you are never again going to mistake it for anything but the torture it is.

When you are ready to end this exercise, allow yourself to move on to a second, more pleasant one.

Alarm

Many habits occur primarily outside conscious awareness. You are not aware of doing it at the time, and so you are unable to decide not to do it. This exercise alerts you to the fact that you are engaging in the habit so that you can choose to stop yourself. For variety, the habit in question is eyelash pulling.

Settle back, peaceful and comfortable, and as you do, imagine experiencing in your mind some kind of a warning or an alarm. It might take the form of a ringing bell or a buzzing in your head. It might take the form of a crackling static. It might be visual. It might be a red light flashing or a strobe light pulsing. It might be some combination. Whatever it is, this is your personal alarm system.

And you need this alarm because you need to be protected. You need to be protected not against burglars or thieves, but from your habit. You've spent many years practicing your habit, many years pulling out your eyelashes. It was second nature to you that you did it so much. Without any thought at all, your hand would go up to your eyelid and pull out an eyelash. And now you know, now you've decided that you are not going to do that anymore. You've decided to change. You're not going to do that. But sometimes that part of you that does it out of habit will try to do it again. If you knew that you were doing it, you would certainly stop yourself. But you've been doing it for so long that you can do it without even trying. You could practically do it in your sleep.

You need to be protected. You know that if you were aware of reaching up for your eyelashes, you would protect yourself. If you know that you're doing it, you will take care to stop it. But you have to know about it.

And that's where the alarm comes in. If your body should find that your hand is going up, it will self-protectively trigger the alarm. When the alarm goes off, you will know that your hand is approaching your eyelashes and you need protection from the part of you that is used to pulling your lashes and still wants to. And by alerting you, the alarm will allow you to protect yourself, to break the cycle of the habit.

Bring your hand up toward your eyelashes. As your hand gets close, become very aware of your alarm. Become very aware of the signal being sent. And as you become aware, you realize that you need to protect your eyelashes, that you need to tell yourself that you may not pick at them, that you may not pluck them. Bring your hands back down and hear the alarm cease its warning. Now try it again. As your hand comes up, the alarm signal begins. As it approaches your eyelashes, it gets stronger and stronger, more intense and more demanding. It makes sure that your hands, that your fingers, do not approach your eyelashes without your knowing about it. And once you know about it, you take charge; you take command of your hands.

Sometimes your hands come up toward your face for some innocent gesture. You might be bringing your hand up to brush a wisp of hair off your forehead. Or you might be bringing a Kleenex up to blow your nose or to wipe away a tear. In this case, of course, the alarm will not go off. This is not the habit trying to sneak in like a thief in the night. This is your body doing what it should. As long as your hand is going about some legitimate business, it does not set off the alarm. If, however, your hands, having got into the neighborhood, try to take advantage of the proximity by reaching for an eyelash to pluck, the alarm will go off immediately, intensely, demanding your attention.

If you find your hand going off and triggering the alarm, one good way to deal with it is as soon as the alarm goes off, as soon as you become aware of the urge to bring your fingers up to your eyelashes, transform the motion into touching your cheek. As soon as you do, as soon as you switch from reaching from your eyelashes to touching your cheek, the alarm ceases and you know you are safe.

In particular, if you find that you are tense and you are using the exercise of touching your cheek to relax, there will be no confusion at all, no alarm because the alarm is to warn you that a part of you, the habit, is in danger of hurting you. You do not need to be warned when you are allowing yourself to take good care of yourself.

When you are ready to end this exercise, open your eyes and bring yourself back to the usual waking state.

Flower Garden

Habits are typically nurtured by an attitude of "a little bit won't hurt." A destructive behavior is tolerated because each particular bit causes only minuscule damage. This exercise focuses attention on how small destructive behaviors add up. Hair pulling is the habit treated. Some people pull so much they have large bald patches.

As you settle into a state of deep relaxation, you think about the fact that when you pull a hair out of your scalp, you feel as if it's only one of so many that it doesn't matter. It's been hard to take seriously the effect of plucking a hair. But now you settle back and imagine yourself walking through a garden. It's a beautiful garden filled with every variety of flower. Look around. See all the beautiful colors. Look at all of the different types of flowers: beautiful white daisies, their centers matching the yellow of some nearby black-eyed susans, perhaps some fragrant lavender phlox or tall scarlet hollyhocks or graceful pink roses—all the beautiful flowers all around growing in carefully ordered array.

And as you walk along through the garden, looking at all the beautiful flowers, you absentmindedly reach down a pluck a petal from a flower. But it doesn't matter. It's just one petal. You continue to look at the flowers. And you notice that again your fingers have a flower petal between them. You must have plucked another one, or two or three as you look at the petals on the ground. But you know that it doesn't matter. It's a big garden. There are lots of flowers with lots of petals. The person whose garden this is will never notice, will never know the difference. So you continue to walk along enjoying the beauty, smelling the fragrance of the blossoms, feeling the warmth of the sun, enjoying the play of light and shadow on all the beautiful colors, and so what if you seem to have plucked another petal or several more petals. They're small. They don't really matter. The garden is so full; the flowers are so many.

And you continue to appreciate the beauty of the garden, not paying attention to your fingers as they pluck a petal here and there. It doesn't really matter. You're just enjoying the beauty of the garden. It gives your fingers something to do. You're not hurting anyone. You're just enjoying the garden.

Suddenly, your reverie is broken. Someone is coming. You're about to greet them when you look around aghast at what has happened. You are in the center of a large area of stalks and branches. The ground is littered with the bright colors of the flowers, but not a single flower remains in bloom. Every stalk, every stem has been denuded and plucked bare. You've destroyed a whole patch of the beautiful garden.

And a sick feeling settles down like a lump of lead in the pit of your stomach. The sick feeling tells you that you've done it, and there's no excuse. Bit by bit, petal by petal, you've managed to destroy a large plot of beautiful garden. And you feel so horrible. You feel so awful. You feel such remorse, such shame, such despair.

But as these feelings sweep over you, a small ray of hope comes burning through the gloom. The flowers are gone, but the good soil remains. The roots of the flowers are still there, safe in the earth. You've plucked the petals, but you haven't destroyed the life.

It's too late for this year. These blossoms are well and truly plucked. They'll never fill a vase; they'll never again be admired by someone walking through the garden. What you did is not nothing. You destroyed a patch of garden for an entire growing season. But it's not the end either.

Next year these flowers will grow back, once again bringing beauty to the world. You can't make these petals go back on the stalks, on the stems, but you can commit yourself to never harming this garden patch again. Not even "just one petal."

When you are ready to end this exercise, open your eyes and bring yourself back to the usual waking state.

Warning. Discretion advised. *The following is one of four highly unpleasant hypnotic exercises in this book. You may prefer to skip them unread. That would be fine. However, some people do very hurtful, repulsive, and grotesque things to themselves. They engage in behaviors that can be extremely self-destructive. One way they do so is by masking the harsh reality of what they are really doing. These exercises are designed to force them to recognize a painful truth in order to change.*

The Stable Hand

Like "The Torturer," this is an aversive technique focused on why you don't want to bite your fingernails. It also should be followed by a more positive exercise.

Biting your nails is inherently unpleasant. You have had to do something to make it mentally possible to bite them. You had to detach yourself from your hand. It had to feel not like your hand, which feels pain when the nails are bitten to the quick, but just "a" hand, a hand which was not sensitive to the pain, a hand which in some ways was not your own.

And as you settle into this relaxed state, more and more you begin to feel detached from the hand. And as you do, you begin to imagine yourself biting fingernails in that familiar fashion, working the fingernails into your teeth, biting on them. That's right. Working off bits of fingernail, softening them with your saliva, biting on them with your teeth. And as you do, you begin to notice how bits of nail are getting stuck in your throat. You may be noticing a bit of fingernail getting stuck inside the gum at the tooth line. And you reach back with your tongue and try to free it, try to get that bit of nail out. It's stuck just as that other bit of fingernail is stuck in your throat.

Oh, well, no matter. You have a good nail here to work on. That's right. A good fingernail to chew on, to peel off, to bite off.

But then you look a little closer and see that this time it is truly not your own hand you are biting. You're biting the fingernail of a stranger. You're biting the fingernail of someone you don't even know. You have this stranger's finger in your mouth, and you are chewing at the nail with your teeth, sucking at the nail with your mouth. And then you look a little closer at this stranger. And what your eyes tell you, your nose confirms. You are chewing on the fingernail of a stable hand. In your mouth, you have the fingers of somebody who spends his time mucking out horse's stables. You think about where those hands have been. Probably the cleanest thing he's done all day has been to groom the horses, getting bits of dirt and horse hair and dander beneath the nails. And that's the clean part. The hands are covered, the nails caked, with horse manure and urine-soaked straw. And you've been chewing on that. A nail encrusted in that is stuck in your throat. Another is jammed beneath the gum. Worst of all, you still have that filthy fingernail in your mouth and are chewing on it.

You pull your head away and spit, cleansing your mouth as best you can from the revolting experience. You go and brush your teeth and gargle to clean your mouth out. And you resolve never to do that to yourself again.

When you are ready to end this exercise, go on to a more pleasant one.

The Magnets

Commonly, habits happen when an individual's mind is elsewhere. One does not sit down for a good session of picking at oneself. Instead, it happens when one is doing something else.

This tendency is especially true of people whose habits involve something which is always available. Nails to chew or hair to pull, for example, are always at hand, and it is very easy to begin absentmindedly pulling or chewing when attention is engaged in reading a book, driving a car, or watching television.

———•◆•———

Imagine yourself settling down into your chair with your book. You're settled in and relaxed, ready to begin to read. You know, however, that this has been a time when it's been easy to slip inadvertently into your habit. So before you begin to read, you're going to go through an exercise. Your hands are turning into powerful electromagnets. That's right. Each hand is becoming a powerful electromagnet. The book, meanwhile, is turning into a piece of iron. It's a very light piece of iron. It's no heavier than an ordinary book. You're easily able to hold it while you read, but it is a piece of iron, and the powerful electromagnets which are your hands clamp onto the book. Your fingers are clasped to the book. Your hands are not unusually tense or tight. You don't have to work hard at holding the book, it's just that as they are in contact with the book, it would take a great deal of effort to remove them.

As you are sitting and reading, your hands are not going to drift idly away toward your head, toward your face. They are going to remain just where they belong. Your hands are stuck to the book. Without even thinking about them, without any effort on your part, they're going to remain attracted to, attached to, the pages of the book.

As you reach the end of a page, you are glad that your fingers are electromagnets. When you need to turn the page, you momentarily interrupt the power and turn off the magnetic field. While they are doing their job of turning the page, your fingers easily leave the book and perform the appropriate action. As soon as that page is turned, however, the power is on. The magnets are on; your fingers are staying where they belong. When you are ready to end this exercise, open your eyes and bring yourself back to the usual waking state.

Overdo It

People with self-destructive habits often fool themselves into thinking that they're just doing a little bit at a time, as described in "Flower Garden." Often they tell themselves they will do just a little bit more. If they knew how much they might do, it would help them to stop. In this exercise you're going to free yourself from the delusion that just a little damage doesn't hurt by focusing in on how much you're doing. It will also deal with the way you've learned to ignore the pain of doing the habit.

◆ ◆ ◆ ◆

As you settle back comfortably and peacefully, while leaving your hands in the resting position, think back to a time when you were biting your fingernails. In particular, go back to a time when you were telling yourself you were just going to do a little bit more. And as you think about that time, you feel yourself going back, remembering exactly the way it felt, remembering how you told yourself that you were only going to do a little bit more. You told yourself that you were going just to finish this little bit. Then you would stop. You know from experience that you didn't stop. You know that you kept doing it, and you're going to go back now to the way you felt then, that you'll just do a little more.

But this time you're going to change it. You're going to catch your attention. You're going to say to yourself, "Who am I kidding? Just one little corner more? That's absurd!" You're going to get all ten of them. You're going to chew all ten of those suckers all the way down till there's nothing your teeth can manage to work loose. One little bit more indeed. You've got ten fingernails. Now go for it!

You have that little corner of a nail that you've managed to get your teeth around. Give it a good yank. Feel the satisfying sensation as the nail tears across. Feel it give as you pull with your teeth, peeling the nail back from the quick. That's right. You feel it this time. So often when you've bitten your nails, you've managed to numb yourself to the sensation. Too often, you haven't felt it until later. You haven't felt it until it was too late. But not this time. This time you feel every torn bit of flesh. You feel the sensitive skin under your fingernails as their protection is peeled away.

But there's something so satisfying, so tempting about biting your nails. There's nothing left on that finger. So go on to the next one. The first finger is bleeding, hurting. It's time for a fresh one. So you take that nail in your teeth and begin to soften it up with your saliva. That's it. Get it nice and pliable, soft and ready to rip. But you can't really wait long enough, so you take a bit of nail and bite right into it. Feel the satisfying click as your teeth meet. Now feel the horrible sensual feeling as the nail tears, as the grain of the nail makes it rip deeper than you intended, right across the quick. You don't even think about fooling yourself into believing that you're just going to finish this nail, that you're just going to fix this last little bit. You've got eight more to go after this one, and you're not going to stop this until there's nothing left to chew.

That's right. It hurts. You're mutilating your fingers, but you can't stop now. You still have more to do. You still have further to go. You have to get every last available bit of nail. Who knows? You may stop biting your nails, and then you would lose the chance to do this. Then you would lose the opportunity to get this nail.

And then, in horror, you listen to what you've just been saying. You look at your nails. You've been not only torturing yourself but mutilating yourself. You've been hurting yourself. You've been cannibalizing yourself. At least a real cannibal could wait for the victim to be dead before beginning to eat. You've been biting and chewing at yourself while you're still alive.

And you're treating this as an opportunity. You're treating this as a chance to do something. This is something horrible, and you realize the sooner you stop it, the happier you'll be. The sooner you stop it, the safer you'll be, the sooner your body can begin to heal, heal and grow.

When you're ready to end this exercise, open your eyes and bring yourself back to the usual waking state.

There's No Time Like the Present

You can deal directly with the temptation to "finish just this bit off" in a slightly different way. This variation can be done either as a part of the preceding exercise or whenever you find yourself having begun to bite your nails.

◆◆◆

As you settle back, you once again find yourself, whether in reality or imagination, in the midst of biting your nails. And you feel an urge to finish just this nail, to smooth just this corner, and you immediately recognize this tactic for what it is. It's a disguised way to keep on going without stopping. It's a way to sneak in a bite.

And you realize that you can't change the past. What you have done, you have done. The nails that you have mangled have been torn.

But the present and the future are yours to command. You've bitten your nails in the past. But you have the power never to bite another nail again. You have the power to see to it that never again will one of your nails be bitten. And you're going to seize that power. You are going to take charge, take command. You are going to do it.

The first thing you do is to pull your finger away from your mouth. That's right. There's nothing good that your teeth can do to a fingernail. In fact, there are many bad things they can do to your nails, but nothing good. You need to protect your nails from your teeth. Perhaps there is a rough corner or a torn edge of a nail. It's not going to be helped by your teeth. You need to do something else. If you can, you should get a nail clipper or an emory board and properly repair that loose bit. Or it may be that it's not convenient to do so at this time. That means that you're going to have to take special care to protect that delicate bit of your body. You have a small bit of your body that's in danger, so you're going to have to take especially good care of it until you can give it the sort of attention it deserves.

And it makes you feel very good, proud, and happy to know that you are treating your body, treating yourself the way you should.

When you are ready to end this exercise, open your eyes and bring yourself back to the usual waking state.

Other People's Reactions

This exercise is going to focus on how other people respond to your habit. Sometimes the main reason or the only reason people want to stop an otherwise harmless habit is because of the way it looks to other people. Sometimes people find this useful in dealing with harmful habits because they are more motivated by the responses of other people than they are by such basic behavior shapers as pain.

Get yourself nice and relaxed and imagine yourself sitting in a room with several friends. And as you're sitting there, so relaxed, you find yourself reaching up and playing with your hair. That's right. You begin wrapping a lock of hair around your fingers. But as you do, as you become aware of doing it, perhaps because your alarm has gone off, you realize how it makes you look. You know that you are in charge of yourself. You know that other people can't make you do something you don't want to do. You know no one can force you to change your behavior.

But you don't like the way it makes you look. As you sit there, twirling your hair around your finger, you realize that one of your friends is thinking how nervous it makes you look. You're not really nervous, but your friend thinks you are. That's the impression you're giving.

And then you look at another friend, and you realize that she doesn't think you look nervous. She thinks you look extraordinarily vain. You can almost hear her muttering to herself, "Who does she think she is? A character on an Aaron Spelling show?" And you realize that she thinks you look not only extraordinarily vain but also monumentally brainless. She's sitting there thinking that all the important stuff must be on the outside of your scalp, not inside it. And you know that's not true, but you hate to look that way.

And then you look at your third friend. His look is the most upsetting of all. He knows you're not nervous. He knows you're neither vain nor an airhead, but with a slightly sad shake of the head, he acknowledges what he does know. You don't have any control over this. You don't have any choice about whether to play with your hair. The habit has taken control.

But with a deep meaningful smile crossing your lips, you give your head a shake and bring your hand down to a resting position on your lap. And you leave it there. Because not only are you not nervous, not vain, not stupid, you are also not a slave. You are in charge. You decide what to do, and you decide to control your appearance. You decide to keep your hands out of your hair. And while you don't do things that you don't want to do, it is very satisfying to see the look of enhanced respect on the faces of your friends. When you are ready to end this exercise, open your eyes and bring yourself back to the usual waking state.

11

Smoking

The real dilemma of people who want to stop smoking is that in fact they are ambivalent. If there were not a part of them that wanted to stop smoking, there would be no problem. They would just keep smoking. Or alternatively there would again be no problem if there weren't a part that wanted to keep on smoking. They would just stop. The problem comes from the fact that the person simultaneously wants both to stop and to smoke. Two opposing factions are struggling for control of the person's actions.

In a way, then, you can think of smoking or not as like an election in which different parts get to vote on the decision to smoke or not to smoke. When we vote for president of the United States, we realize it's not necessary for either candidate to get every single person in the country to cast a favorable ballot. Instead, the majority rules. Those who voted for the losing candidate may be disappointed and may not like it, but their candidate lost and the opponent is the next president. They must accept the decision of the will of the majority.

During an election year, a great deal of energy is spent not in running the government but in running for office. Think of how disruptive it would be if right after the general election the backers of the losing candidate were to say, "Wait a minute. Let's have a new election." The country would be in chaos because all the attention and energy would be focused on the election process and none on the governing of the country.

A smoker who is considering becoming a nonsmoker, then, needs to begin by realizing that he or she has a decision to make. You need to decide whether or not to continue to smoke. The U.S. Surgeon General, your family, your friends, your doctor—none of these can make the decision for you. Sometimes, in fact, the pressure of others can interfere with a person's own wish to stop. In these cases, because everyone else is pushing in this direction, you cannot hear the voice inside you which agrees and wants to stop. Instead all you hear yourself saying is "You can't tell me what to do. You're not my boss, and I'll smoke to prove it."

When we think of the different parts of ourselves, it's clear that they are not all the same. Some parts of the mind are conscious and intelligent and are entrusted with leadership and decision making. Some parts are more representative of the animal side of humans. Just as laboratory rats can be conditioned, so also people learn habits. The problem of physical addiction takes place on this animal level.

For the person who wants to stop smoking but is having trouble doing so, it's reasonable to think of this problem as a situation where the leaders of the person's mind have a good idea but have to persuade the majority of the masses to go along with it. In order to accomplish this task, they need to go on a campaign along different fronts—educating, persuading, and modifying attitudes, as well as making behavioral change as easy as possible.

Throughout the process, you should remember that you do not need fanatical, unanimous devotion to the nonsmoking cause. The president is the candidate who receives the most votes, even if many of them are lukewarm. All you need to do is convince a majority of yourself to agree to vote against smoking. The die-hard prosmoking element need not be eradicated—just outnumbered.

Remember also that once this decision is made, it does not need to be revoted every fifteen minutes. Instead, once the decision to stop smoking has been made, it is final. When the animal which had been conditioned to smoke starts whining, it can be told, "Shut up. We've already decided this." These harsh words can then be followed by milder ones which can ease the difficulty while making it clear that there is no new voting on the horizon.

Mechanics of Stopping Smoking

Use this exercise not only in the beginning of stopping smoking but also as a base to which you come back time and again. It is helpful in organizing your thoughts and orienting yourself to why it is you are choosing to give up cigarettes.

Enter a state of trance. Now that you've got into this deep, comfortable state of relaxed concentration and imagination and attention that we call hypnosis, you know that you have decided to go through these exercises not simply to relax but also to achieve a goal. You wish to stop smoking. Or more to the point, a part of you has chosen to stop smoking. In the past, it has been that a part of you wanted to stop, but the majority wished to continue. You're going to use techniques that you will learn in order to tip the balance. It doesn't have to be a total tipping, just enough to change the actions from those of a smoker to those of a nonsmoker. As you think about it, you realize that you've really enjoyed smoking. Nobody has forced you to buy cigarettes and smoke them. In fact, you've put up with ever-increasing prices and mounting social disapproval. Clearly there's been something about smoking that you've liked.

Part of what has pushed you to continue to smoke has been physical addiction. We'll deal with that a little later. That's not really the hard part. Another thing is habit. That's a little more difficult, but we'll deal with that also. First of all, we have to deal with the hardest part of all, the fact that you like it.

That's right. You enjoy smoking. Cigarettes taste good, or at least some of them do. They give you something to do with your hands. They mark time for you. They give you a format for relaxing. You're not sitting and doing nothing. You've just stopped for a cigarette break. Smoking gives you a way of interacting with people—offering and accepting cigarettes and lights. And it's a convenient prop. It helps define your identity. It makes you one with a fictional character, be it the Marlboro cowboy or the liberated Virginia Slims woman. It does all these wonderful things. Of course you like smoking.

There is, however, a down side.

Cigarettes are poisonous.

That's right. Cigarettes are a poison to your body. It's really a shame that anything so enjoyable has to be poisonous, but it's true. You know that it is. You know that the U.S. Surgeon General has published proof that smoking hurts your body. It hurts it in many ways. It increases the likelihood of getting cancer, not just of getting lung cancer, but of getting every type of cancer. It increases the risk of heart disease. It not only raises the likelihood of having a heart attack, but it also makes every sort of circulatory disorder more likely. It raises the risk of stroke. It also increases the likelihood of every respiratory illness. It makes you more likely to get emphysema. It even makes you more likely to catch a cold. It makes you sick.

And it's not just the scientists and the doctors and the U.S. surgeon general who are saying this. You know in your heart that it's true. You know what too many cigarettes do to your throat. You know how they make you cough. You know that they are hurting your body. You may try to kid yourself, but you know the truth. They're poison.

Maybe you didn't know it was poison when you started, although as you think back, you realize that the clues were there. Remember how that very first cigarette made you feel kind of sick to your stomach and queasy? Your body was trying to tell you something. Remember how it made you feel green? Your body was trying to tell you that it was being poisoned. Remember how you had to learn to smoke? Think of how it would have felt if you had sat down and smoked a whole pack of cigarettes the first time you ever smoked. You would have become acutely ill. You could only smoke a little at first. You had to learn to tolerate the poison, to ignore the sick feelings. Though you learned to tolerate the sick feelings, the poison didn't become any the less poisonous. Instead, you just learned to ignore your body's warning signals.

But it is a poison. You would like to have it both ways. You would like to have the pleasure and enjoyment of smoking, and you would like to have the pleasure of being healthy. It's kind of like somebody who would like to buy something and also have the money that certain something would cost. Of course you would like both. But you can't have both. So now what?

Now you have a choice. You can have the pleasure of smoking at the cost of hurting your body or you can take care of your body at the cost of giving up the pleasure of smoking. And when you put it that way, you realize that this is a very easy decision to make. In the past you've been asking yourself the wrong question. You've been asking yourself, "Do I want to give up smoking?" Now you realize that if it's simply that question, the answer is "No." But another question goes with it: "Do you want to take good care of your body?" The answer to that one is an overwhelming "Yes." And it happens that taking care of your body includes not poisoning it. So the whole question is "Would you rather poison your body with a mildly pleasurable toxin or take care of your body?" And put that way, you realize you would no more smoke than you would swallow some rat poison. So you have decided what to do. You want to stop smoking.

Now lift up your hand and touch your cheek. As your hand touches your cheek, take a deep breath and exhale. That's right. And as you exhale and touch your cheek, you feel the muscles of your body become so relaxed, and you think about the fact that smoking is a poison for your body. And you think about how you want to take care of your body. And you realize that the choice is clear. Even though you want a cigarette, you want your health even more. And a sense of peace comes over you. You are not warring with yourself. You're not having a part of you that wants to smoke fighting with the part that doesn't. All the different parts agree that you want to take care of yourself even though that involves not smoking.

Whenever you get the urge to have a cigarette, you are not going to fight against it. Instead, as soon as you become aware of it, you are going to reach up, touch your cheek, take a deep breath, and, as you let the breath out, feel your muscles relax. Think about how smoking is a poison to your body and how you want to take good care of your body. And you find yourself relaxing and able to be at peace with yourself.

Now that you have made the decision to stop smoking, you need to know what's going to happen, what you can expect. You're going to experience waves of desire to have a cigarette. Part of the experience of wanting a cigarette will show up in your muscles. They will tend to become tense as you physically act out ambivalence between wanting to reach for a cigarette and wanting to stop yourself. When these waves come, first of all, you're going to remember that you have a choice of how to deal with them. What you're not going to do is to light up a cigarette because that would be to poison yourself. Instead, if the urge is very strong and you feel that you need help and support, you will have the option of putting yourself into a state of hypnosis. If you do this, it will relax your body. As your body is relaxed, you will stop fighting with yourself. Your mind will become relaxed and clear. You will be able to see that this is a fight within yourself that can hurt only you. And you remind yourself that self-preservation demands that you protect and care for your body, and as you do, you let go of the urge to smoke as you would let go of any urge that you knew would really hurt you. In this hypnotic state, you can add whichever other exercises are helpful to you at that moment.

There's no sense in saying you don't have time to hypnotize yourself unless you're also going to say you don't have time to decide to have a cigarette either. You've put far too much energy into stopping smoking to throw it all away just because you can't spend five minutes to hypnotize yourself, five minutes to keep yourself safe.

Or you may decide the urge is not quite so strong as to require full hypnosis. If this is the case, then as soon as you become aware of the urge and of the tension, that's right, you bring your hand up to your cheek and take a deep breath, and as you exhale, you feel your body becoming relaxed and you feel yourself motivated to protect your body from the poison.

You're going to find that the desire for a cigarette is not a

constant, steady state. Instead, the desire is going to come as a series of waves. When you get a wave of urge to have a cigarette,
it's not a condition you are going to have to endure forever. Instead, it is going to build up, reach a peak, and then fade away.
And when it goes away, you are going to feel good, proud of
yourself, happy that you stuck to your resolve and protected
your body.

That won't be the last wave, of course, but you can get
through these waves one at a time.

As you go along, you're going to discover a pattern to them.
For the first two or three days, the waves are going to be the
strongest and the most frequent. After that they're going to begin
to change. It's going to be like the tide going out. The waves are
going to be weaker and weaker. They are going to come less and
less frequently. Just as when the tide is going out, sometimes a
large wave will come along, so every once in a while, you might
get a stronger urge for a cigarette. But just as the overall effect of
the outgoing tide is a pattern of smaller and smaller waves, so
also you will find the desire to smoke gets less and less frequent,
less and less strong.

At first, you should hypnotize yourself at least three times a
day for twenty minutes at a time. If you need to do it more often,
that's fine. This is not a drug to which you develop a tolerance.
Instead, it is learning, and like any learning, the more you practice, the better you know it. As the waves become weaker and
less frequent, you can begin to cut back on the frequency of hypnosis if you are comfortable doing so. You should continue to do
it at least daily for the first six weeks. After that, if you're comfortable, you can continue to cut back more, but you should hypnotize yourself at least once a week for the next year. That's
work, but it's work that not only gets you the important reward
of a healthy body, but that makes it easier to get that reward.

It would be foolish to go through the work of making your
body healthier by not smoking if you were simultaneously to
make your body less healthy by gaining unnecessary weight.
Some people think that because they are stopping smoking, they
deserve a reward of candy or some other extra food. The real reward of stopping smoking is a healthy body. That's the only re-

ward that really matters. Adding unnecessary calories isn't a reward; it's a punishment. You've had enough and too much of hurting your body. You're not falling for that trap. You're going to take care of yourself to keep your body healthy. Besides, there never was a piece of candy which satisfied the urge for a cigarette. They are two separate things, two separate appetites.

Often, when people stop smoking, they find their body begins to weigh more even though they have not increased their eating. Two side effects of nicotine are responsible for this gain. First, nicotine is a diuretic. It makes your body lose fluid. Second, nicotine is a stimulant to the digestive tract. It makes food go through your intestines more quickly. When you first began smoking, your body had to learn to cope with these side effects. Your body learned to try to retain fluid to counteract the diuretic effect. Your body slowed down your digestion so that the speeding up effect of nicotine would merely bring it back to where it should be. Now you've stopped the nicotine, but your body is still trying to compensate for it. While your body was able to learn to live with nicotine, it's even more easily able to learn to live without it. It will just take a little time. Your body will stop retaining fluid. It will allow your digestive tract to speed up. Sometimes this happens very quickly. Sometimes it takes as long as three months. However long it takes is OK. You have the rest of your life, and stopping smoking means that you'll have a longer and healthier life span to enjoy after your body has reequilibrated. That false weight gain will go away.

Someone for whom smoking is only an occasional sort of a thing will find many different ways of stopping work well. However, for someone who is a moderate to heavy smoker, smoking has become a habit. A part of you has become psychologically conditioned to have a cigarette just as Pavlov's dogs were conditioned to salivate at the sound of a bell, just as laboratory rats are conditioned to press a lever to get a food pellet. That's right. The animal part of you has been conditioned like a laboratory animal. It's a very strong habit that you're dealing with. Unlike the laboratory rat, however, you have a mind, and you can use this mind to decondition yourself. As you decondition yourself, though, you have to keep in mind that the animal part of you has learned like an animal and has to be retaught as an animal would be retaught.

This means stopping cold turkey. Obviously any way of stopping smoking eventually leads to completely stopping. Oddly enough it is easiest to get to the point of stopping by the direct route.

You know that animals learn by rewards and punishments. If a behavior is rewarded, it will be encouraged and will happen more and more often. If it is not rewarded, eventually it will wither and disappear. It will extinguish. When the animal part of you asks for a cigarette and is given one, it is rewarded. As a result, it will have learned that bothering you and asking for a cigarette gets a reward. Every time you have a cigarette, you strengthen the urge to have another. In fact, if you only occasionally give way, you'll strengthen it the most. It will learn not to take "no" for an answer. So it's necessary for your ease and well-being to be very firm, to let yourself never again reward that part of you that asks for a cigarette. To do so is to condition the animal to keep asking again and again. And you, not the animal, should be in control.

In addition, any heavy smoker knows that there are a few cigarettes in a day that really taste good. And if you just have the good ones, it makes them all seem better. "Cutting back" means rewarding the animal with the most enjoyable cigarettes of the day; it means saying that it is all right to poison yourself occasionally; it means you are still a smoker. And smokers who cut back are smokers who increase later.

So that means the decision is simple and straightforward. You never have another puff of a cigarette again. First of all, this makes sense when you realize that cigarettes are a poison to your body. You don't want to have any poison, not even just a little every once in a while. Also, you don't want to condition your body, you don't want to train the animal within to keep on asking for cigarettes more and more and more. Even an occasional puff, especially an occasional puff, will teach that nuisance that it will be successful if it keeps asking and asking and asking. As with a whiny child, occasional encouragement will keep it going to what seems like forever. The fastest way to train it is never to reward it again.

Now, you know that nicotine is an addictive drug, that smoking is more than just a habit. That is particularly why you need to stop and stay stopped. Rewarding the animal by giving it some of the drug that it's used to will keep it continuing the addiction. Just as the alcoholic, who is addicted to ethyl alcohol, cannot drink in moderation, so the nicotine addict cannot smoke in moderation. It reawakens the addiction to have a dose of the drug.

Let's think about addiction. The word *addiction* has to do with the way your body develops a chemical habit. But just as your body can develop such a habit, so it can also break it. Sometimes people who are severely injured are treated with morphine for pain while they are healing. Morphine is a powerful drug related to heroin. They become addicted to the morphine while they are recovering. When they no longer need the drug to control pain, they discontinue it and go through a withdrawal. While it is not enjoyable, it is not the hell described by street junkies. Much of the torment of narcotic withdrawal is based upon myths and legends that lead a person to expect that torment.

There are lots of stories around about how hard, how impossible it is to stop smoking. Tobacco companies love to hear these stories because they discourage people who want to quit smoking. Many of these stories are told by people who continue to smoke. Since they did not conquer the urge to smoke, they need to say that this urge is an overpowering, unbeatable force, because the alternative would not make them look very good. Some people who have stopped like to describe how horribly difficult it was to do so. They like to boast. They like to make themselves heroes of their own myths.

The reality is that stopping smoking is something that you can do. People no better or stronger or determined do so every day. Millions of ordinary people have done it already and they are not heroes.

In many ways it's easier to learn to stop smoking than it was to learn to tolerate smoking. That involved learning to tolerate hurting your body. This involves giving up a minor pleasure. You're going to be taking care of your body, getting healthier all the time. And unlike with more powerful drugs, there's no need to withdraw gradually. No one ever had an epileptic seizure from stopping smoking. It's a discomfort, but one that you can bear. It's work, but a job that you can do.

And throughout it all, three thoughts help you to forge ahead. First, you realize that you are choosing health, life, and not poisoning yourself. Second, you realize that as you go on, it will get easier and easier, that you're looking forward to a task that becomes less and less difficult as time goes on. And third, you know that however far you have gone, however long it has been since your last cigarette, you've put in a lot of good work. You would hate to waste it by smoking and then knowing that you had to start all over again. You don't wish to waste the excellent progress you've made.

There are a number of other techniques that you are going to learn that will help you with different parts of the urge to smoke. Some of them will be very appropriate for you, others less so. You just use and take advantage of the ones that suit you best at any particular time. It may be that the ones that help most in the beginning will be different from the ones that help you later. You will always keep as your base, however, this exercise that reminds you why you are in control and why you are doing what you're doing.

When you are ready to end this exercise, count backward from 3. At 1, open your eyes and find yourself relaxed, refreshed, and fully alert.

Social Poison

This exercise is often particularly helpful for those who are less bothered by the effects of cigarettes on their own bodies than they are by other people's responses to smoking.

You know that people's attitudes about smoking have been changing. It's no longer something that everyone does. You may or may not have started smoking because everybody else did it, but you certainly are not stopping just because everyone else stopped. You are not just responding to social pressure. If anything, there's a part of you that might feel like continuing to smoke just to defy others. Of course that would be foolish. Of course you wouldn't really do that, but you do live in the world, a world populated by other people.

Go back to a time when you were smoking and see yourself with a cigarette and how you were treated. You see how in a restaurant you would be herded off to a special place. You weren't allowed to sit with everyone else. You were put in the smoking section. You were treated like an inferior being. Think of when you were in public enjoying a cigarette and seeing people turn to look at you, wrinkling their noses with displeasure, coughing to indicate the smoke sickened them, sniffling and letting it be known that the odor was offensive.

And you look down, and you see the yellow stains on your fingers from holding the cigarette, and you see how unattractive, how unappealing, those stains are. And you look in a mirror at your teeth, and you see the yellow, the staining from the smoke you've pulled in. And as you look in the mirror, you see the lines in your face and realize that they were deepened by smoking. The cigarettes you smoked not only affected your circulation in catastrophic ways, like possible strokes, but also produced subtler, long-term changes. Your blood supply had to deal with increased carbon monoxide from the cigarettes; nicotine changed your circulation. It helped to age your skin.

And you see yourself in public lighting up a cigarette, and you realize that people don't want to be so near you. See people inching away from you, from the smell, people not wanting to associate with you. When you suggest going to lunch, some people don't want to go with you because they don't want to sit in the smoking section. They may be rejecting smoking, but what you experience is they are rejecting you. Some people insist that you leave their house and stand outside if you're to have a cigarette. You're treated like a pariah. And you can hardly blame them. If they get near you, they're going to have to inhale your secondhand smoke. They're treating you like poison because your cigarettes are poisoning them.

And you realize how much it hurts to put yourself outside of society this way. It makes you very sad. You see people looking at you, and you realize that some of them are looking with pity. They're saying, "Look at that poor person—the one who can't stop smoking," and they shake their heads sadly. And you hate that pity, and you hate being looked down upon.

You know that you are a good person and you want to be treated like one. You know that you're capable of taking good care of yourself. You know that you're capable of changing. You started smoking without really realizing what you were doing to yourself. You started smoking not appreciating what the outcome would be. But now you know and you don't like that outcome. You're not going to hold onto leper status. You don't want to be treated with pity, contempt, anger, or disdain. You want to rejoin healthy society. You want to walk into a restaurant and be welcome at any table in the house. You want to be able to go anywhere without being treated like a second-class citizen. You don't want to have to look around and see if there are "No Smoking" signs. That will be a prohibition that's irrelevant to you. People will eat with you without concern about smoke ruining the taste of the food. The stains can fade from your fingers. You can go to the dentist and have your teeth cleaned knowing that you're not just wasting your time. You're not going to deposit another layer of yellow. You're going to look your best. And it feels good.

When you're ready to end this exercise, open your eyes and bring yourself back to the usual waking state.

The Same Old You

Sometimes people have difficulty changing a behavior because that behavior is part of how they picture themselves. This exercise helps you bring to mind situations in which you used to smoke but enables you now to see yourself in the same situations without a cigarette.

━━━━━●◆●●━━━━━

Sometimes it seems very hard to think of yourself as not smoking. Perhaps you've smoked for years. Perhaps you've smoked for your entire adult life. It feels as though smoking is part of your essence. Now, as you relax and settle comfortably into hypnosis, picture yourself doing some familiar activity, any familiar activity which you often did while smoking. Perhaps you'll see yourself having a cup of coffee and a cigarette. Or perhaps you'll see yourself at your job doing your work and smoking. Imagine it like a motion picture, like a movie. But as you do, imagine that the picture on the screen isn't made of just one single piece of film. Rather it's multiple pictures of the same thing superimposed on each other. And one of these images has you holding the cigarette. In all the other images, your hand is empty. That bit of film that has you holding a cigarette is you the smoker. That's the smoker part of you. And as you watch, you're going to see your body remain where it is, doing what it has been doing, but the smoker is going to stand up and step aside. It's going to look the way it looks when in the movies a translucent figure of a ghost leaves the body behind. That's right, the smoker stands up and, as he or she continues to smoke, becomes smoke. The smoker becomes smoke and is blown away and dispersed by a fresh spring breeze.

But as you look, you're astonished to see that you are still there. You are there, just as substantial and real as you have ever been. Getting rid of the smoker still leaves a complete you behind. If you were having a cup of coffee, you are still there having a cup of coffee. Your ability to drink coffee was not a special skill possessed by the smoker. In fact, you're a better coffee drinker without the smoker. Now that your taste buds aren't being coated with tar, now that your taste buds and nasal passages haven't been burned and made insensitive by the smoke, you can really taste your coffee. When you're doing your job, you realize that it was not the smoker who knew how to do your job, it was you. It still is you. In fact, the smoker made it harder to do your job. It was more difficult because you simultaneously had to do your job and smoke a cigarette. It was a distraction. Just before fading into smoke and being blown away by the breeze, the smoker may say, "But you needed that distraction. You needed me to distract you to allow you to do your job." And you chuckle to yourself. The smoker is so transparent, still trying to ensure his or her own reality.

You never needed the smoker; the smoker needed you. When you don't smoke, the smoker doesn't exist, but you do. You don't really do your job better for distraction, and besides, if you did, you could certainly come up with a healthier, less self-destructive diversion. You could chew on a toothpick. You could sip at a cup of water. You could tug at your ear lobe. You could doodle on a sketch pad. The list is endless.

Now, you may find it helpful to go through many, even all, of the different situations in which you habitually smoked. Going through all of them will allow you to remove the smoker from each of them. It lets you see with your own eyes how it's you, not the smoker, who handled these situations.

When you are ready to end this exercise, open your eyes and bring yourself back to the usual waking state.

The Happy Nonsmoker

This exercise, like the one before it, is meant to help with the feelings of strangeness or differentness you may experience in the transition from smoker to nonsmoker. By visualizing past times when you were not smoking and did not miss it, you can recognize that you are essentially the same you even without a cigarette.

Feel yourself settling down, and feel yourself moving through time and space, leaving behind the present and going back, back into the past, back into your past. Go back to a time when you were happy and content, feeling good and competent when you weren't having a cigarette. And as you think about that time and remember that time, you feel yourself begin to bridge back to that time. Perhaps this will be a time when you were at a movie or a play and were very much enjoying it. Perhaps it will be a time when you were working with your hands in the garden. Perhaps it will be a time when you were going for a walk or perhaps when you were at church or in school. Perhaps it will be when you were playing a sport.

And as you think about that time, it becomes more and more real, more and more present, until you really feel yourself right back there. Feel yourself in that activity, happy, content, enjoying yourself. And it occurs to you that this is in fact you. This is you, yourself, and you are a nonsmoker. Back at this time you may be a nonsmoker only for brief periods of time, but you are a nonsmoker. And as you think about this, you realize that being a nonsmoker is not to become someone new, someone different. It's instead to emphasize a part of you that has always been there, and you realize how familiar and how good this feels. And you may want to keep exploring your past to find other times, different times when you have been happily nonsmoking, until it feels so familiar and so comfortable, until you regain your identity as a nonsmoker.

When you are ready to end this exercise, open your eyes and bring yourself back to the usual waking state.

Warning. Discretion advised. *The following is one of four highly unpleasant hypnotic exercises in this book. You may prefer to skip them unread. That would be fine. However, some people do very hurtful, repulsive, and grotesque things to themselves. They engage in behaviors that can be extremely self-destructive. One way they do so is by masking the harsh reality of what they are really doing. These exercises are designed to force them to recognize a painful truth in order to change.*

Bucket of Tar

This exercise is designed to point out most vividly how smoking hurts your body. It can be useful as a way of moving from the American Cancer Society's dry statistics to a gut-level physical experience.

As you settle back and relax, becoming deeply and comfortably settled in, you're going to begin to do something difficult. It's going to be hard, but it's never going to be more difficult than you can manage.

Imagine what it would be like if there were a large bucket of tar in the middle of the room, right in front of you. Think about what it would look like. Look at the shiny, slick surface. Watch the bubbles form as the tar boils, and as each oily bubble bursts, it sends a whiff of chemical into the air. Just smell that tarry smell. You've smelled it before. You've smelled it when road crews had a bucket of tar melting to fix the highway. You've smelled it when roofers have been heating up tar to apply to a leaking roof. You remember seeing mops that have been used to spread the tar. How ruined they look. And you think about how terrible it would be if that bucket were to spill and dump even a fraction of its contents on the floor. You think of how awful that would be, of how that would ruin the floor or the rug, of how you would never get it up.

Imagine dipping your finger into it. How it would burn. How torturous it would be. It would be like a fraction of being tarred and feathered. And you know that if you were to get it on your finger, once the tar had cooled and you had peeled it off and washed it, even so a stain would have permeated your skin, would have sunk down deep into the cells of your finger. You realize that your body can cure itself, that your finger will not be stained forever, but it would take a long time for it to heal itself.

But as bad as it would be on your finger, suppose there were a long, white straw, stuck into this vat of boiling tar. Imagine how awful it would be to suck on that straw. Suppose you got some in your mouth. How awful it would be, how it would burn and coat your tongue. But at least you could spit it out and minimize the damage.

Now suppose you were to suck on that straw and suck that tar into your very lungs. Imagine what it would do, how it would choke you, how it would seal off those airways, how it would burn and damage delicate tissues. They couldn't pay you enough to do it. No one would be able to force you to do it. Even if it were just a little bit, that would make no difference. A tiny bit or a huge amount, you wouldn't do it. You know better than that.

Then you realize where you've seen that straw before. That's what a cigarette is. A cigarette has its own source of heat to melt the tar. It has its own tar. It doesn't have so much as a bucket, but it has more than enough. In the past when you used to smoke, every time you lit up a cigarette, you were distilling and melting small amounts of tar in the tobacco. And you were sucking it into your lungs. That's right. Each time you did, you brought more tar into your mouth and into your lungs.

You remember times when you smoked more than usual and how your mouth tasted. Smoking more than usual made you aware of how you had coated your tongue with tar and other chemicals. And as you think about your lungs and how their capacity has been diminished, you realize it's because those fragile, delicate air sacs that transfer oxygen to the blood have been coated with tar, and you know how a coating of tar makes everything air-tight. No wonder you can't breathe. No wonder cigarettes have made you cough. You've been trying to get the tar out of your lungs. Your body has been trying to protect itself. Your body was trying to protect itself from you.

You're never going to be able to look at cigarettes in quite the same way again. You're not going to be able to look and see them as harmless. In the past, they tricked you. In any given puff, the amount of tar was so small that you didn't realize it. But it doesn't matter that the amount was small because it wasn't just one puff. It was puff after puff, bit upon bit upon bit of tar. And you realize what this has done, how it has hurt you. And in the future when you think of a cigarette you're going to realize that even a small amount is coating your delicate lungs with tar. And you won't want to do it. You'll feel—not just know, but feel—that this indeed is a poison. This indeed is something destructive, something hurtful to your body, and you're not going to do it. If someone suggested cutting off the tip of your little finger, you would not say, "Well, that's only an unimportant bit." Instead you would say "no," that you were protecting your body. So also, if the idea came along of having just one cigarette, you're not going to say, "That won't cause too much damage." You'll say, "No. I don't want to do myself any damage."

Never again will you fall prey to the fact that the damage is done in small, hard-to-detect amounts. If a burglar were to enter your house and steal everything you owned but did it one piece at a time, you would not say as she or he went out the door with a silver fork, "Oh, it's only one fork. It doesn't really matter." In particular, you would not say that if you knew that this was the burglar's fiftieth trip to your silver chest, and if you knew that she or he had every intention of continuing to make trip after trip, each time with only one of your possessions, until you had nothing. You would not allow a thief to pick your pocket with the proviso that it be done one dollar at a time. So, too, you have learned that you need to care for and protect yourself, even from things that seem too small to do much damage.

And as you think about this, it makes you feel very good, very strong, and very healthy to realize that you are taking good care of yourself. You are doing the right things for yourself, and it strengthens your resolve to keep doing these things.

When you are ready to end this exercise, open your eyes and bring yourself back to the usual waking state.

The Miserable Smoker

When people start thinking about quitting, they may forget all the negatives of smoking. Instead they experience stopping as though they were giving up something purely wonderful. This exercise reminds the new nonsmoker how nice it is not to be a slave of cigarettes.

———◆•◆•◆———

While you're so relaxed, you think about how much propaganda you have swallowed about how wonderful smoking is. You think about how teenagers experimenting with smoking for the first time will inhale, feel sick, nauseated, and disgusted, then look at each other and say, "That tastes great. There's nothing like a cigarette to relax with," because they know how "cool" it is to smoke. And you think about how you've been taught to believe that you can't do without a cigarette, that it is pleasurable to smoke and painful to stop.

Imagine yourself lighting up a cigarette. But instead of just having a puff and putting it aside, you're going to let yourself see just what this smoking experience is like when you do it intensely. That's right. As soon as you exhale, you put the cigarette to your lips again and suck in long and hard. Feel the smoke burning its way through your lungs. Feel the light-headedness as the drug hits your system and as your brain suffers a mild degree of anoxia, or oxygen deprivation, as you're breathing in carbon monoxide. Feel your lungs rebel and want to cough. And as soon as you've exhaled, draw in another big lungful. Really smoke that cigarette. You're not going to waste any of that precious smoke. You're going to suck it all into your body. And as you do, you realize that this isn't really a very pleasant habit at all. But keep it up. There are plenty more cigarettes in the pack. You really want to see what it's like to smoke. You really want to see what your body is being subjected to when you smoke, puff after puff, lungful after lungful, cigarette after cigarette. Your tongue becomes raw, burned, and coated with a thick yellow stain. You're feeling sick. This is what you've been doing to yourself.

And it is a habit. A habit that you drag along with you. Imagine that a ball and chain are fastened to your ankle, a ball and chain of the type convicts used to wear. Think what it would be like if everywhere you went, you had to drag that ball and chain with you. And you realize that's what cigarettes have been to you. They've been a ball and chain. Think about how you couldn't leave the house without checking to see if you had your cigarettes with you, without making sure you had enough to smoke. You realize that you gave up your freedom to those cigarettes. You realize that you became their slave. They were the master. They told you that you couldn't go somewhere without stopping at the store to get more cigarettes. You think about times when you were in a nonsmoking situation, about how that habit made you nervous and uncomfortable. You think about being in a movie theater, and instead of being able to enjoy the film, you were getting fidgety, wishing you could have a cigarette.

And you remember times when you've left enjoyable events to go out in the lobby and have a smoke, even though you would have enjoyed the performance if your habit hadn't distracted you. Your enjoyment was ruined.

And you think about how the urge to smoke asserted itself at times when it forced you to go out in the middle of the night to get more cigarettes. You think about times when you wouldn't have gone out to get anything else, but you would go out for cigarettes. And you think about the time you were out of cigarettes and how you were ready to go through the ashtray to look for long butts to relight. And you realize how pathetic they made you.

And finally, the scene changes. There you are in the doctor's examining room. You're sitting there by yourself. You feel the cold paper of the examining table beneath you. You shiver inside the skimpy johnny, and you feel the sweat rolling down your sides and arms, from your armpits, and the doctor comes in and looking at her solemn face you know what she's going to say even before she says it. That's right. You have cancer. And you're in for a long series of operations, of chemotherapy, of losses of part of your body, perhaps the loss of a lung or of your vocal chords or the roof of your mouth. And you realize what these cigarettes have done for you.

But now change the scene. You're no longer in the doctor's office. You're no longer sick. You are no longer fettered with a ball and chain. You're free. You're free, walking in the sunshine. But you realize where it is you're walking. You're in a cemetery. You're here for a funeral. But it's not your funeral. You're alive. You're here for the funeral of your cigarettes. They are dead. You have killed them. And you see the coffin. And you know that in the coffin is the image of your smoking. Perhaps inside the coffin is a large cigarette. Perhaps it's the image of a large carton of your favorite brand. Perhaps the Marlboro man is in that coffin. Perhaps it's the woman in the Virginia Slims ad who pretends to be liberated but is really a slave to the tobacco industry. And as at any funeral, you're sad. You're sad at the loss. You're sad that you have to give up what was nice about the one who was lost. But on the other hand, you know that no matter how nice, how attractive, that other one is, you're not going to climb into the coffin and share the grave with the corpse. You've chosen life. You've chosen well.

And now the funeral is over. I'd like you to imagine holding in your hands a fresh pack of your favorite cigarettes. You can even open it up. Take out a cigarette. Feel the familiar weight and texture. Smell the aroma of unburned tobacco. And you recognize this is something you've enjoyed in the past. And you touch your cheek and take a big deep breath, and as you let it out, you feel your body relax, and as your muscles relax, you think about how, even though they are enjoyable, cigarettes poison your body. And you've chosen life. And you see how easy it is to take that cigarette and throw it in the garbage. You're not worried about waste. If you had lit it, it would have been reduced to a pile of ashes. Then it wouldn't have been any good, but it would have poisoned you before it was thrown out. This way, you know it isn't really any good, and it's thrown away before it can hurt you. And this sense of pride of accomplishment, this sense that you can do anything you need to do, anything you set your mind to, remains with you.

When you are ready to end this exercise, open your eyes and bring yourself back to the usual waking state.

12

Weight Control

Alcoholics, drug addicts, and smokers know the solution to their habit is never to have another drink, fix, or cigarette again. Total abstinence, however, is not a possible alternative for the person with a weight problem. One can live a whole lifetime without alcohol, drugs, or tobacco, but one cannot live long without food. What an overweight person must learn is how to have a healthy and moderate relationship with food.

This chapter is by far the longest in this book and contains the greatest variety of hypnotic exercises. Overeating is the most complex of all the habits and so warrants the use of the greatest number of treatment strategies. Also, the problems inherent in controlling eating behavior are relevant to the problems involved in taking control of other types of behavior. There are lessons to be learned in this chapter which can be translated to a variety of problems. For example, the exercise entitled "Chains" can be readily adapted to most habits.

Changing eating patterns is not easy. Since bodies try to preserve equilibrium and resist changes, weight tends to be fairly stable. To change weight is *work,* and the most effective and permanent weight loss demands slow, steady change. It is, however, a piece of work which is possible, and the tasks of changing your relationship with food, establishing a new, viable eating pattern, reducing, and controlling weight are made easier through the use of various hypnotic suggestions.

You need to decide, first of all, how much you want to weigh and what you are willing to do in order to achieve that weight. One of the most important aspects of deciding how much to weigh is that it is a personal decision. Your physician can advise you about the range of weight that experts would consider ideal for your height, frame, and lifestyle but cannot make your choices for you. While your health should be monitored by a physician during any major reduction, your weight is your business. It's your body and your decision. The motivations that your family, friends, doctors, coaches, fashion designers, or "society" have for you to lose or gain weight are really irrelevant. Provided it is not inherently unhealthy, "proper" weight is whatever weight suits you and your lifestyle.

For most people, there is a range of weight, a variance of about ten to twenty pounds, that is healthy. Within this range, the choice of actual weight is often a matter of decisions about values. Different people have different tastes about their appearance. Some people think they look best when slender, while others prefer a more Rubenesque look. Within the healthy range, some people find it just isn't worth the work necessary to lose a final few pounds. Thus they choose to weigh a little more than they would ideally like in order to enjoy life's pleasures.

There is, however, an unfortunate and very common tendency among those who are at the upper end of a healthy range to spend months or even years wishing they weighed five pounds less without actually making the changes in lifestyle needed to produce such weight loss. These people would be much happier deciding either that a five-pound weight loss is important enough to *do* what is necessary to achieve it or else that the pleasures of eating are too great to give up. If they choose to live with a bit of extra poundage, they get to eat what they want. If they choose to eat a bit less food than they'd like, they will slim down. Regardless of which decision is made, *some* decision is made. The person who can make a choice can be content with what he or she is doing, rather than living in a state of constant frustration and dissatisfaction with himself or herself.

Many people who try to lose weight find the process of "going on a diet" to be a torturous exercise in futility. For them, the word *diet* is defined as a short-term course in self-deprivation, somewhat akin to holding one's breath under water. What happens when a person who has gone through life eating in a fashion that results in excess weight, be it 10 or 110 pounds, decides to reduce? All too often, he or she learns a way of eating that is designed to produce fairly quick weight loss. Through semistarvation, a certain magic number on the scale is reached. Immensely relieved to be at a good weight, such a person decides the special diet is no longer needed and surfaces for a good meal.

Now, at the time when the diet is stopped, the dieter knows two ways of eating. The first is a pleasant, well-established, maybe lifelong pattern. The other is a "diet" that is tolerable in the short run, but unlivable for any length of time. What this person, like many others, then does is to go back to the only viable way of eating he or she knows—the one which led to the extra pounds in the first place and is guaranteed to do so again.

What these people do not know is how to eat in a healthy and comfortable way that they can maintain for the rest of their lives. Those who struggle with a weight problem do not know how to have a moderate relationship with food. Often they report spending the entire day preoccupied with food. When in a weight gain mode, such people are constantly eating, shopping for, preparing, or thinking about food. When they are dieting, they are obsessed with deciding whether to keep to the diet or "cheat," with thinking about what they will eat when they go off the diet, and with feeling proud or martyred because they are keeping to it. Nowhere in this scenario does food fit into life as a minor but necessary part. Rather than something that one must have to maintain life and that can provide a small but real pleasure, food becomes the overwhelming focus of existence.

This overinvestment in food is frequently accompanied by a rather complicated "morality." People are "bad" when they don't stick to a diet, "good" when they do, sinful if fat, virtuous if slender. There is virtue not only in slimness, but also in suffering, since an unpleasant feeling state seems to be connected with successful weight loss. This view of reducing is like the theory that only unpalatable medicine can be good for you. It is not the antibiotic but the suffering of swallowing the evil-tasting stuff that counts. There are even foods which develop clear moral value. Chocolate is "bad," probably the worst. Ice cream is similarly evil. Potatoes are quite wicked, as are all starches. Salad is "good," especially if you leave out the things you really like. Sugar is "bad" unless it is ingested in the form of fruit or in some other "natural" guise. Anything labeled "organic" is good. Margarine is good; butter is bad. In general, diet morality goes something like this: whatever foods you like are bad; the more unpalatable the food, the better it is for you.

In truth there is no such thing as a food which is intrinsically good or bad, though some foods are specifically bad for certain people. High-cholesterol foods are not indicated for the person who needs to lower a cholesterol count, strawberries are not good for someone who is allergic to them, and too many sweets can be harmful to a diabetic. Certain food additives, the poison in Snow White's apple, for instance, or carcinogens in cake mixes, benefit no one, but then again, they are not really *food*.

Most people simply find themselves more likely to eat large quantities of the foods they like than of those they do not like. A chocolate bar and three cups of boiled turnips have roughly the same number of calories (100), but one is less likely to have eight or nine helpings of turnips than one chocolate bar. The tastiest foods are just easiest to overeat. In reality, this fact does not mean they should never be eaten, but simply that it takes *work* to see that they are eaten only in moderation.

For *losing weight* to be a meaningful term, *weight* must first be understood as having a number of major components: bone, nervous system, muscle, fluid, and fat. The first two are constants, contributing a stable amount to a person's total weight. Although muscle weight can be lost, doing so does not usually contribute to healthy physical fitness. In fact, muscle weight may increase as a person becomes thinner and more physically fit. Fat and fluid, the last two components of weight, are both changeable. Water weight is continually subject to temporary fluctuations and can be varied by going to a sauna, sweating, or not drinking adequate fluids. However, not only can too much fluid loss result in an unhealthy state of dehydration, but the weight will be regained as fast as it was lost. Many quick-loss diets are based on losing fluid, and although the loss may be quick, it is not permanent.

Meaningful weight loss is loss of fat, the last component of a person's total weight. Now, a certain amount of fat is essential for good health. It provides insulation, padding, and a viable source of stored energy. However, not only can too much fat be a source of self-hatred and emotional distress, there is, as well, a certain point beyond which fat becomes seriously harmful to physical health (for men, fat composing over 30 percent of total weight; for women, over 40 percent). The enlargement of body size makes continual extra demands on the respiratory and circulatory systems. Fat tends to pack itself around veins, interfering with their smooth operation. Furthermore, an undesirable increase in cholesterol, which clogs and obstructs veins and arteries, is associated with fatty buildup. This extra fat is best lost.

Although at times it seems that fat has a mind of its own, Newton was actually right. Matter is neither created nor destroyed except as changed into energy. Both fat and food are primarily sources of fuel to provide energy for the body. Our bodies require fuel in order to be active. Everything we do burns up energy. Sleeping burns up a small amount of energy; vigorously exercising, a great deal more.

Just as any activity can be described in terms of the amount of energy it uses in order to be performed, so can foods, the fuel for our bodies, be described by the amount of energy they produce when burned. This amount of energy is measured in units called *calories.* Each activity burns up a certain number of calories, and every food provides a certain number of calories.

A person who is doing something is one who is burning up fuel. The fuel can either be food which is freshly taken in or fat, which is food that was consumed and converted to a different form to be stored because it was not needed at the time. A person who is burning up fewer calories than he or she is taking in by eating will convert the excess to fat, storing it up for the future and thereby gaining weight. A person who is taking in fewer calories than he or she is expending uses fat as a source of energy, thereby losing weight.

More specifically, a pound of fat has the fuel capacity of 3,500 calories. If a man eats 3,500 calories more than he burns up, whether in one day or over one year, he will gain 1 pound of fat. If he burns up 3,500 more than he takes in, he will lose 1 pound of fat. A 150-pound sedentary woman uses about 1,500 calories a day. If she were to decrease her food intake by a third, lowering it to only 1,000 calories per day, it would take her seven days to lose a pound of fat ($7 \times 500 = 3,500$). If she were to go on a total fast, she would lose 3 pounds of fat in one week.

People who start diets expecting weight loses of five, ten or twenty-five pounds in the first week or two can only get those results by losing fluids. While it may be encouraging to see the numbers on the scale change, fat just does not come off in such large quantities so quickly. On the other hand, it is comforting to know that it is not really possible to gain five pounds of fat from one large meal. In fact, to gain a single pound of fat, a person needs to take in an extra 3,500 calories (which equals half a gallon of the richest ice cream), over and above normal consumption. For you to lose weight, for you to lower the amount of fat in your body, you need to decrease the number of calories of any type you take in, increase the number of calories you burn up, or both. Anybody whose lifestyle remains stable and consistent will burn up roughly the same number of calories each day. When you eat about the same amount every day, keep a fairly consistent activity level every day, and weigh about the same every day, the number of calories you take in is the number of calories you burn up. This amount is called a maintenance number of calories.

It should be noted that as your weight changes, the number of calories needed to maintain that weight also changes. The 150-pound woman who burned up 1,500 calories a day in her sedentary lifestyle, for example, might lose 30 pounds and so weigh 120. If her lifestyle remained sedentary, her maintenance caloric intake would no longer be 1,500 calories per day, but about 1,200 (because her lighter body is easier to carry). Even when she was through losing weight, she would have to continue to eat less than she did previously in order to maintain her new weight.

It should be clear that in order to lose weight, you need to change your fuel intake and energy output equation. You can (1) take in less food and so be forced to use fat for fuel; (2) maintain your current eating habits but increase your exercise so that more fuel is needed and is drawn from your fat reserves; or (3) do both. These tasks can be eased with hypnotic suggestions.

The strategies that follow are the ones which have been found to be the most helpful in actual practice. Some tactics deal with the technicalities of weight loss; others with physical, emotional, or social aspects; and still others with how to maintain a desirable degree of fitness. The person who goes through these hypnotic exercises and follows the strategies will certainly lose weight and will most likely find it less difficult than expected.

Learning to Eat Right

Anybody who needs to slim down has developed a variety of well-entrenched eating habits that contribute to weight gain. Engaging in some other activity while you eat, eating quickly rather than slowly, and cutting up all your food at once instead of just before each bite are habits that encourage overeating.

Although hypnotic exercises vary in usefulness to different people, this one should be done, and done first, by anybody who wants to lose weight. It will allow you to practice eating the right way without all the calories you'd get if you were to practice with real food.

━◆◆◆◆━

Now that you are feeling so comfortably relaxed, you are ready to begin working to teach yourself a new way of eating. As you know, you have spent your whole life eating in a way that leaves you weighing more than you wish. This old way of eating is a deeply ingrained habit, a habit that it will take work to change. You know that when you try to change the way you do some activity, you have to concentrate to do it the new way. Further, you have to practice doing it the new way. If a pianist had learned to play a piece with a certain fingering and wished to learn a new one, he or she would have to work intensely to learn the new technique and learn it so strongly that the old one was overruled. So it is with eating. You need to learn a new method of eating and learn it so completely that this new way, not the old one, becomes the habit. The new orders must be in a stronger voice than the old ones.

This requires concentration. It means that for some time you will not be able to eat and do something else at the same time. If you try eating while doing something else, such as watching television or reading the newspaper, you will naturally fall back into your old habits. In order to concentrate, you can do nothing while eating but eat.

Part of dining with other people involves social interchange. Talking and interacting are an important aspect of the dining experience. Because of this, you will be able to talk and interact with your dining companions while you eat, or rather during the meal, but not at the moment you are actually eating.

This requires effort. It is not easy to give up watching TV while eating or reading while eating, especially for people who dine alone. However, doing so makes how you eat be the focus of the difficult job of changing your eating pattern. Instead of having to feel you may not eat, you are forced to choose. Would you rather eat or watch TV? Would you rather eat or read the newspaper? Either is permissible, but both cannot be done at once. As you go on, you will learn that many choices have to be made. This is your first choice.

Now, settle comfortably into your chair and imagine yourself seated at a table with a beautiful meal spread out before you. All of your favorite foods are there. As you are choosing the meal, you can put anything on the table. You might wish to put the meal that you are next going to have on the table, or you might wish to choose a more imaginary meal. Suppose you choose roast chicken, mashed potatoes, gravy, and green beans.

Dessert will be apple pie. As you sit down at the table, take a moment to settle in and relax. You are dining, not entering a feeding frenzy. No one will steal the food. You need not wolf it down to protect it. Take the time to admire the presentation and to decide which foods and how much of each is right for you. You decide that you would like a small portion of each.

Put a small portion of the chicken on your plate. Now put on a spoonful of the potatoes and pour a little gravy on them. Help yourself to a few green beans.

As you look at your plate, pick out the very best-looking bit of food. You know that your taste buds are fresh, and so you will taste the first bite better than you will taste any subsequent bite. Now, pick up your knife and fork and cut that small piece; put it on your fork and bring it up, and place the piece in your mouth. Now, *put down your knife and fork.* Focus all your attention on the food in your mouth. Savor, taste, and enjoy it. That's right. Keep the food in your mouth as you chew and taste it. Continue to do so until you've extracted all the goodness, all the flavor, all the pleasure to be had from that bite. Only then do you swallow.

You know that if you had continued to hold your knife and fork in your hands, you would have been paying attention to your plate and carving the next bite. All your attention would have been focused on the bite that you were preparing, even though you could not taste or enjoy that bite while it was on the plate. It is so easy to forget that you can never taste food unless it is in your mouth. It is foolish to pay attention to food on your plate, which you cannot taste, when you have food in your mouth that you can taste.

If you were holding your knife and your fork, you would be getting the next bite ready and anticipating it. This would have made you want to swallow the food in your mouth to get rid of it so that you could taste the food on the plate that was ready to go. But that would never have been tasted either because you would have been busy preparing the next bite. Your old way of eating is more suitable for a factory worker being paid piecework rates. You would think that there was an advantage in preparing bites as quickly as possible so they could be disposed of.

Because it is new, you find it is work to force yourself to put down the knife and fork between bites, or to put down the sandwich between bites, but as you practice you realize that you gain a great deal of satisfaction from the pleasure of enjoying and tasting your food. You realize how little pleasure you used to get when you ate, and you know that led you to substitute quantity for quality. You were always looking to the next bite for pleasure, not realizing that the secret was to enjoy the bite that was in your mouth already.

Now pick up your knife and fork and select your next bite. Cut it and bring it to your mouth. Now again put down your knife and fork and focus all your attention on savoring, tasting, and enjoying the food in your mouth. Pay attention to the blend of flavors that makes the food taste so good. Notice the texture and consistency, notice the pleasant changes that occur as you continue to chew. When you have exhausted the pleasure of that bite, you allow yourself to swallow it.

If you are thirsty, have a glass of water before you that you can drink. If you wish to have another beverage with your meal, you have that in addition to the water. Water is for thirst; the other beverage, like any food, is to be sipped and savored, tasted and enjoyed.

Continue to eat what is on your plate, concentrating your attention on the food in your mouth while it is there. If you do not dine alone, you can stop and chat with your companions between bites. But only between bites and after you have put your knife and fork down. Talking with your mouth full not only is bad manners but distracts from the pleasure of your food. There is no need to swallow prematurely. If you have something to say, you will be able to say it after you have swallowed your food.

As you continue through the meal, you begin asking yourself before each bite whether you truly want more or if you would merely be eating out of habit. Now, you became overweight by learning to eat when your body was no longer hungry. You have temporarily lost the ability to know when you are full. In time it will return. In order to relearn the sense of fullness, for a while you are going to have to eat according to what your intellect, not your belly, tells you. When your brain says, "Stop," that's enough. Pay attention to the way your stomach feels at that point. That sensation is what people call "having eaten enough." Eventually you will learn to recognize this sensation as a signal to stop eating, though for the time being you will have to count on what your brain tells you.

You, not the plate, must decide when you are done. The plate does not know how you feel, so you should not eat until the plate registers that you are done by being empty. Instead, you actively choose to stop when you wish.

In order to make it clear to you who decided that you were done, you leave some food on your plate. This can be difficult, and you will work on ways to do that later. When you are done, you will probably wish to clear away your plate quickly so that you do not have to deal with remembering that you are done eating. If you are at a restaurant or in some situation in which you cannot take away your own plate, you will discreetly do something to the food that will make it unappetizing and allow you to see readily that you are done eating. You might mix foods together in ways that you don't like or perhaps sprinkle on an excess of salt or pepper.

Now you know how to eat to allow yourself to enjoy eating a reasonable amount. This needs to be practiced two ways. First, you must put in the effort to eat this way every time you eat. Constantly remind yourself that you are a civilized person who is dining, not a ravenous beast who is feeding.

As in learning any new habit, you need practice. It would be self-defeating to practice by eating eight or nine meals a day. However, you could enter this state of hypnosis or relaxed concentration eight or nine times a day and vividly imagine dining the new, correct way. The more you practice vividly imagining eating, the more it will become second nature. You will probably do well to practice this exercise before every meal, imagining yourself with the meal you are about to have. Before each mealtime is a minimum. More practice won't hurt you.

When you are ready to end, count backward from 3, and at 1, you'll be fully alert, relaxed and refreshed, and quite aware of the lesson that you've learned.

The Choice

Using the image of a balance scale, you work on understanding just what you are deciding when confronted with the option of eating. Here you learn to focus on the nature of food, what it can do, what it cannot do, and what it will do, so that you can comfortably make a decision about how much to eat.

━━━━●◆●━━━━

Now that you are comfortably relaxed, focused on thinking about the ideas of this exercise, you visualize in your mind's eye a pair of balance scales, the kind where you put weights on each side and see which is the heavier. As you look at this, you realize that you are about to work on making a decision, on making a choice.

Food has served many purposes for you in the past. You've used it as a solace when you are unhappy, as a comfort when you were lonely, as a celebration when you were glad, as a substitute for company, as a way of reducing anxiety, and as something to do with your hands. It has been a reward when you have done well and a present you have given yourself. Sometimes you ate because it tasted good; sometimes, even though it tasted bad. In each of those situations, though, you overlooked the most important reality of food.

Food is a fuel for your body.

That's right. Most basically, food is a fuel for your body. Your body uses food to supply energy for its activities. Food can taste good or bad, be fresh or stale, but it is always *fuel*.

You know that if you take on more fuel than your body can burn up, it will be stored. For storage tanks, your body has fat deposits. That's right. If you take on more fuel than your body can use at the present, that excess gets stored in fat deposits. When your body takes on less fuel than it is burning up, it will call on those reserves and burn them up as fuel. Food that you ate long ago when your body did not need it will be used as an energy source.

And too much fuel hurts your body.

Food is a fuel that your body needs in the proper proportion or right amount. Too much fuel hurts your body in several ways.

Carrying around the fat reserves is extra work for your body. Your body has to work harder to do anything. Even sitting still requires more effort the more fuel reserves your body has stored. The weight puts a strain on your muscles which carry the extra weight. It puts a strain on your heart and lungs, as they must supply oxygen to a larger and heavier body than they were designed to do.

And it hurts your body in others ways too. It makes your body unattractive. It makes your body *look* as unhealthy as it *is*, just as your body would look unhealthy if it had too little or no fuel reserves.

And what happens to your body happens to you.

If your body is out of shape and unattractive, the repercussions are felt by you. If your body is slowed down by excess weight or tired because of carrying around too much weight all the time, you are going to be the one who is going to be unable or too tired to do things. If your body is unattractive, you will be the one giving a bad first impression to people. If the effect of too much weight over the years shortens your life, you will be the one who dies before your time.

If your body is fit and healthy and does not carry the physical and emotional weight of excess fuel being stored in it, then you will be the one to reap the rewards of a healthy body which can do the things you want to do.

When confronted with food in the past, you have always asked yourself, "Do I want to eat this or not?" When you put it that way, you all too often answered, "Yes, I want to eat that." The question was asked all by itself, as if there were no consequences involved. You are now going to focus on changing the question from "Do I want to eat this?" to asking instead, "Do I want to eat this enough to do so, knowing how this fits into my life's plans?"

Every time you have to decide whether to eat, what to eat, and how much of it to eat, you will see that set of balance scales in the back of your mind. You will realize the question is not simply "Would it taste good to eat that food?" or "Can I fit that food down my throat without being too stuffed?" Instead, you will see that you have a choice between two alternatives.

Many factors go into the decision of what and whether to eat. Many elements are balanced in the scales in your mind. When confronted with a tasty food, you will not lie to yourself and say you wouldn't want to eat it. You'll be able to admit that of course you want it. But you will know that this is not the only thing that you want in your life. One factor in the decision, something you put in one side of the balance scales, is whether it would taste good. Another is how much fuel your body has had that day. Another is how much fuel your body will be getting the rest of the day. And yet another is how much fuel your body needs today. You'll be able to take into account whether something is too much fuel or not.

If it is not too much fuel and you want it, you can happily eat it without guilt. You know that this is good fuel that your body needs for its energy expenditures.

If it is too much fuel, you know that you have a choice. You have to choose between the pleasure of eating with the pain of hurting your body and the pleasure of taking good care of your body but giving up this food. You can weigh these factors in deciding. You see that the choice is not simply "Do I want to eat or not?" It is rather "Would I like to eat, knowing it hurts me, or shall I choose the greater pleasure of caring for myself by caring for my body?" The choice is between immediate pleasure and long-term happiness.

You face decisions like this all the time. For example, there are times when you wake up in the morning and it's comfortable under the covers, and you are tempted to sleep late. You also know that you have an obligation to get up if you want to get to your job on time, make breakfast for your family, or do whatever else it is that you have set as a task for yourself. If you choose to get up, it is not because staying in bed is uninviting, but because doing what you feel you should do is even more important to you. You do not take your car into the garage for a tune-up because you enjoy seeing your mechanic. You take it in so that you have a car you can depend on.

That's right. Before each time you eat, you will think of the factors that go into your *choice.* You know that food is not really a reward, a friend, a solace, or any of those other things. Food is a fuel for your body. You need the right amount of fuel. Too much fuel hurts your body. What hurts your body hurts you, so your choice is not simply "Would it taste good?" but "Is this the best thing for me?" This is an idea that you will remember every time you go through an exercise. It will be an idea that you think of each time you make a decision to eat or not to eat. The picture of the scales will be available in your mind's eye to remind you that you choose between things, that to choose one is to give up the other.

When you are ready to end this state of relaxed concentration, do so in the way that you have found to be most comfortable for you.

Learning What You Really Do

People have all sorts of ideas about when they do or don't eat and how much or how little they eat. Frequently, they are not aware of the times when they do themselves the most damage. Sometimes they think they are eating only a little bit when in fact they are eating a great deal, a little bit at a time. There are other times when in fact they are eating only a tiny bit, but they feel as guilty about it as if it were a huge amount.

You can learn to write down how much of which food you are consuming so that you will be able to know exactly what you really did eat. You will then be able to use your record to see what you were eating when you lost weight and what you were eating when you did not.

As you settle in, peacefully relaxed, focusing on this lesson, you realize how important it is that you change the way that you eat. As you think of this, however, you realize that you do not really know what your eating behavior is. You *think* you know, but you really do not know all the details of your eating that affect your weight.

There are times when you eat and feel very guilty and so

overestimate the amount that you ate. There are other times when you eat and are hardly aware of it at all. Perhaps you sometimes try to fool yourself into believing that calories don't count if you ignore the fact that you are eating them, or that calories don't count if no one else sees you, or that they don't count if you're sampling as you cook or taking a bite from someone else's plate. Perhaps you think that food does not have an effect on you if it's eaten at the store before the checkout line or if you eat it before you get home, or if you eat it while exercising.

Many people chronically, constantly, habitually eat more than they think they do in small, regular ways. Also, people often have a problem that starts by eating something which is moderately more than they need but is not too disruptive of their eating plan. Once they have done so, however, they feel so guilty about "ruining their whole diet" that they go and eat a great deal more. Overestimating that first slip makes them feel there is no sense in further moderation. But really, it is the continued eating, not the first bit, that leads to overweight.

If you knew the right way to eat for your body, knew what it required, and knew what you gave it, you would not need to be doing these hypnotic exercises. To learn to change your eating, you must learn what you eat, when you eat, and how you eat.

You need to get a little notebook. At the top of the page write the day and date. Every day you will write down *everything* you eat when you eat it. That's right. When you choose to eat some food, you get out your notebook and write down the time of day and the food that you are about to eat. Be specific. Do not write "Lunch"; rather, write, "Four ounces of chicken, one slice of bread, and tea with one teaspoon of sugar." Do not write, "A handful of nuts," but "Eleven peanuts" if that's how many you eat. Eleven peanuts is less than fifteen and more than five.

So, write down the time, the specific food, and a note that will help you to understand what was going on. If it is your set mealtime, mark that down. If you are eating between meals, mark where you are and what is going on that leads you to eat at that time. If you are at a meeting and someone is presented with a birthday cake and you accepted a piece, mark that down. If you just had a fight with your mother and are feeling upset and have half a dozen donuts, write it down. If you are talking on the telephone and munching M & Ms from the bowl that you keep by the phone, write that down.

You will probably find that there are places and situations in which you habitually eat. Perhaps sampling the sauce as you make it is your downfall. Perhaps you finish up the leftovers as you clear off the table and wash the dishes. As you learn that these are times that you tend to overeat, you can devote special attention to controlling yourself then. As you recognize that certain types of emotional situations lead you to overeat, you can learn to identify and begin to deal appropriately with the feeling that you have improperly been calling hunger.

For the next few days, you are to write down everything you eat without necessarily trying to change what you do eat. You are going to be providing for yourself a baseline for what your eating behavior usually is. It will be hard.

Even people who are not trying to change their eating behavior, who are not interested in losing weight, find it very difficult to write down what they eat. But just because it is hard does not mean that you cannot do it. In the past you have been on many diets which caused all sorts of distress or discomfort. Now you are learning a system of eating that should not be so unpleasant but does require effort. One of the efforts is keeping track of the food you eat.

Accurately knowing what you eat will not make the calories of those foods take effect. If you swallow it, it's in your body. Putting it on a piece of paper will not make it any better or worse. The real deed is the swallowing of the food. Allowing yourself to know about it will not make it worse and eventually will make it much better as you learn more and more to think through and decide what to eat.

You may find that you do not have time to write it down. That is fine as long as you say to yourself that if you do not have time to write down the name of the food, you don't have time to eat it either.

Later, when you have learned new ways of eating, and when you have learned to identify particular problems for yourself, you'll be able to use this record of your food habits to keep track of the kind of job that you are doing and to help you to learn to control or eliminate those things which are a problem.

You'll repeat this exercise whenever you find that you are having trouble writing down what you eat. You will find that as keeping a record continues, it will be an easier and easier habit.

When you are ready, you can end this exercise or go on to another.

Your Body

When people decide to lose weight, they often have in mind either what others would like them to weigh or a number on a scale. Instead you can define for yourself the reasons you want to reduce and choose a suitable body for you out of a series of imagined possibilities. Practicing visualizing a thinner you, not some skinny stranger, can help keep you comfortable with yourself as your body changes.

Let yourself become relaxed, keeping your attention focused on the following. You know that you want to change your weight, so you need to take the time to think about what you are trying to do and why you are trying to do it. You start with your body. It is your body. It is your body, and you can decide what it will be and what you will do with it. If some important person in your life wants your body to be different, the solution isn't to please him or her by changing your body, just as if someone doesn't like your career or choice of spouse, you don't deal with that disapproval by changing jobs or getting divorced.

Nobody else lives in your body. Nobody else controls your body. If fashion magazines say you should be different, that doesn't mean you need to obey them any more than you are required to raise and lower your hemline as each clothing designer dictates.

No one else is going to lose weight for you. If others want to lose weight, they must do it on their bodies. You are in charge of your body. And now comes a time of decision. Just what do you want your body to be, and what are you willing to do to get it there?

Most students would like to get 100 percent on every test. They would also like to go out and have a good time rather than study. They have to decide how much do they want the better grade and how much time are they willing to devote to studying. They usually come to a compromise that reflects how much work they're willing to do and how high a grade they need to have.

You are not willing to put in the kind of total dedication to fitness that's required of an Olympic athlete. You are also unwilling to let your body be completely shapeless and let yourself yield to all temptations to eat. And so now you have to decide. Just what is your goal? What are you looking to obtain? What kind of a body are you willing to do the necessary amount of work to have?

Picture in your mind's eye a series of people, all of them you. They are ordered in sequence by size and degree of fitness from most obese to skinniest. Each of them is a little less fit than the one to the right and a little more fit than the one to the left. Each of them has a way of living that includes how much to eat of what kind of food, how much and how regularly to exercise. Each has a slightly different lifestyle, each looks slightly different, and each body feels slightly different. The more fit bodies are physically better able to do physical tasks without tiring as easily as the less fit. They also require more work, in the form of exercise, to maintain.

The different bodies enjoy food in different ways. The heaviest get their pleasure from large quantities of food. The thinner enjoy the quality of each bite. All get pleasure, but of different sorts.

As you look over the range you realize that the bodies at the extremes are not the ones for you. And you realize that you and only you choose which of the bodies in the middle you will make be your real body. And it gives you a wonderful sense of power and freedom to know the choice is yours.

When you have chosen, visualize yourself in a large mirrored room, such as a ballet studio. There you stand at your chosen weight. If this is a weight you had in the past, you recognize the shape, but in an older self. Just look at yourself. Look at the shape of your body. Move around. Feel how your body feels. Your body weighs less, so your arms and legs are able to move with less effort. You're stronger. You run out of breath less easily.

It feels great.

And you like the way you look, too. You like the fitter, trimmer person whom you see in the mirror. You like the way it feels to be that person, and you like the way you look being that person. And as you watch, you realize that that can be you, that that *is* you. That is you as you soon shall be. And as you begin and continue to lose weight, when you look in the mirror, you will not see a stranger. Instead of feeling that you are turning into someone else, you will feel that you are becoming visible, that you can be seen, that you are no longer hidden beneath a layer of fat.

You can end your state of relaxed concentration now or go on to another exercise.

The Bankbook

Imagine your daily food record and calorie count as a checkbook register. It's OK to eat moderate amounts as long as you stay within the limits of your calorie budget.

Settle back, and get nice and relaxed. You know how every day you keep track of the food you eat and the number of calories in them. Now you are about to follow a procedure that can teach you to use that information in a helpful way.

Visualize in your mind's eye a bank book, like the register in your checkbook where you keep track of deposits and withdrawals. But this is a special one, because instead of keeping track of your money, you are going to keep track of your calories.

If you haven't already decided how many calories per day you can eat in order to lose weight as fast as you want, do so now. You know that 500 calories less than you burn up a day will produce a loss of a pound of fat a week. Suppose you decided that you would budget yourself for 1,100 calories a day. That's right. Every day, you could eat 1,100 calories of tasteful, nutritious food and lose weight at the rate you intend.

Today is Day 1 of your bankbook. You start off by crediting yourself with a deposit of 1,100 calories. Those are your 1,100 calories to spend however you want. You can freely spend them in any way without having to feel bad about it. They are yours. You have given them to yourself.

But that is all you have given yourself for today. You do not have infinitely many calories to spend, just 1,100.

This allowance gives you much freedom. If you wanted, you could sit down and drink 1,100 calories worth of hot fudge topping for breakfast and not have to feel at all bad about it. That's permitted. Unfortunately, if you did that, you would have spent all your allotted calories for the day, and you couldn't have anything else. You know that 1,100 calories worth of hot fudge sauce wouldn't be a healthy, well-rounded diet, but it's OK because in time your body would develop cravings for nutritious foods if you ate nothing but fudge sauce. In the past, you have not denied yourself nutritious food, but now you realize that you are dealing with choices.

So as you start your day with 1,100 calories, each time you eat, each time you take out your pad to write down what you are eating, it's like writing out a check. The food is like the "Pay to the order of" on a check. The circumstances are like "Memo," or why you are writing the check, and the number of calories is like the amount of the check.

If, for example, you decide to have a cup of coffee with one spoon of sugar (16 calories), you deduct 16 from your 1,100. Now you have 1,084 remaining calories to spend for the rest of the day. You decide you will have a slice of dry toast with it (100 calories). That leaves 984 for the rest of the day. You realize that you don't have to feel bad about eating this toast. You chose to spend the first 116 calories of your daily allowance this way.

As you go through the day, you keep realizing that you are becoming a value-conscious consumer. You see things that you would like to eat, but you say to yourself, "I don't want to spend that many calories on that food. I would rather save them for something I want even more."

As the day draws to a close, you may find that you have not eaten quite 1,100 calories. You may have 50 left. Instead of running out and quickly finding something worth 50 calories to spend it on, you go to sleep knowing that you are 50 calories ahead, that you have a little extra for tomorrow.

The next day, when you wake up, you make a deposit of another 1,100 calories to your account. Altogether that gives you 1,150 to spend today. This bonus makes you feel happy that you didn't waste those 50 calories at the end of the day but saved them for another day.

Sometimes you may find that you are eating more than your allotted amount, that you are eating food that does not fit into your budget. You are overdrawing your account. If that is the case, you will recognize it and realize that it means that you will have to pay it back in the future, though perhaps not all in one day. For example, if you eat 1,000 calories beyond what you have allowed yourself for one day, that means that you are going to have to repay it by eating 100 calories less every day for the next ten days.

When you start to binge, the realization that in the future you are going to have to pay back every bite that you are taking now will help you to get control of yourself. Whenever you feel ready, go ahead and end your state of relaxed concentration.

Weekly Weigh-In

People trying to lose weight may get so preoccupied with the process that they take scale readings as often as once an hour. Even if you do so less frequently, you probably check your weight's ups and downs more often than is necessary. This exercise is designed to teach you that hourly and even daily fluctuations in weight are really insignificant. Instead, learn to weigh yourself once a week to give yourself a *realistic* sense of your progress.

Allow yourself to become peacefully relaxed, and focus your attention on these ideas. Your body makes changes in itself all day long. Your temperature is not the same when you are sleeping as when you are awake. Your heart beats faster and slower at different times. Your weight changes over the course of a day as well. If you engage in physical exercise and break out in a sweat, you lose weight. After going to the bathroom, you lose weight. Right after eating or drinking, you weigh a little more. Some of the variations in your body's weight are predictable from day to day, like the tides. There are times of day when your weight will tend to be its highest, and times it will tend to be its lowest.

In the course of a week there are cycles as well. There are days of the week that you will tend to weigh less, and those when you will tend to weigh more. Some people weigh more on Monday because they eat more over the weekend. Some people get so much exercise on the weekend that they lose weight, which they regularly regain as their sedentary work week progresses. For many women, there is the additional factor of their weight predictably changing during the month as they retain and lose fluid.

When you think about it, you realize that you put yourself on an emotional roller coaster when you watch every little up and down of your weight. You lose a pound and are ecstatic. You gain a pound and get depressed. Worst of all, your reactions are not reactions to real, significant, important changes. They are reactions to the kinds of fluctuations that only mean that human weight is not a perfectly stable, unchanging constant.

Imagine yourself on a beach watching gentle waves come rolling in. You watch them break, roll up the sand, and recede. Wave after wave comes in and goes out. Imagine trying to say where the water line is if you get caught up in each wave. Just picture yourself frantically running up the beach as a wave comes in, saying, "Here's the water level, no here's the water level," and then, "Oops, there goes the water level," as you go chasing the wave back into the ocean. You would soon be exhausted and depressed because the water level kept changing.

On top of that, you would be so busy chasing each wave in and out that you would completely lose sight of significant changes, like the tide coming in and the tide going out. On a lake, you would miss slower events like the change of water level as the countryside gets more or less rain, as feeder streams swell and dry up.

So it is with your weight. As you weigh yourself and see your weight going up and down, thinking that this change means anything important, you make yourself needlessly unhappy or unjustifiably pleased. Many of the weight changes that you notice from day to day have more to do with what day it is than with what you had for breakfast that day. Changes within the day have more to do with the time of day than your eating habits.

And you are going to be freed—you need to be freed—from this nonsense.

From now on, you are going to weigh yourself only once a week. Pick a day. Any day will do. And pick a time of day. This will be your official weekly weigh-in time. At this time you will get on the scale. You will make sure that if you are dressed, you are wearing clothing that weighs about the same amount each time, so you don't lose weight by taking off your rubber boots. You are going to get on the scale, see what the scale reads, and write it down. Make sure the scale is in the same place from week to week, as many home scales will vary by several pounds depending on where they are placed. Similarly, make sure you stand on the same place on the scale. You can put your feet where the scale will read the least or where it reads the most. It doesn't matter as long as it is the *same* each time you weigh yourself.

Now go and mark your new weight on the sheet that you are keeping of weekly weigh-ins. That's right. You have a piece of paper on which you have made a list of dates seven days apart, and next to each date, you write down your weight.

You can use this sheet to let yourself see how the way you cared for yourself over the last week has affected your body.

This is not evidence against you, nor should it be cause for guilt, despair, or wild celebration. Instead, it's merely a source of feedback to let you know whether you are on track or not.

If you lost a pound or two during the week, then you know that the way you took care of yourself and ate over the last seven days was beneficial. You know that you lived up to the expectations that you set for yourself. If you did not lose, or even gained, then you have learned an important lesson as well. You know that you need to change from what you did last week if you are to reach your goal.

As you do this, you see that you need not get so taken up with every bite you do or don't take. Skipping dessert once does not make you lose weight, and having a bit of cake once does not make you gain. It is what you do hour after hour, day after day, that makes a difference. If you eat more food than your body needs at one meal, you will know that that meal is not going to be the only thing that will determine your weight at the end of the week. You will remember that it is one of many, many occasions you will have during the week to eat, overeat, or not eat. Knowing that, you will be able to see to it that you do not continue to eat more than your body needs. If you eat a healthy way at one meal, you will know that that does not ensure anything about the rest of the week.

You might be tempted on the night before your weigh-in to starve yourself so that you will look better on the scales in the morning. But who are you kidding? You could set up a pattern where you needed to starve one evening a week in order to make progress. What would be important would be that you continued to make progress from week to week. The effect of the weekly starvation would just be to see to it that your weigh-in time was the lowest weight of the week. And you know from watching the waves at the beach that what is important in determining water level is not catching any particular wave at any particular second, but finding the general depth of the sea.

When you are ready to end this exercise, take a deep breath and open your eyes. You will find yourself fully alert and refreshed.

Eat Anything, Not Everything

Provided it is not medically contraindicated for you, there is no such thing as a forbidden food, a food you can never have again. Instead a healthy eating pattern should involve choices of how much of which food, out of all foods, you want to eat.

————.⬛◆◆◆◆————

Settle back, get comfortably into a relaxed state of concentration, and, as you do, imagine spread out before you all the foods you might eat today—not just the ones you will eat, but all the ones you could eat if you choose to do so. They are grouped according to time of day, from breakfast in the morning to snack at midnight.

There, at the start, right before you, you see all the different breakfasts possible: coffee, danish, doughnuts of every flavor, eggs, bacon, cereal, toast, muffins, yogurt, juice, fruit—all of them spread out before you. And you walk along this table, as though passing through time zones, seeing the foods that you will think of eating later on as a mid-morning snack: more coffee, pastries that go with it so well, even candy bars. As you go by each food, take the time really to look at it, to see what is there. Don't imagine tasting each food, but see just what it is and know how tempting it could be.

Continue into the next time zone and see all the lunches you might choose. Look at the salad bar. It has not only lettuce but also pasta and beans, salad dressings, croutons, bread, olives, tomatoes, onions, bacon bits—all the different things that are available. Now look at the array of sandwiches: the deli-style sandwiches piled high with meat, the fast-food burgers loaded with sugary dressings and special sauces, or homemade sandwiches. You see yogurts, soups, quiches, bagels—that's right—and even leftovers. And there is plenty to drink as well. Diet soda, soda with sugar, milk, milkshakes, beer, even martinis. And lunch is also a time for desserts. See, perhaps for the first time today, the array of cookies, brownies, pies, and cakes available to you.

As you continue down into the next time zone, you see a lot more snack food for that mid-afternoon snack: little bags of potato chips, pretzels, snack cakes, candy bars, cookies, fruits. It's also a time when you might stop for a cocktail and have a drink and perhaps some of the accompanying nuts or crackers and cheese.

And as you move on to later in the day, you see the foods you might snack on as soon as you come home from work. There are snack foods and samples of the food that is being prepared for supper. Look at the ingredients being readied for dinner, the ones that you could just pop into your mouth. Look at all the dishes being prepared that could be sampled, that could be tasted. And now move along to dinner itself. It's almost overwhelming as you look at the huge variety of dishes: meats, fish, pasta, potatoes in all the different ways they can be prepared, vegetables, rich salads, hors d'oeuvres, and drinks. And then there's dessert. All the desserts are there: your favorites, those you like only marginally, and those you have only on special occasions. And now you move down to the after-dinner snacks, through the midnight snacks: an extra piece of pie, a sandwich of the food you had for dinner, a bowl of potato chips or popcorn, some frozen cake. All are there; all are available to you.

And as you look over this vast array, wandering up and down the table, seeing all the different things that you like, a sense of great happiness and joy comes over you as you realize that you can eat anything you want. Any food or drink on that table, any food or drink you can imagine, is yours. You just can't eat everything. Or at least you can't eat everything today. There is nothing forbidden to you, nothing to tantalize you, nothing to regret that you can never eat again. You can have whatever you want.

You just can't have everything today.

If you have a craving for something, you can choose to satisfy it, choose to eat that food. It will take up a certain number of your calories for today, and that's fine. You are allowed to eat your proper number of calories every day. It is fine to eat your daily allowance of calories. You can choose to spend them as you wish.

If you wished, you could eat nothing but hot fudge sundaes everyday. You could not eat a great many hot fudge sundaes every day, but you could eat nothing except hot fudge, ice cream, and whipped cream within the limits of your daily allowance. If you did, you would soon find that you would develop a craving for some green vegetables, starch, and protein. Your body will not for long give up healthy food in favor of sweets or junk food. The problem is not that you want junk food or sweets instead of healthy food, but that you want them in addition to your healthy food.

Now, instead of feeling deprived because you cannot have ice cream, you know that you can have ice cream, but you might have to give up your grilled cheese sandwich in order to afford it. Also, it might make you realize that you don't want that whole ice-cream cone but just the first three licks. Understanding that you can either finish the cone or have something else, but not both, may make you choose to throw away the rest of the ice cream and have a nice salad later on.

This realization makes you feel very good, very happy, and aware of your ability to choose whatever you want. There's no deprivation because there's nothing forbidden.

You can eat anything, just not everything all at once. Whenever you are ready, you can either go on to another exercise or simply end with this one.

When to Eat, When Not to Eat

You have an internal clock that tells you when to be hungry. Yours may be set to "once an hour," "mid-morning, mid-afternoon, midnight, and mealtimes," or "all the time." This hypnotic exercise teaches you how to reset that clock.

Once again relax, comfortably settle into a peaceful state, and, when you are ready, concentrate on the following information.

Over the years you know you have learned a number of unhelpful habits about the way you eat. Many of these habits have to do with the amount of food you eat, the lack of attention you give the food as you are eating it, and the way you wolf it down. Today you are going to work on *when* you eat your food.

Your body has an internal clock. At different times of day, it tells your body to do different things. For example, your body's temperature goes up and down in a particular pattern every day. There are times of day when you get sleepy. There are times of day when you are quite wakeful. You do not decide, "My temperature will now rise one degree, and I guess I'll have it drop down again in ten minutes" any more than you have to say to yourself each night, "Now I think I will get sleepy." All of these automatic fluctuations are part of a pattern or cycle that has a very regular rhythm.

Hunger is also subject to this kind of rhythm. Although your brain does monitor whether or not your body feels hungry, hunger is not something that brains usually check on all the time. In the middle of the night when you are asleep, for example, your brain does not check to see whether you have recently eaten or need food. It knows that this is a time for sleep, and it does not even bother to check to see if you are hungry. For most people, there are times of day when they eat and times when they do not. Shortly before you are used to eating, your internal clock signals to your brain that it is almost eating time. Another part of your brain, deep inside it, is then activated to see whether or not you need food.

If you are in the habit of having danish and coffee each day at ten, then a little before ten your internal clock will signal that it is almost time for your danish and will appropriately prepare your body. It will get your stomach ready to digest food, make you aware of the fact that it is almost time to eat, and make you feel hungry.

If you try to change your pattern or habit by skipping this danish, or if it's just not convenient to have it at that time, your internal clock will strongly signal for that food. However, if you do not eat soon thereafter, in perhaps half an hour or so, your body will stop looking for its ten o'clock danish. It's not that you ate, but that, as time has passed, your internal clock is no longer set to a time when it should look for food. It's not that you have eaten, and it's not that your body is less hungry; it is just that it is no longer a time when you expect to eat.

When people travel great distances quickly, they suffer jet lag. It takes time for their internal clocks to synchronize with local time. But when people move faraway to different countries, they do not spend the rest of their lives experiencing jet lag. They adjust to the time change. Your body routinely resets your internal clock twice a year at the beginning and end of daylight savings time. So also you can change the times that your body is aware of hunger and is checking to see if it is time to eat.

If you are in the habit of snacking at a certain time—say, at a coffee break at ten—you will of course find yourself getting hungry at ten. Now, at that time one of two things can happen. You can have something to eat, an action that teaches your body to continue expecting to eat at that time, or you can not eat. The first time you don't eat, your body will treat it as a problem to which you need to be alerted. Your brain will say, "Hey, it's time for your cheese danish. Did you forget?" This part of your brain doesn't understand that you are trying to change your life. It's just an alarm clock. The next day at ten, if you don't eat, your brain will issue the same red alert. If you do eat, your brain will say, "Oh, I guess yesterday was just some unusual interruption." If, on the third consecutive day, you don't eat, your brain will again say, "Hey, aren't you going to eat?" but it will begin to wonder. It will begin to think perhaps the clock is being reset. Perhaps ten is no longer going to be a mealtime.

Day by day, the brain will begin to think it increasingly likely that ten is no longer a time to eat. If you consistently do not eat every day at ten, it will not be long, perhaps two or three weeks, before your brain's internal clock has learned that ten is not a time to eat, and so it will stop looking for food then. At that point, you will not feel hungry, and you will not feel an urge to eat.

However, this two- or three-week transition is a time of great importance. As each day passes, the feeling grows stronger that a change in eating time is occurring. But there is still a strong question inside. If you eat at this point, your body will then say,

"Oh, it's been a mistake that we haven't eaten at this time. I should keep the alarm set." Eating once isn't the end of the world, but it does convince your body that this is a time that you are supposed to eat, and it resets the alarm. If you don't eat at ten for a week and a half and then eat "just this once," it will put you back almost to the beginning of the readjustment. You have to go back and again, day by day, reestablish that ten is not a time when your brain should remind you to eat.

If you have trouble because you are used to eating at mid-morning or mid-afternoon, or if perhaps you're in the habit of having a late-night snack, you know that you need to make a change by not eating at those times. When that time comes, you will say to yourself, "Oh, that internal clock in my brain doesn't yet know that I have decided to change my eating habits. It's looking for food now because it doesn't realize that I have made a shift." It will help you to know that it won't be long before your clock has been reset. It's very encouraging to recognize that in a little while this hunger will not be a problem for you, that you won't feel an urge to eat at that time any more than you feel a strong urge to eat when you are sound asleep. And it will particularly help you to remember that if you don't eat, the clock will soon reset itself, but if you do eat, you will be setting the clock to the old way, setting yourself up for future days of wanting to eat at this time.

For some people, the problem is that they eat at any time of the day. For such a person, "all of the time" is time to eat. These people are always asking themselves, "Shall I eat now?" "Well, how about now?" If you are one of these chronic, habitual snackers, you are constantly struggling with deciding whether or not to eat at any particular moment. Your continual questioning makes life very difficult. Think about how nice it would be not to need to struggle with this question all day long. Think how nice it would be to go through the day not needing to decide not to eat but finding yourself unmindful of food, naturally not overeating. This natural temperance can be yours.

You do have an internal clock. It's just that it is set to look for food at all waking hours. But such a clock can be reset. In fact, it is no more difficult to reset than anyone else's. If this is you, you need to decide what times of day you will consider eating. You might decide to eat three meals a day. If you do, decide what times your meals will occur. You might choose breakfast at 8:00, lunch at 12:30, and dinner at 6:45. Your task for the next few weeks will then be to teach your internal clock when it should look for food and when it should not. It's important to make sure that you eat when you have chosen to and to eat nothing at all in between. If you do, it will not be long before you find yourself getting hungry at mealtimes but unconcerned about food between meals. You will have freed yourself from the agony of having to decide whether or not to eat at every moment of the day. You will have reduced the number of times you ask yourself, "Shall I eat now?" But you must remember that you don't want to go back and add extra times to check, "Shall I eat now?" Just continue to think about how nice it will be to free yourself from this aspect of food's tyranny. It will make you feel very good indeed. And you will continue to feel good about it as you end this exercise.

The Shrinking Stomach

"Hunger pains" signal people to think about eating. For some people, however, it is almost as if these stomach contractions are felt as an alert to a serious problem, a real emergency that can't be ignored. This exercise can help you understand the sensation in your stomach not as hunger, which demands immediate satisfaction by eating, but as a good feeling that tells you you are making progress.

Settle back peacefully and relax. Pay attention to your body, its feelings and sensations. Notice how you can move your awareness to different parts of your body. As your attention shifts, you notice whether your hands are warm or cool, moist or dry. You might shift your attention to your feet and feel whether your shoes are loose or tight, comfortable or not. You realize that you can shift the focus of your attention on your body, and you notice how you can change perceptions. Pay attention to the fingers on your right hand. As you do, decide whether you would like to make them feel a little bit warmer or a little bit cooler. And now, imagine how it might feel if the temperature of your fingertips were to change. Take the time to focus on this change and feel as your fingertips become more and more warm or cool. See how, by thinking about a feeling, you are able to affect it.

Your body has two ways of assessing whether it's hungry. Today you are going to work on one of these to give you the ability to change it. One way your body tells if it wants food is by checking the tension of the muscles of your stomach. If your stomach is full and stretched, it sends a message saying, "I'm full," to the brain. If the muscles are able to contract and meet no resistance, it sends up a message, "I'm empty. Fill me up." People who swallow balloons that are then inflated report feeling full when the balloon is inflated and hungry when the air is let out of it. In deciding whether it's hungry, your stomach can't tell the difference between an inflated balloon and a filet mignon. For your stomach, volume is volume. This is not the kind of sophisticated part of your body you would like to have run your life. Instead, your brain is going to learn a way to take charge, to control the demands of your stomach.

When you have not eaten and your brain checks with your stomach, you are going to feel that your stomach muscles are able to contract and pull in and out and not find anything inside. Now, if you haven't eaten lately, concentrate on your stomach, and feel how your stomach muscles contract to see if there is food inside. Feel these muscles pulling in, contracting, testing to see if your stomach is full. In the past you have identified this feeling as "hunger." However, all it really is is your stomach registering that it is contracting and pulling in. Your stomach is signaling that it is contracting and growing smaller. This is exactly what you want. This signal, that your stomach is empty, is not a sign that there is something wrong. In fact, it means that things are right. This is exactly what you are trying to do. Your stomach is supposed to be empty. And you realize that this signal says that you are doing a good job.

You realize that you used to identify sensations that were telling you that your body was burning up fat as a sign that something was wrong. You used to think that just because your body did not have food at that moment there was something wrong, and you used to think that you needed to do something to fix this problem. Recall how it felt to think that this sensation of hunger was a sign that there was a problem. Recall how it used to feel that this meant there was something wrong, that you were "dying" of hunger.

But now you know differently. Now you know that this is not a sign that something's wrong, but quite the contrary. You recognize that this means that you are doing things correctly. Nothing is wrong. Things are right. This is how it should be. Your body is getting healthier and fitter. It's not a sign of danger, but a sign that things are right. An athlete getting in shape feels sore muscles but knows this soreness is not because of doing something wrong in working out. The athlete recognizes these sensations as a sign of something done right, of muscles getting healthy, fit, and in shape. Just so, the sensation of hunger you experience as you become healthier, fitter, and more in shape is a sign you are doing something right.

In the past, the real problem was not that you would starve, but that you would overeat. The real danger was too much weight. Now you know you are not going to die of malnutrition. Now you recognize your sensations of hunger as a sign that you are doing something right.

Your stomach is signaling that it is growing smaller. It is shrinking, and if you continue this good work, soon not only your stomach but your whole body will shrink and grow smaller and more compact. It will shrink to a smaller, stronger size. That's right, this sensation in your stomach is not a signal that something is wrong, but a monitor that is assuring you that things are right. You have not overeaten, you have not become stretched, bloated, and distended. Your body is becoming smaller, harder, healthier.

You like this feeling. Your stomach is signaling that what your brain wants is what is happening. In fact, it is such a good feeling that even when you eat, you want to be careful not to eat so much that you lose this good feeling, this signal that all is well.

That's right. Even as you end your state of relaxed attention, hold onto this feeling of success, this feeling of reassurance that you are doing a good job. Every time you feel your stomach, you feel a sense of satisfaction at a job well done.

Twenty Minutes

Often people start by having a small snack but then continue to eat until they no longer feel hungry at all. A little while later, they realize they feel stuffed. In this exercise you learn something that can help keep you from accidentally overeating when you snack.

One way that your body senses that it is hungry is by the contraction of your stomach muscles, but that is not the only way. Now it's time to learn another part of how your body senses hunger. Settle back into a state of relaxed concentration, and allow yourself to learn and develop images that help you to understand how your body asks for more food.

You know that when you eat, food does not go to your stomach and just sit there or pass solely through your intestines and supply them with food. Your digestive tract is not the only part of your body that requires fuel. When you put food in your mouth, you begin the digestive process. Your teeth and your saliva begin to change the food from its original state into useful fuel for your whole body. When you swallow the food, the process continues, and your digestive tract goes about the business of transforming the food to a useful form and putting it into your bloodstream. Your blood then carries the fuel to every cell in your body, including your brain. In the center of your brain is a small area which has the job of seeing whether or not there are adequate nutriments in your bloodstream. If not, you feel hungry. If so, you feel sated.

This process does not occur instantaneously. It takes about twenty minutes from the time you swallow food for it to reach your bloodstream and get to the relevant spot in your brain where it registers its presence as fuel.

Think back to a time in your past, before you ate moderately, when you were hungry. Suppose you decided to ease your hunger by eating a cookie. You'd take the cookie, put it in your mouth, and swallow it. But your brain would still be registering hunger. You knew what to do with that. If you are hungry, have a cookie. So very quickly a second cookie joined its friend, followed by a third and a fourth. Soon there was a whole cookie convention in your stomach. After about twenty minutes of solid cookie eating, your brain registered that there was again plenty of fuel in your blood.

Then, as even a little more time passed, your brain began registering the fact that you weren't just full. You were stuffed, bloated, and kind of sick. You said to yourself, "How could I have eaten a whole bag of cookies?" and you were confused, because you were hungry when you ate every one of those cookies.

But now you know that time is a factor in easing hunger. You know that back then when you decided to have a cookie, you swallowed it and were still hungry. But as you think about it, you realize that the reason that you were hungry was that even though the food was in your mouth, then in your stomach, there was still no extra fuel in your blood. Your brain was still registering a shortage of fuel in your bloodstream.

Now, the second cookie was not going to get to your brain any faster than the first one, and the third would not beat either of them. What your body needed then, and still needs, is time, about twenty minutes to be specific. From the time you swallow food to the time it reaches the relevant spot in the center of your brain is about twenty minutes.

If you have one cookie, you will still be hungry for about twenty minutes, and there is nothing that can make you not feel hungry for that time span. No additional food will shorten the time. And in twenty minutes, the fuel from that one cookie will register as available, and you will not feel hungry. You can spend that twenty minutes eating cookie after cookie after cookie, or you can spend it doing anything that you like other than eating. Either way, you will spend twenty minutes being hungry, and then you will no longer be hungry.

Now, you are not used to thinking of being satisfied by a single cookie or by a small portion of much of anything. You are used to thinking it takes as many cookies (or anything else) as you can eat in twenty minutes to take the edge off your hunger. People with greater weight problems are ones who devour many cookies in twenty minutes. People with less trouble with their weight eat fewer cookies in twenty minutes.

People eat for many reasons. As far as physical hunger goes, however, there are only two relevant parts. One is the contraction of the stomach, which is satisfied by a balloon as well as by food, and with which you have already learned to deal. The other is that part of your brain which doesn't require a great deal of food, just one cookie, to bring your blood fuel level up.

When you are feeling hungry and decide that it is a time to eat, you will be able to use this exercise in two ways. First of all, you will remember that no matter what you do, you cannot make the hungry feeling go away instantly. You might visualize in your mind's eye an alarm clock which is set to go off in twenty minutes, an alarm clock that does not have controls that allow you to reset it. No matter how hard you stare at the clock, it will be twenty minutes before it rings. If you eat an appropriate bit and are still hungry, you will not make the mistake of thinking you did not eat enough. Instead, you will say, "Of course I ate enough. My brain is just a little slow to find out about these things. But it will. It will soon know that I've eaten."

This knowledge also helps you to recognize why, when you are eating a meal, you are going to eat slowly. Not only does eating slowly allow you to savor, taste, and enjoy each bite, but it also allows your brain to register the fact that you have eaten before the meal is over. If you gulp your food down in ten or fifteen minutes and dash from the table, your brain will be leaving the table unaware that food has even been consumed. You will be tricked into thinking you left the table hungry.

This information helps you to recognize all the more what food is. It is a fuel for the cells of your body. It is a fuel that takes time to be delivered. Just as if you were to call up a wood supplier and say, "Please send out a load of firewood," you wouldn't expect to be warmed by the fire as you spoke on the phone. You would know that it would take a while for the wood to be loaded on the truck, unloaded, put in the fireplace, and lit.

And it helps you to distinguish in your mind between food and other kinds of comfort. Food is a fuel that takes time to go to work. It is not a lot of other things. Just as putting a cookie in your mouth does not make you instantly not hungry, it also does not make you not lonely, not sad, not anxious, not alone, not anything. That's right. Food is simply a fuel which takes time to be delivered. And you really don't want to build your life around something as trivial and slow as that.

As you end your state of relaxed concentration, you remain aware of what you have just learned.

"Wasting" Food

While you are learning to eat less, you may continue to feel pressured to eat more. The following strategy is designed to help deal with the well-entrenched stricture that you should eat food rather than "waste" it.

Settle back and, as you do, visualize in your mind's eye yourself sitting at the dinner table having just eaten a nice, satisfying, healthy dinner. That's it. Look and see what nice dishes you had. Feel the good feeling that comes from knowing you've eaten just the right amount, not too much and not too little. Savor the aftertaste of that good food. You should feel great.

But there's a problem.

You left food on your plate. And this makes you feel very, very bad. You hear that familiar voice saying, "Don't waste food. It's sinful to waste food. It's bad to waste food." Without even trying, you can think of at least three spots on the globe where there are hungry people, including children, who would just love to have that good food that you are wasting. You've had years of training in how awful it is to waste food, in how bad you are if you do. You know you are supposed to finish everything on your plate. It doesn't matter whether you are hungry or full; you are supposed to finish what's on your plate.

And then there's the matter of the food that is sitting on the serving dish and the final bits that remain in the pots. It would be wasteful to throw them away. Do you know how many people go to sleep at night hungry? Waste not, want not. There might come a day when you are going to wish that you had some nice food such as what you have in front of you right now. Some day you might be in the mood for some of that and you are not going to have it. Maybe there's a nice piece of chicken sitting there on the serving dish. You know there'll be a day when you'll think, "Gee, I wish I had a nice piece of chicken, like the one that was on the dish the other day," and you won't have it. Not only will there be hungry people all over the planet, but also there you'll be, with an unsatisfied yen for a nice piece of chicken.

And as you listen to this voice in your head talk about wasting food, something strange begins to happen. You begin to giggle.

You suddenly realize just how absurd the load of guilt that you have been given all these years really is.

You have extra food on your plate. If you don't eat it, children who are starving will go to bed hungry tonight. But if you do eat it, they are still going to go to bed just as hungry. There are many *real* ways to help hungry people. Donating to a charity or working in a soup kitchen are two of them. If you don't eat that chicken, at some day in the future you'll wish you had it. Of course, if you do eat the chicken now, there will still come a day in the future when you'll wish you had that piece of chicken and it will be gone. In fact, if you don't eat it today, there's an outside chance it may be waiting in the refrigerator for you tomorrow. Or then again, it may spoil before you want it. In any case, eating it now is not somehow going to feed hungry people, and eating it now does not make it available for some future occasion.

The fact is that once food has been purchased, prepared, and served, it is not going to be available to hungry people elsewhere, nor necessarily to you in the future. The food that is placed on the table, the food that is put on your plate has no purpose but to feed you. There is nothing else for which it's good.

You've learned that food is a fuel that your body needs. It's something that helps your body and something that can give you pleasure. You've also learned that too much of it hurts your body. There's too much on this plate. Some of the food that was put on the plate was food that you needed, food that was healthy for your body as a source of good fuel and pleasure—the right amount of food so that you could enjoy it and get pleasure from it. When there's more food than that, the rest of it is waste. If there is more food than your body needs, that excess is waste. It's garbage. And where does garbage go? It goes in the garbage can. If it's more than your body needs, it's garbage, and garbage goes in the garbage can.

When you say to yourself, "I'll eat this now so it won't go to waste," you are saying that your mouth is the garbage can, that you are the garbage can. More food than is good for your body is garbage, and if you swallow it, you are the garbage can.

The usual garbage can, the one that's made of plastic or metal, where most people throw their garbage, is not hurt by having garbage put in it. It's made to be a garbage can, so putting garbage in it does it no harm. Your body was not made to be a garbage can. If you put the garbage in it, you'll hurt your body.

Imagine you are driving your car and you are low on gas, so you pull up at a gas station. Suppose you have a coupon that entitles you to up to fifteen gallons of free gasoline at this station. And when the attendant fills up your tank and says it took twelve gallons, you hand him your coupon and say, "I'll get the other three gallons next time I'm in." But he says, "No, you only get as much gas as your car can take, up to fifteen gallons, at this one time. If your car will only hold twelve, that's all you get." If you drive away, you will have "wasted" three gallons of gas. But what would you think of a person who, deciding not to "waste" those three gallons, rolls down his window and says to the gas station attendant, "No problem. Pump those three gallons right back there into the back seat." And when the attendant hesitates, that person grabs the pump and pumps those three gallons into the back seat. That person didn't "waste" gas.

But he did waste gas. That gas wasn't helpful. His gas tank didn't need more gas to supply fuel. In fact, those three gallons hurt the car. If you eat that extra food, food which is more than your body needs, it's still being wasted. It's not only wasted, it's hurting you because it will be turned into fat and stored in your body. And you don't need to build up extra fat deposits.

So as you look at that extra food you're able to say, "This food was wasted from the moment it was prepared, because too much was purchased, too much was prepared, and too much was served. Once it's on my plate, it has no function other than to feed me. If there is more than my body requires, that excess is waste, is garbage. The only way that eating it now will keep it for me for the future is the bad way. If I eat this garbage, it will turn to fat, and some other day I will have to use that fat for energy rather than eat some nice fresh food for that day."

When you are ready to end this hypnotic exercise, do so however you like.

You, Not the Plate, Decide When You Are Done

Like the preceding one, this exercise helps you deal with the guilt that goes along with wasting food.

When you are nice and relaxed, visualize before you a plate of food. It's an appealing selection, a nice meal, perhaps the next meal you are going to have. As you picture this food, think about not only what food is on the plate, but how it tastes, how it smells. That's right. Vividly imagine that meal before you. See it, smell it, taste it. Using small bites and putting your fork down between each, eat, taking time to savor, taste, and enjoy. Feel yourself grow pleasantly full. Stop eating.

You've eaten the right amount of that food. Just taste the good aftertaste that lingers on your palate. Feel the good feeling in your stomach that comes from knowing that you've eaten just the right amount, not a bite too much. You know that you can feel good about the amount you've eaten because it's the right amount. There's no need to feel guilty because you haven't overeaten. There's no need to feel bad because you've done just the right thing. You've eaten the right amount of the right kinds of healthy food. It feels good and you are satisfied.

But there is still food on your plate.

And as you look at the food on your plate, a strange and funny image comes to mind. You imagine that plate beginning to talk, saying, "You are wasting food." Listen to the voice for a second. It's a familiar one, isn't it? Yes, that old familiar voice is telling you that you shouldn't waste food, that you should eat what's on your plate, that you should finish, that you should clean your plate.

And as you listen to this voice, you begin to chuckle. You see just how ludicrous it is that a plate should tell you when you are finished. You have many ways of knowing when to eat and when not to eat. You have got into some habits of eating too much, so you don't just trust your instincts; you've learned there are several ways to tell when you've had enough. One way of knowing that you've had enough to eat is by checking the number of calories you've consumed against your total of allotted daily calories. Another way you have is by feeling the sense of proper fullness that you can feel in your stomach when it is as full as it should be, not fuller. Another way is by noticing that you no longer have a taste or yearning for the food. None of these reasonable methods includes a plate telling you that you should eat more.

You really are far too smart and far too interested in your body's health and well-being to listen to a plate or a container or a bag or any other inanimate object telling you whether or not you are done with your meal. You are done when you say you are done. You are done when you decide to stop.

In fact, in order to make it perfectly clear that the decision to stop eating is yours, you will always leave a little food on the plate. When you are eating a meal, you will always leave at least one bite of each different kind of food on your plate untouched. These small bits will serve to point out and remind you that you have stopped eating not because the plate said, "There's no more of that food on me so you can stop eating now," but because you have decided that you are done. If you are eating from the container, you will always stop when there is still, at the very least, a little left. This remainder will be your signal, your way of telling yourself that you, a rational human being with a mind of your own, have decided that you are finished.

And it gives you a very good feeling to know that you have freed yourself from a former enslavement. You no longer need to force yourself to consume the amount dictated by an inanimate object that knows nothing of how you feel inside, knows nothing of how you are learning to take charge of your life.

When you are ready, let yourself become fully alert, but remain aware of the ideas you have just reviewed.

The Garden

In this exercise you can use the image of a garden to help you accept and feel how the process of changing your body is a slow one that requires steady, patient effort.

As you settle back and once again enter a special state of concentration and imagination, picture in your mind's eye a plot of land. It is rich, fertile land that has been planted. It is a garden. It's your garden.

Take the time to look at this garden with its vegetables and flowers. Look through it row by row, plant by plant. See your favorite plants here. Bend down and smell the flowers. See the variety of colors as the blossoms look so pretty and sway in the breeze. Smell the rich earthy smell. Feel the warm sun beating down on you, giving life and energy to your plants. Pull up an offending weed. Feel the earth between your fingers. This is your garden. You've worked hard to get it to this state.

It is not perfect, and you have not made it as good as it will be, but it is far better than the uncared-for plot you began with.

As you look at the garden, you think about the importance of patience, the time for growth and the time of ripening that cannot be speeded up. Look down at a plant whose first leaves have just broken through the soil. Someday it will display a large, beautiful flower. But right now it shows just the first leaves coming up to the sun. No matter how much you wish it, you cannot make that tiny plant suddenly be full-sized. If you were to try to encourage it and speed it up by grabbing the tips of the leaves and pulling, you would not stretch it into a flower, you would instead tear it in half or pull it up by the roots. As you look at a green tomato, you know that no amount of wishing or rushing will make it ripe today. Even if you painted it red-orange, nature would not be fooled. It would still be an un-ripened tomato.

Things happen slowly but steadily in this garden of yours, and the work required of you is regular and steady. You need to water your plants regularly. If you do not water them for a long time, they will die no matter how much water you give them later. You cannot give them a whole summer's water the first week in June and none thereafter. Steady, regular work in small amounts is what's needed. You need not do much every day, but you need to do some. You need to do a small amount of work for a small amount of progress that only later shows up fully.

If you neglect your garden for a few days, all is not lost. The garden will not have gone all the way back to weeds, and the plants will not all be dead. They will have lost some ground, however. They will not have grown as much or as well as they would have had they been tended. They missed being watered. They had to compete with weeds. They needed their fertilizer. It's not too late for the garden, but the sooner you resume tending it, the better it will be.

You could hurt your garden. You could go and tear up plants by the roots. You could trample on them. You could cut them down. You could watch swarms of insects come and eat your plants and do nothing to stop them. Or you could abandon your garden for a long time. You could leave it unwatered until the plants had withered and died. You could let it be overgrown with weeds. Whether quickly or slowly, you could undo good work.

But even if you did this, all would not be lost. All is never lost. You always have the soil, the earth itself. Plants that have been trampled on can be encouraged to grow again. Ones that have been cut can be allowed to grow again. Seeds can be collected and planted. Weeds can be pulled up. If insects have been eating the plants, they can be controlled so that the rest of the plants will be saved. If all the plants have died from lack of watering, new ones can be planted, nurtured, and watered.

It's never too late. No matter how much damage, whether from active abuse or neglect, has been done, it's never too late to start rescuing the garden. The sooner you stop hurting it, and the sooner you start caring for it, the better it will be. If half the plants have been pulled up, the remaining half can be saved. Their flowers and fruits can be enjoyed this year. If all have been destroyed, the sooner you get started weeding, cultivating, and planting, the sooner new growth can begin.

So it is with your body. You cannot speed up the burning of fat beyond certain limits of exercise any more than you can speed up the growth of a plant by pulling on it. Sunshine, water, and fertile soil will make a plant grow as quickly as it can. Proper eating with plenty of exercise will make your body burn up fat and become smaller as quickly as possible. No matter how much you wish it, there is a pace and a timing to the growth of fitness in your body.

When you do not do your exercises and do not eat the way you should, the effect is like not tending your garden. Just as the garden gets worse the longer it goes untended, so your body gets worse the longer you go on eating the wrong way and not exercising. But no matter how long you go, it is never too late to reverse things. It is never too late to go back to caring for yourself and your body. And the sooner you resume, the better. The more quickly you get back on track, the less your garden will have gone to seed or your body to pot.

You'll find these images will stay with you and be particularly strong at those times when you naturally wish you could get to your ideal weight and be done with it rather than have to go through the slow process.

And finally, you recognize as well that just as a perfect garden does not stay perfect untended, so your body will also require your loving attention for all your days. Once established, a garden needs only the easier care and attention to keep it nice, but it does need that attention. Once you have got your body fit and healthy at the right weight, you will not need to do the difficult work of changing, but you will need to maintain the effort of keeping it that way. But you can look forward with confidence knowing that by then, you will be an expert and able to live naturally the way that will do that.

When you wish to end this exercise, you will do so however you like.

Exercise through the Year

Against the backdrop of the changing seasons, you visualize both the slow but steady changes that will take place in your body and the important role of physical exercise in making these changes possible.

———◆●◆●———

Settle back once again. Get yourself comfortable and relaxed, and let yourself go off through time and space to a beautiful country lane. There you are, on this lane. It's early summer. You are going for a walk. As you move along, it's taking a great deal of effort to keep on walking. You are finding that your muscles are out of shape, that you are easily tired. It takes a great deal of effort to carry on. But you force yourself to keep on going. You keep on walking even though your lungs are pumping and your legs are tired. You keep on going even though you don't really feel like it.

You walk along the lane, and as you do, you notice that the days are beginning to get a little bit longer, the sun a little higher in the sky, the air a little warmer, and it's hard, but not quite so hard as before, to keep on going. It's getting to midsummer and you are starting to feel a little bit better. Your muscles have become stronger as they've gotten used to the exercise, and, if the truth be told, it helps that there's less of you to carry around. You realize that walking is not so much of a burden. It's really quite pleasant. You realize that as you walk, you can look around and see the wildflowers in bloom, listen to the birds chirping, smell the freshly mown grass.

As you go on, you begin to feel more and more fit, more and more healthy. Your stride has picked up quite a bit, and as you look around, you see the leaves are beginning to turn colors, beautiful reds and oranges and yellows. You can smell the fragrance of apples and maybe the smell of wood burning in a fireplace. You are really striding along through this autumn, more and more healthy, more and more fit.

The sky clouds over and snow begins to fall. It's winter. And now you are on your cross-country skis. Last year it would have been hard to imagine yourself skiing along a snowy trail. But now it feels natural. Your heart and lungs are pumping away, keeping your more fit body active. You are able to exercise so much now, that you can really burn up a great many calories. You really realize that being able to exercise so much takes the weight off faster, faster because you burn up so many more calories while it allows you to be comfortable with the food you do eat. Most of all, it feels great to have your muscles do so much, to be able to slide along on the snow, mile after mile.

And now it's spring. The birds have returned from the south and are singing. The buds are blooming. You can smell the rich wetness of the moist earth. And as you go running along the path, you feel yourself as part of this new birth, this new life. You think back with pleasure and pride to what you've accomplished in the past year. You think about how hard it was even to walk a reasonable distance last year compared with the way you can run smoothly and easily now. You know it took hard work and dedication, and sometimes the progress wasn't so apparent. Sometimes you wondered if it would be worth the price. But now you realize that being fit, being able to exercise, and getting in your daily exercise is a part of your life that you are glad you have, a part of your life that will be yours forever.

When you feel ready to end your state of relaxed concentration, do so however you like.

Slow but Steady

This exercise presents another image designed to help you deal with the long time it takes to lose weight and some of the feelings that are bound to occur as you do.

As you settle into your special state, imagine yourself traveling along a road. It's a long and winding road but an interesting one, marked with variations in the landscape. It winds its way up hills, down valleys and through a countryside that shows the seasonal changes of fall, winter, spring, and summer. It's a road marked by milestones. As you travel along the road, every mile along the way, you can see just where you are. Every mile there is a marker identifying how far along the road you are. Each milestone marks your weight at that point. As your weight changes, you move along the road, one mile per pound.

You are walking along the road, walking at a steady pace. In the past, you've occasionally tried sprinting along this road, running as fast as you humanly could. Unfortunately, it was not long before you collapsed in a breathless heap, unable to go a step further. You may even have tried different schemes that really made you go fast. You were kind of like the cartoon coyote trying to go fast enough to catch the road runner. You found that fad diets and diet pills were, in the long run, about as successful as strapping a rocket to your back.

So here you are, traveling down the road, slowly but steadily. You see now that this is the real way and the best way to go. It will take time to get to your destination, to the milestone that is your ideal weight, but you can get there. And you feel yourself making progress.

When a time comes that you get turned around and move in the wrong direction, perhaps by going on an eating binge, your image of the road helps you in several ways. First, you know that you cannot gain fifty pounds overnight, no matter how much it feels that way. You know that you may be headed in the wrong direction, but you are not traveling at the speed of light. It helps because you are able to see each bite as a step in the wrong direction. It helps you to realize that it's a great fallacy to say, "Well, as long as I'm eating, I'll eat everything today, and I'll go back on my diet tomorrow." You know that at every instant, you are at a point on the road. If you spend the rest of the day running down the road in the wrong direction, tomorrow's dawn will find you with more distance to go to reach your destination than you will have if you stop right now. The image of the road makes it clear to you that even though standing still does not get you closer to your destination, it's still better than moving away from it.

Most of the time, you see yourself moving slowly, steadily forward. As you do, you see that the scenery gets a little nicer, there are more songbirds in the trees, and you are able to walk with more of a spring in your step. It's nicer with each step you take. Even before you get to your destination, even though you are not yet reaping all the benefits to be had, you at least are finding that each step along the way is a little nicer, each mile is a little better than the one before it.

Sometimes you've read articles about how a tendency toward obesity is inherited or about how being overweight in childhood makes it more difficult to avoid being overweight as an adult. It's made you discouraged. It's made you feel as though you were condemned to a life of being overweight by your very genes. But now, as you go marching down the road, you realize that while you may have harder road to travel than some other people, and while you may have started much further down the road than some other people, you can travel the road. You can keep on going. You have your free will, and you can use it to choose to take step after step after step.

Of course you get discouraged sometimes. Of course you sometimes feel like saying, "I'll never get there. Why do I have to travel this road? Why is it so hard?" But when you do, you will think about the road, think about your destination, and think about how it is you, not someone else, who has chosen your goal. And you realize, both now and after you are done using this exercise, that it is a reasonable goal, an attainable goal, one that you can reach with slow, steady traveling, step by step, day by day.

When you are ready to end this exercise, you can go on to another, or you can return to the usual waking state.

Do You Want It, or Is It Just Available?

Assume that, in the absence of supermarkets or other reliable sources of food, prehistoric people needed to eat whenever they could get their hands on food. The strategy in this exercise is designed to help you realize that just because you are present-ed with food does not mean that you have to eat it.

◆●◆●◆

As you settle back, visualize in your mind's eye a scene from the distant past. Gathered around the campfire is a small band of early humans. It's the Ice Age, and these ancestors are sitting around the fire. They live in a world without grocery stores, freezers, restaurants, or Twinkies.

Today the hunters killed a deer, so they will have venison tonight. They did not wake up that morning and say, "We're in the mood for venison. Let's go get some at the store." They woke up that morning hungry and with no food. Members of the tribe then went hunting, searching for any source of food.

They were lucky today. They killed a deer, and there is plen-ty of meat for everyone. So now they are sitting around the fire eating all the venison that they can. Everyone eats to the point of being full and then keeps right on eating. Even though hunger has been sated, they keep on eating every last bite they can force down. In a world where you can't go shopping and buy just the right-sized portion, where you can't even be sure of being able to get more the next day, in a world without freezers and zip-lock bags, the best way to store fuel is in the body. They eat all that they can so that the excess calories will be stored in their bodies as fat. What they don't eat today will soon spoil. Next week, they won't be able to eat this deer, but they will be able to live on the fat that they have built up from eating too much venison at this meal.

The next day, they get up and are hungry again. The hunting party goes out, but today it is not successful. There's no food to-day. Today will be a day that the people do not eat. When you must live by hunting or foraging, you have days when you eat too much and days when you do not eat at all.

The next day, in their wandering, the tribe comes upon a bush which is covered with ripe berries. They know what to do with these berries. They eat them. They know that if they do not eat them now, or at least within several days, they will not be able to have them at all. Berries are available only when they happen to be available. Too early in the season, they are not ripe; too late, they are rotten; and when mature, they are prey to other hungry animals. These people cannot say, "I'm not in the mood for berries today. I'll have them some other day." Instead they say, "This is the only time that I can definitely have berries, so I'd better have them right now." And they know exactly how to figure out how many berries they should eat. They gobble as fast as they can, and when there are no more berries left, they have eaten the correct amount. However many they could get was how many berries they should have eaten.

You are not one of them. You do not live in a world where food can be stored safely only as fat in your body. You do not live in a world where you need to eat whenever you can in case there is no food the next day. You do not live in a world where treats are available only when they happen to be found and so must be snatched whenever they can be.

Too often, you've been in a situation where some food that you liked was available, but you really weren't hungry or you really weren't quite in the mood for it at that time. You didn't really want that food at that moment. Perhaps you were at a restaurant after a satisfying meal and the dessert cart came along. You were not hungry. You had had enough. But you thought to yourself, "I must have this now, while I have the chance to eat this dessert." So you ate it.

The next time you are faced with this kind of situation, as soon as you begin to reach for that food, an image will come to your mind of yourself clothed in fur and carrying a stone-tipped spear. And as a primitive hunter, you know that you eat whenever you can. That's right. Don't let that dessert escape. Who knows when you'll track down the next one. If you do not eat this one, you may get to a point where you are too weak to hunt up another. As a primitive hunter, you may someday be dying of starvation, wishing you had eaten that extra dessert so you could have stored its energy as fat.

And then you realize how ridiculous it is for you to be treating food the way a Neanderthal would. You're eating not because you really want it, but because it's there. You realize that if you want dessert on some future day, you'll be able to go out and get it without worrying about whether you will die of starvation before you find it.

You realize that you do not need to store calories as fat to keep you alive on the days when you are not successful in your hunting. You have a refrigerator and access to supermarkets. You are not living your life like a bear who stores up a layer of fat for hibernation.

After you have ended this exercise, whenever you are confronted with food and find yourself instinctively reaching for it, the image of yourself dressed in furs, using a stone-tipped spear for a serving utensil, will come to mind. As you see that primitive human, you will remember that you can ask yourself a question that the primitive people could not use. You ask yourself, "Do I *really* want this, or is it just available?"

Just Say "No"

Managing to deal with the forces compelling you to overeat when you are trying to cut down can be difficult. This exercise teaches you to imagine and deal with the social pressures to consume more food than you should.

As you relax, think about a dilemma in which you've often found yourself. If you eat too much, you feel guilty. If you don't eat too much, you will be made to feel guilty by the person who cooked or supplied the food. That's right. You've been caught between Scylla and Charybdis, two monsters, each with its own burden of guilt. In another exercise, you will work on dealing with the guilt that you feel about your eating, because guilt is not helpful to you in changing your eating patterns. Today you are going to work on handling the pressures that other people put on you to eat the old way, in ways that they find satisfying.

Think back to a time when you were eating a meal that was cooked by another person, whether friend, spouse, or relative. Perhaps it was your mother. Let's use her as an example.

Your mother likes to see you eat. It makes her feel good to

know that you like her cooking. Perhaps she feels that your love for her is in direct proportion to the amount of food you eat. She wants to know that you love her. She wants to see you eat a lot. But you know what food really is. It is not love from her nor an expression of love to her. It is not a means of communicating your feelings toward each other at all. You used to use it as a means of communicating, but not anymore. Now you know that food is a fuel for your body. When you look at the plate, you know that you are looking at fuel, and that if you eat too much, it will hurt your body.

Your mother may not understand this. She may not realize that you have decided that you want to become more fit and healthy. She may not realize that eating too much food would hurt you. But you do.

You have two jobs, dealing with yourself and dealing with your mother. The first job is to see to it that you eat the right amount of the right food. You decide what goes in your mouth. It is your body; those are your muscles; you are not a baby who can have food pushed into its mouth. You are in command. No food can enter your mouth unless you put it there. You know how to take care of yourself, and you want to take care of yourself, so you can and do take care of yourself. You will not let yourself take refuge in falsehood such as "She made me eat it." No one makes you eat anything. It's your body, and you are in charge of it.

Your other job is dealing with your mother, who is pushing you to eat. You don't wish to hurt her feelings. If you wanted to, you could say, "That's all for me. I'm trying to lose weight." While you could do that, it's probably not the best idea. If you say that, she will think you really want to eat more but feel prevented from doing what you want by some vague enemy called weight loss. In fact, though a part of you might wish to eat more, your total decision, your final choice, is that you do not want to. If you say, "I can't have more because I want to lose weight," you are leaving yourself too open to responses like "Oh, you don't need to lose weight. You look perfect just the way you are," or "One little bit won't hurt you," or "You can go on a diet tomorrow," or "But I made it especially for you."

Besides, you've learned that the degree of fitness that you

wish to maintain, the amount that you wish to weigh, is a personal decision. You are not intending to open up a discussion on what you and your mother and everyone else thinks you should weigh. Talking about your weight and whether or not you can eat something makes it seem as though you are encouraging a discussion about what you will weigh. *You* decide because it's your body.

So you must say something else. You know that if you say something with uncertainty or indecision, you will leave yourself open to an argument. So you know you must speak firmly and with conviction.

You might say, "No thank you. I'm full." You might add, "It was really very nice of you to make such good food, and I really appreciate it. Thank you very much." When pressed to have more, you remember that there are two messages you wish to get across. The first is that you will not eat more. The second is that you wish to communicate expressions of feelings in a way other than by eating. Words don't add weight, and they can express sentiment much more clearly than a piece of pie can. So you can follow with two-part statements like "Really, I wouldn't like any more, but I really do enjoy coming to visit you," or "That's all for me, but I really appreciate your going to the trouble of making my favorite dishes for me." You keep in mind that the expression of sentiment can be made without keeping it in the language of food.

If pressed, you can ease the situation with some tricks. You know that you are in charge of your body, and you determine whether you eat or not. Sometimes it helps to say such things as "Perhaps you could wrap some up and I could take a piece home and freeze it to eat later." If you do this, you will be free to use it as a leftover or to throw it out as soon as you get home. You know that throwing away a piece of your mother's cake that does not fit in with your eating plan is not the same as throwing away your mother or throwing away her love. When you are told, "Well, you always used to eat more," you can say, "Oh? Well, I guess I've changed."

Sometimes a situation is complicated because you asked for something. Perhaps you requested some dessert that took a little effort to get, or perhaps you asked for seconds, intending to eat only a little bit more, and found that you were given a huge helping. Now you're in the position of having wanted a small bit and having been given a large amount. You know that if you don't finish it, you are going to be blamed for not eating what you requested.

The first thing to remember is that you do not have to eat more than you choose. You know that you wanted only a small amount. You don't have to take responsibility for the larger quantity. Remember the exercise about wasting food. You know that what you choose not to eat is best left uneaten. But you know that other people might not understand this lesson. Perhaps you can help them. Perhaps if they see your example, they will learn that it sometimes is OK, even good, not to finish food. And perhaps they will learn that if you ask for a small helping, they should not give you a large one in hopes that you will eat that much.

As the food is put in front of you, you say, "Oh, that's far too much. I won't be able to finish that." Whatever she says, you will have established your position in advance. Eat as much as is good for you; then feel free to be quite effusive in the praise of the food without eating more. Say how good it is, how wonderful it tasted. Do not eat any more.

When pressed to eat more, repeat how good the food is and how grateful you are that she went to the effort to get that food for you. Then say it's enough. You may be pressured further. At this point you can pull out your secret weapon. Say, "I really wanted it, and it really tasted great, and it made me very happy. But if I eat more, I will feel too full, and it will make me feel sick rather than good. I'd rather stop while I'm enjoying it than eat more and ruin it. Thank you, though." Now, as you've defined it, if she presses you further, she will be trying to make you sick. If she does, you can feel very free to refuse, because no one needs to cooperate in helping someone make her or him sick. What's more likely is either she will relent and not pressure you to eat more. Or she may have trouble understanding what you just said, in which case you need to repeat it clearly.

You may get a lecture about wasting food. You will simply

say, "That really is all I can eat comfortably." In time, she may learn through experiences like this that piling your plate higher and higher does not necessarily mean you will eat more.

Both while imagining and later, out of trance, living through these experiences, you remember that even if nobody else knows it, you know that there are ways of expressing love that do not have calories. You know that to reject food is not to reject a person. You know that you can talk about feelings rather than prove them by eating. And the bottom line is, you know that you make the final decision to eat or not to eat. It's your body. You can just say, "No."

Holidays

A variation on the exercise above can be done by focusing on holidays or parties, when the social pressure to eat is great. Since food often plays a big part in celebrations, people sometimes make the mistake of thinking that the food is the holiday and the holiday the food. Imagining a choice between eating a badly cooked, meager Thanksgiving meal with people you love or an appetizing Thanksgiving feast with total strangers may help underscore the idea that the essence of the holiday isn't the food. It's the company. It's a holiday of community, of people being together.

Sometimes people aren't happy with the company, and they try to make up for it by replacing it with food. Remember that doing so doesn't make you any happier, it just makes you miserable in two ways.

Sometimes people are tempted to skip a party altogether because they aren't altogether sure they can control their eating. A good strategy is to decide in advance whether or not you'll eat and, if you will, how much you'll eat. Remember that you cannot, at this point, eat and do other things, and that if you ate as you did in the past, the holiday wouldn't be a time of joy and pleasure but one of sadness and self-recrimination. So, resolving to eat in the way you've now learned, realize that this year you can truly and without regret celebrate the holidays.

Warning. Discretion advised. *The following is one of four highly unpleasant hypnotic exercises in this book. You may prefer to skip them unread. That would be fine. However, some people do very hurtful, repulsive, and grotesque things to themselves. They engage in behavior that can be extremely self-destructive. One way they do so is by masking the harsh reality of what they are really doing. These exercises are designed to force them to recognize a painful truth in order to change.*

"I Can't Believe I Ate the Whole Thing"

Even if you don't recognize the relevant commercial, you do, no doubt, recognize the sick, bloated feeling and the regret that follows eating too much. Using the following hypnotic exercise, you are reminded of how awful this feeling is. If you imagine feeling sick from overeating before you go to the table, you are less likely to overeat once you are actually there.

When you are comfortably relaxed and in a state of special concentration, imagine yourself about to sit down to a big meal. Perhaps it is Thanksgiving or some other family get-together. There you are, sitting down at the table with all your relatives before a real feast. The food is plentiful and appetizing. All your favorite dishes are there. And as you sit down, you reflect on how good you've been. You have been doing such a good job of eating moderately, eating the right amounts of good foods, and you decide that you deserve a break. You've suffered and worked hard and long, so you owe it to yourself just this once to eat without control. Besides, your mother's feelings would really be hurt if you didn't eat the way you always ate. That's right. Everyone is used to seeing you pile your plate. You know their feelings will be hurt if you don't. They'll ask you, "Don't you like it, dear?" So just to be nice, just so you don't hurt anyone's feelings, you'll revert and let yourself have a really good time.

And besides, since you don't often get to eat this way, you might as well take advantage of it. Take advantage of this golden opportunity to really stuff yourself.

Now, you know if you stop and think, you're liable to re-

member how good it felt to be taking control of your own life
and of your own body. You're liable to recall how good it feels to
be fit and healthy. You might recall what you've learned; putting
down your fork, savoring, tasting, and enjoying, eating anything, just not everything. So don't stop and think. If you think,
you won't have this chance to enjoy yourself. And besides, if you
think, you'll end up hurting Aunt Sadie's feelings.

So you sit down and pile up your plate. It's easy to do.
You've spent years learning how to do this. You've gotten very
good at it. You're an expert at eating this way, and you see how
easily you slip back into the routine. Pile up the plate. Now dig
in! You know that special kind of pleasure that comes from swallowing as fast as you can. Don't stop to talk, or, if you do, make
sure your mouth is full. People can understand you well enough,
especially if you point at a dish while you're saying it, so they'll
know to pass it to you. That's right. Just eat everything. And as
you finish your plate and someone says, "Do have seconds," let
them see how much you appreciate the work they went to by
having seconds or even thirds, chewing and swallowing as fast
as you can.

You're starting to feel full now, so you'd better ignore the
feeling. If you think about it, you are going to be tempted to stop,
and how often do you get a chance like this to eat everything you
want? If you think about it, you'll stop having such a good time.
So instead, you just let this awareness of fullness stay in the corner of your mind's eye, where it makes you feel guilty. It makes
you feel you are bad for doing this, so bad that you deserve to be
fat. So dig in.

You're feeling quite full now. It feels as though you could
hardly eat another bite. But there's food on your plate. It mustn't
be wasted. There are probably starving children somewhere who
would love it, so your moral duty, as a citizen of the world, is to
finish it. And then someone says, "Oh, there's only a spoonful
left in this bowl. We can't let it go to waste, and there's not
enough to save." You know that every family member must do
his or her part for the good of the family, so you take your share,
even though you're pretty full. And now it's time for dessert.

Everybody knows that "full" from dinner isn't "full" for

dessert. You're supposed to eat dessert. It goes in a different place. There's always room for Jell-O and pie and cake and ice cream. And besides, how often do you get to have such a nice selection? You'd better have a little of everything. You don't ordinarily get to eat this way.

You're feeling kind of queasy by now. You've belched and brought up the taste of something half-digested, and it really is gross. You need to eat something else to get that taste out of your mouth. You feel so full that it feels as if not only is your stomach full, but there is food sitting all the way up to your throat with no place to go. As you swallow another bite, it feels as though you are constricting your throat muscles to squeeze the food down, packing it in a little tighter because you have to make room for the rest of the dessert on your plate. You wish you had taken a little less because it's making you feel sick, but you are going to finish. You have to. Besides, how often do you let yourself have a chance to eat so much good food?

The meal is finally over. You feel sick. Your stomach feels as though it is full of Portland cement. You feel bloated. You barely have the energy to walk out to the couch and rest your heavy belly by lying down. And worst of all, you pick at leftovers as you're clearing the table. As you lie down, you feel sick and unhealthy.

And then you start to realize with horror just what you have done to your body. You've hurt your body. Your body feels sick. Your aunt is happy, your mother knows you have a healthy appetite, and everyone knows you liked the food. But while they are happy, you are stuck with this overfilled carcass. The only thing you can wish and hope for is the passage of time, for hours to pass for your body to deal with this heavy load that you took on. You wish it were hours from now. And it feels familiar. You know this feeling from your past. Just as it felt so easy and familiar to pile up the plate and wolf it down, so also it feels unpleasantly familiar to feel so sick. And you feel so sad, so unhappy at the pain you've given yourself.

But then you realize that this has been done in imagination. The overeating scene is like a videotape you made in your imagination. And you hate how this one ended. So rewind the tape.

You're going to do this scene over again. Go back all the way back to the beginning.

There you are, sitting down with all your relatives and all your favorite foods. You know that you've been eating well, and you know that that makes you happier than your old way ever did. And you know that the way you eat is going to affect your body. You are not eating to please your mother or Aunt Thelma or to show your Uncle Harry how grown up you are. Making a pig of yourself is not really a compliment to the chef. And even if it were, the chef would just have to live with verbal flattery only. That's right. Think of the exercises you've done: eating slowly; savoring, tasting, and enjoying; and putting the fork down between bites. And think of the exercise on why you want to eat the new way, on why you wish to become fitter and healthier. Think back to any of the exercises you've learned that will be helpful. You need to get the help of these exercises because you find that everyone is expecting you to eat the way you always did. Everyone, including you, would find it easy to slip into the old ways with the old familiar consequences. And you remember your new lessons, including the newest lesson: knowing how sick and bloated it makes you feel to overeat.

And you go through the meal again, eating the right amount of the food on your plate and leaving the rest, dealing with the pressures, eating a way that's good for you, using all you've learned. And at the end of the meal, as you leave the table, you feel extremely good. You feel good that you have taken charge of your life, and you feel good because you genuinely enjoyed the meal. You feel happy with yourself, satisfied and contented. As you contrast the way you feel with the logy feeling of before, you know that if you think about the consequences of overeating before you do it, you'll never do it again.

When you wish to end this state of relaxed concentration, do so in whatever way works best for you.

Buffet

A variation on the preceding technique is to visualize a dining room with a buffet table set up in it. Everything in the room is perfectly symmetrical, one half being the mirror image of the other. There are even the same number of people lining equal lengths of the table on both sides. From the center to either side, to the right and to the left, are laid exactly the same foods in the same order.

Starting at the center, you walk down the left side of the buffet table, forgetting moderation. Think of eating in the old way, heaping a large plate with huge amounts of every dish. Notice that all the people here are overweight, and see yourself in a distorting mirror getting fatter and fatter as you continue in this direction down the table. Remember how sick and bloated overeating makes you feel. Drop the too-loaded plate and run back to the center of the table.

Now walk down the right side of the buffet, taking moderate portions of some foods. See yourself surrounded by diners who are fit, and know you belong with them. Watch yourself approaching a mirror that reflects a trimmer you with each step you take toward it. Be glad you have chosen this way.

Chains

When confronted with a bag of potato chips, a bowl of nuts, or some M & Ms, it can be difficult to stop eating once you have started. The following exercise can help you break the "I can never eat just one" behavior that can result in an eating binge.

Get yourself in a nice relaxed state, peacefully ready to concentrate. Visualize in your mind's eye a large iron ring. Now, you want to pick it up, but you see that running through the middle of this ring is a chain, a big, thick, heavy chain. The end of the chain where the ring encircles it is set in concrete, so you can't take it off that way. The other end lies loose, stretching straight out for some distance. If you want to free the ring from the chain, you have to pull the ring down the entire length of chain until you get to the very end. Only when you have gone all the way to the end is the ring free.

Sometimes when you start to eat, you feel just as though you have picked up the ring and must continue down the entire length of chain to get it free. You feel that once you have started eating, you need to continue eating more and more, more and more, until you get to the end of the food. For example, if you start eating a container of ice cream, you feel as though there is no stopping until you reach the bottom of the carton. When you begin a bag of chips, it is as though that first chip means that you must eat every chip down to the last one. When you begin an eating binge, you must eat and eat and eat until your stomach can hold no more.

Think of these situations. Think of times that you have begun eating and felt there was no stopping. As you do, visualize the chain. See how you felt. Once you had begun, you could not stop until you got to the end. Think of the last time that you ate too much. Recall that feeling, that voice in your mind that said, "I don't know why I'm still eating this. It doesn't even taste good anymore. Oh well, there's hardly any left. I'd better finish it." See how that was just like the ring as you tried to pull it free of the chain, how you wouldn't stop until you'd got to the end, how you felt unable to say, "This is enough."

Sometimes in the past you succumbed to the feeling that since you had started to eat the wrong food at the wrong time, somehow it didn't matter how much you had. The weight would come from the crime, not from the amount eaten. But now you have learned that regardless of how you feel, eating less is really not the same as eating more. You now know that your weight is the result of how much you eat. You know that half a bag of potato chips has only half the calories of a full bag. You know that ice cream gives calories for each bite taken, not for each carton opened.

You know that if you could end that chain sooner, you would be able to eat less; you would lose weight.

Let's take a closer look at that chain. As you look, you notice something very peculiar about it. You notice two things which make you feel not so good, perhaps, about the mistake you've made in the past. But forgiving yourself allows you to look closely enough to see the secrets of the chain. The first secret is that these links are not heavy, welded steel. They are simply big paper clips. It wouldn't take a hack saw or an acetylene torch to cut through them. They could just spring apart. They could be slipped off each other. Now you know. You can break this chain at any spot, at any point.

And as you look even closer, you discover the second secret of the chain. You see the chain that has been lying there has never really even been a chain, but a series of individual paper clips that weren't even connected. What you've been doing as you went along the chain was not following an unbreakable length to its bitter end. Instead, as you came to the end of each link, your left hand carried the ring toward the end while your right hand would clip another paper clip onto the end. That's right. It's your right hand that's been lengthening the chain, link after link, yard after yard.

A part of you says, "No, that chain was so strong, so powerful." But you know. You recognize the fact that it was a part of you that wanted to keep on eating that convinced you that the chain was long and strong and unbreakable.

And you realize that it really is lucky for you that this chain is merely a collection of paper clips. This won't change what has been, what you've already done, but it frees your future.

From now on, when you start to eat, particularly when you start to snack or when you find yourself beginning to binge, or find yourself starting to eat and having difficulty stopping, immediately to your mind's eye will come the picture of the chain. And as it does, you will immediately look closely and see that each link is merely a paper clip, a paper clip that hasn't even been connected yet.

If you are eating a bowl of peanuts or M & Ms, you'll realize that each one that you eat is a separate bit of food that need not be followed by another. As you finish one, you will be able to say to yourself, "Is my right hand going to hitch another paper clip onto the chain, or shall I stop now? Is my chain already long enough?" And you will realize that you have the ability, the option, of choosing to make any single one your last peanut or M & M. If you are eating a slice of pizza, you will see that each bite is a separate link. Having a big piece of pizza in your hand is like having a whole fistful of paper clips in it. They are nice and con-venient, ready to be hooked on one after the next after the next, but they are not yet clipped together. At any point you can drop the paper clips, and the ring will be free. You can put down the slice and the binge will be over.

You might find it helpful to go and brush your teeth when you stop eating. Changing the taste of your mouth and getting it clean can serve to put a final end to the chain. When you are ready to end this exercise, you will do so however works best for you.

Monster

As you change your eating behavior, the urge to binge or eat uncontrollably weakens. Using the following hypnotic proce-dure, you conceptualize the urge to eat in an out-of-control way as a hurtful monster who is strengthened as you give way to it.

—————◆•◆•◆—————

Get yourself nice and relaxed, comfortably settled. You're going to do an hypnotic exercise that will help you to deal with and control some of the urges that you get to eat. Visualize in your mind's eye a short, nasty little creature. He looks somewhat like a human, but not exactly. He is distorted. His face reminds you of a malicious, cruel monkey. He looks like a bad imp or gremlin. He is a monster. He's carrying a whip and wearing spurs. He is a monster, and he is on your back.

That's right. This nasty bit of business is on your back want-ing to poke you, whip you, dig his spurs into you.

He doesn't like you very much.

This monster wants to hurt you. He wants to hurt you by making you eat more than you should. This monster wants you to overeat and become fat. This monster wants to keep you eat-ing more than is good for you, eating the things that aren't good for you.

And the reason he wants you to overeat is because he needs you to mistreat yourself in order to stay alive.

When you start to eat at a time that isn't right, perhaps having an unacceptable snack between meals, that wakes up the monster, gives him life and strength. He knows that if you stop eating, he will lose his power and will sink back into a quiet state. And he doesn't want to be put to sleep that way. He wants you to keep on eating. He wants you to keep him alive and powerful. And he stays alive and powerful by hurting you, degrading you, making you do the things that aren't good for you.

When you are eating foods in a greater quantity than you consider right, you are strengthening the monster. Just think of a time when you started eating too much. Just look at yourself eating more than you should, going into a feeding frenzy, eating too much food. Now, as you look closely, you see, mounted on your back, that monster. See him there whipping you, digging his spurs into your back, screaming at you, "Eat, eat, eat." Watch as he leads you to make a pig of yourself, degrade yourself, hurt yourself.

The only way to kill that monster, to rob him of his power, is to starve him. Just watch the scene as you say, "No," when he yells, "Eat, eat." At first, he will gather up his energy and intensify the assault, whipping you, goading you, hurting you, putting more and more pressure on you to eat, to eat more and more. As you again say, "No," his efforts become even stronger, even more frantic. But as you watch, you realize that his energy is coming from desperation. He is summoning resources to try to beat you down because he knows that if he doesn't, he will become weaker as you become stronger. So you again say, "No." And as you do, you recognize him for the sniveling little weasel that he really is. It's almost as if you had let the air out of a balloon as you watch him deflate, becoming smaller, weaker, and less powerful. You recognize that as you take advantage of your own life, take charge of your eating, you become stronger. And you see that as you do so, that monster, that appetite, that compulsion to eat becomes weaker and weaker, more and more helpless.

In the past, when confronted with a strong urge to eat at a time you really felt was not good, you have made the mistake of thinking that if you just had a "little bit," the urge would go away. If you just stretched your feeding guidelines by a hair's breadth or ignored your strategy for a short while, everything would feel better. Now you realize the fallacy of that thinking. Now you recognize that the "little bit" that you ate didn't quiet the monster. Instead it woke him up and gave him energy. And the more you ate, the more ravenous he became, the more he demanded that you eat.

But now you know. The easiest way to control the monster is to resist the first impulse to overeat, not give in to it. You recognize that this impulse is a faint stirring of the monster wanting to be allowed out, wanting to be able to torment you. And you recognize that at this point, you are strong and the monster is weak. If you give way just a little, you will not feel better; you'll feel worse because you will have the monster to struggle with. Knowing that resisting the first impulse quiets the monster will often be enough to help you not give him that first bite, that "little bit" which mobilizes him.

Sometimes you'll forget and have that first bite, waking up the monster. At those times, you'll remember that each bite you add gives more strength to the monster. The sooner you stop, the less you will have strengthened him. When you first stop, he will make a great deal of fuss and try to torment you into continuing to eat. You will know that this frenzy is motivated by his desperation. If you stop eating, he will lose his power. And so you know that the sooner you stop, the sooner you will weaken him and strengthen yourself.

And it makes you feel so much better about yourself when you see yourself as strong, free, in charge of your own life, rather than making yourself the miserable slave of that tyrannical monster.

Whenever you feel ready to end this exercise, do so however you like.

Guilt Does Not Help

Guilt is counterproductive when it makes you punish yourself by eating too much. You can learn to work on the future instead of helplessly regretting and repeating your past mistake of overeating.

<hr>

Settle back and get nice and relaxed, but as you do, recall a time when you felt that you had done something wrong. Perhaps you had hurt someone's feelings. Perhaps you had neglected a duty. Perhaps you overate the "wrong" kinds of foods. You know the kind of thing that makes you feel so bad, so guilty.

As you feel this feeling grow stronger and stronger, you start feeling that you are a bad person who deserves to be punished. And you know just the punishment. The worst thing that could happen to you would be to gain weight. So you know what you are going to do. You are going to make yourself eat.

And since you're such a bad person, since this food is a punishment, not a reward, you are going to eat, and you are not even going to enjoy it. You are not going to get the pleasure of the taste of the food. Instead, you are going to eat for pain. You eat to gain.

Also, way inside yourself, is a hurt sniveling little wretch who will enjoy eating anything, no matter how truly unpleasant. That part of you is going to take cold comfort from the volume of food that gets swallowed. It's like a big, fat baby that knows it's not being cared for, knows it's not being loved, and so clings to the food, to being stuffed as a kind of comfort.

It feels very familiar, this sense of feeling guilty, feeling bad, and feeling driven to eat. The eating is a compulsion. You're doing it because you're bad; you're doing it as a punishment for yourself. Sometimes it's even a punishment for having enjoyed some food. You have one bite of a good-tasting food, enjoy it, and feel guilty. And the guilt drives you to punish yourself, to hurt yourself.

But deep inside is another part of yourself, a reasonable part, a mature part. This part has long recognized the folly of your circle of guilt and overeating. Until now this part has not had a clear voice to intervene. But now you are able to listen and hear what this mature, healthy self has to say: "You are not really a bad person. You don't need to suffer. You don't deserve punishment. Even if you had done something wrong, the way to correct it would not be to hurt your body by eating too much food.

That makes nothing right. Hurting yourself benefits no one. If you really did something wrong, there is something appropriate that you can do about it. If you neglected a duty, go back and perform it. If you hurt someone's feelings, you can say you are sorry. Eating too much does not help the job get done. If you have trouble in a relationship with another person, you need either to work out that relationship or realize that at this time it can't be worked out. In any case, though, hurting your body, making yourself fat, does not make anything better.

This urge to feel guilt, along with the desire to take it out on your body, is an old and familiar pattern, which is why you must work so hard to break it. When you find yourself feeling bad and eating, particularly when it doesn't taste very good, you must realize what you are doing. At those times, you are not enjoying your food. You are using food to punish yourself. And at those times you're going to search inside yourself for that mature part that says that hurting your body doesn't make things better, that working against your own goals does not solve things.

This is particularly something to watch out for when you find yourself tempted to turn an enjoyable experience of eating a reasonable amount into a full-fledged binge. As you find yourself tempted to binge, you need to remind yourself that it's OK to enjoy the food that you have enjoyed. You are permitted to eat and permitted to enjoy the food that you eat.

In the past you've made the mistake of thinking that guilt feelings were somehow connected to weight loss. It was almost as if it didn't matter what you ate as long as you felt bad enough about it, almost as if suffering would keep the pounds from accumulating. But now you know it's what you eat that changes your weight.

Overeating doesn't solve your guilt, and it doesn't solve your other problems. Instead it *adds* another problem. Eating the right foods in moderation does not solve your other problems either, but at least it results in a healthier, fitter body with which you can tackle them.

When you are ready to end, you will do so and will find that you are alert, refreshed, and aware of what you have just learned.

So It's Not Going So Well

In the course of your weight loss there are times when the weight comes off more slowly than you wish, or times when it seems not to come off at all. There are probably times when you slip and gain and times when you get very discouraged. You don't quite know how to deal with these episodes or how to work your way out of feeling demoralized. So now try some suggestions that should help.

Settle back and get comfortable, peaceful, and relaxed. This has been a difficult period because your weight has not been going down as quickly as it had before. You may feel stuck at a plateau. That's normal. Even if you are keeping your eating under control and doing just what you should be doing, you will be likely to hit plateaus where your weight seems stuck. Your body tries to keep itself stable. It tries to keep many things—temperature, respiration, weight—basically the same. Your body will resist changing until it sees that you are really seriously going in that direction. If your eating and exercising stay constant, you might find you will lose very little or nothing for several weeks, then suddenly lose a number of pounds fairly quickly.

Perhaps you've even had a bad week and have gained a few pounds. That's normal, too. The habits of a lifetime, including the habit of overeating, die hard. What is important is not whether or not you have any slips, but what you do when you have them.

So right now it's particularly important that you do settle back and so let yourself get into the comfortable state of relaxed concentration and attention. This is a time when it's easy for you to feel bad—to feel so bad, in fact, that you prevent yourself from getting hypnotized. So it's all the more important that you put in a real, strong effort to get yourself relaxed, focused, concentrating. Then you can take advantage of what you have learned, of what you know how to do, so that you can help yourself. You know that there is a part of you that is used to eating the old way and wants a return to it. And there is a part of you that doesn't like you very much and wants to hurt you. These parts are going to try to keep you from getting back on track, going to try to keep you from regaining the momentum you once had.

Picture, in your mind's eye, people from your past who have hurt you with their comments or looks about your weight. Think of everyone who has ever rejected you or criticized you. Let them stand for the people who feel better about themselves when you feel worse about yourself. There are some people who feel that if they have you to feel sorry for, they have a role, they are needed. They rather like having someone who needs help. They need you to regain your weight. As you picture all of them, you see that these characters really want you back where you were. They want you to regain your weight. They don't like the fact that you have changed. They resent your progress.

And think of all those "well-meaning friends" who have been busy telling you, "Oh, you don't need to lose weight," "You'll get too skinny," or "Are you all right? Are you sure you are not sick?" And as you see all these characters, you realize that their wishes are not your wishes, their goals are not your goals. You have different goals. You have goals that include becoming more fit and more healthy. Just because they need to feel superior to someone doesn't mean it needs to be you. Just because they need a wounded bird to nurse along doesn't mean you need to break a wing. And you truly realize, perhaps for the very first time, that you have it in your power to change your body's shape, to lose weight and become healthy and fit. That's right. You know that this is a task that you can accomplish. You know that you don't have to yearn wistfully for a fit body. You know you can get it. You know that if you go back, review the previous strategies, and use whichever ones worked for you before, you will be able to regain control of your eating.

When you sit down to eat and find that in the back of your mind it's as if your cast of characters is encouraging you to eat quickly, without putting down your knife and fork, you remember and say to yourself that the food will taste better if you savor, taste, and enjoy it, putting down the knife and fork between bites. When they encourage you to eat more and more, you remember that you have been learning how to tell when you have had enough. When they encourage you to clean your plate, you remember that you, not the plate, say when you are done. You remember that you are not a garbage can into which wasted food is put. You remember that you are not "dying of hunger," but that you are experiencing a sensation that says you are doing well. You remember that you can eat food when you want to, not just because it's available and not just because it is forbidden fruit. You remember all the lessons you've learned, and you remember most of all that the kind of after-the-fact guilty, miserable feelings to which you were prone do not help. That guilt will not make you lose weight or eat less, so it is not something useful to you.

You have been tempted to throw up your hands and say, "I'll never get it right! I give up!" and quit trying. This demoralized voice is the part of you that feels guilty, that feels bad, and that wants to punish you by eating even more. But you know that you are not a bad person and you are not going to treat yourself as if you were. You know that you had been choosing to take good care of yourself; then you slipped, or perhaps hit a plateau. So now, instead of "I'll never get it right," you say, "I don't have it right quite yet, but I'm getting better, and I'll keep getting better."

And you've done a lot. You have lost weight since you have begun. As you think about the weight you've lost, visualize in your mind's eye a pound of butter, a pound of margarine, or a pound of lard. That's right. Just look at that block. Just look how big and fat it is. Now think of how many pounds of fat you have lost already. Think of how many pounds of fat are no longer on your body because you've burned them up as fuel. Just imagine if you were to go to the store and were to buy that many pounds of lard or shortening, and if you were to stuff those packages inside your clothing how horrible you would look. And you realize that you had that much lard or shortening not under your jacket but under your skin. You not only had to carry it and look bad, but you had it clogging up your arteries and generally making you unhealthy. You have done something about that. You have lost pound after pound. You have got rid of so much of your fat, and you can be very pleased and encouraged and proud of this. That's right. You are the kind of person who changes eating habits, who does things differently now.

And okay. So perhaps you've even gained some weight this week. It's probably not as bad as you're afraid. You know that for every pound of fat gained, you have to eat 3,500 calories more than you burn up. It's likely, if your weight went up several pounds, that much of it is water, which is quickly gained and quickly lost.

But even if not, what's most important is that you have caught yourself and have begun moving once again toward fitness.

You may feel like eating more than is right for you. You may feel like continuing to overeat. That's OK. It's normal to wish to do that, normal to feel like doing that. That doesn't mean you need to do it. Wanting to do something does not mean you must do it. And you know that even stronger than your urge to continue overeating, even stronger than your urge to feel guilty, even stronger than your urge to go back to the old ways, are your wish and decision to become fit.

Now you are going to go back, and you are going to use and continue to use the suggestions in this book, particularly the ones which may be the hardest but may, by the same token, be the most helpful to you.

Keeping the Good Feeling

This final lesson is one designed to help you to remember why you are doing all this work and to help you keep on treating your body the good, healthy way you really want.

Settle back, and once again enter a special peaceful state of relaxation and concentration. As you do, let your mind go back into your past and remember how you used to be. You remember the way you used to treat your body, and you remember the confusions you used to have.

Think back upon a time when a well-meaning person, who cared about you, started nagging you about your food. Think back to the way you felt when you were given that disapproving glance when you reached for food. Think back to the time you were told, "You really should take off some weight." Think back to when you were told, "Wouldn't you really rather have the salad plate, dear?" or "You don't really want that dessert you ordered, do you?"

And you remember the way you used to think that you would lose weight for that other person. And you know that dieting for that other person sooner or later always led to a declaration of independence: "I'll show them who's the boss. I'll have two." Because, as you now know, all the motivation in the world makes no difference if it's someone else's motivation.

Now you know that you're not really going to lose weight for your spouse, your friends, your mother, your doctor, or "society." You know that you're not going to change your habits for them, and you know what a mistake it's been when you have eaten more just to prove to them that you were the boss, because now you know that there really is no confusion about who is in charge of your body.

You are in charge of your body. And you are the one who lives in your body. You choose what goes into your body. You enjoy or suffer the consequences of the care you give yourself. No matter how well intentioned they are, those other people never had to do the work of learning new ways for you to eat, never suffered your disability of being overweight, and will never gain your reward of being fit and healthy.

That's right. Controlling weight is something that you have done, and will continue to do, for yourself. Other people are spectators, like the audience at a sporting event. They can yell cheers and encouragement, they can be discouraging or even "boo" you, but still, it's the athlete on the field who performs well or poorly. And you have learned to perform well. You have learned to do your best not because of the watching crowd, but because you want to win.

You realize that different parts of yourself want different things. You know that there really were some pleasures in overeating. But you also know now that these pleasures were not worth the pain. They hurt more than they felt good. You know now that your body paid a price, too high a price, a terrible price. And when your body paid, it hurt you.

You've learned that this weight business is something that happens between you and your body. And you know that the real victory for you, the real reward that you seek, is the kind of life that you can live in a fit and healthy body, the kind of body that you can have. It's not that you don't want some of the things you used to have, but you even more want the good feeling that comes from having taken care of yourself. You even more want the good feeling that comes from having given yourself the special present you are giving yourself, a gift that only you can give: the precious gift of a healthy body that will let you do the most that you can, a fit body that will allow you to do as much as you can. You are no longer going to handicap yourself by making yourself carry around excess pounds of lard.

You know that this fitness does not solve all of your problems. If you could not play the violin before, losing weight will not transform you into a concert violinist. But a person who has learned how to take control of his or her own life, who has learned the pleasure to be had from reaching long-range goals, and a person who has more energy as a result of being fit, is in a better position to learn to play the violin than is someone who feels out of control, who is down on himself or herself, whose life is obsessed with food.

Your recovery is still rather new. There are going to be times when it will be difficult to maintain your new way of eating, when the old habits will seek to reassert themselves. For a long time you are going to continue to use the suggestions you've learned in this book. You should continue to hypnotize yourself daily as long as there is any question of your ability. You won't hurt yourself by working too hard, learning too much, or gaining too much control. As you reduce the frequency, you should do so gradually, going to every other day, then every third day. If you eventually cut down to once a week, you should be certain to use the weekly exercise for a minimum of a year. Your old habits were very well established, and you should not be afraid to keep practicing to make sure the new habits you've learned stay strong. Sometimes it will be difficult. When you are feeling stressed or nervous, you may find yourself tempted to go back to your old way of eating. That's not surprising. And that's why you have these suggestions that can help you to get through these tough times without reverting to overeating. There will be some situations, like the holidays or when you get into certain kinds of fights with people you care about, when you will be tempted to go back to the old ways. That's why you have the exercises that deal with the holidays and social pressures to eat. You'll think of each of the different lessons you've learned as tools, as available resources. Whenever you need one, you'll know where to find it. You will go back to the appropriate exercise and review it. And most of all, when you go back to relearn what you've already covered, rather than thinking of yourself as a failure who has to repeat a grade, you will feel, instead, very successful. You will feel yourself to be someone who knows how to handle problems as they come up. You are the kind of person who has the resources to handle the dilemmas that are, of course, to be expected in any life.

You know that what you have embarked upon is a lifelong journey. The well-established garden needs less work to keep it up than a weed patch needs to be transformed into a garden. But it still needs regular, careful work to prevent it from deteriorating. Your fitness requires regular work and ongoing control of your eating. You have not survived a diet only to return to your old fattening ways. Instead you've learned a new way of living, a way with its own satisfactions, its own pleasures, its own joy.

And as you think about this, now and out of trance, you feel very, very good indeed. You feel a deep, deep sense of joy at what you have done for yourself. And you know that this is a precious prize that you are going to work to keep forever.

13

Physical Problems

As discussed at the beginning of this book, hypnosis works at that intersection of mind and body where thought affects physical reality. In many of the chapters, emphasis is laid upon the body's response to psychological events, such as muscle tension caused by anxiety.

This chapter is devoted to the treatment of physical concerns in which the body itself is the focus. These are not varieties of psychosomatic disorders, where the mind causes a physical illness, but symptoms whose origin is biological. There are a number of assorted physical symptoms that have been proven to be treated extremely effectively with hypnosis. This chapter offers approaches to some of the more common ones.

All of these approaches have been researched and shown to be effective but should not be seen as a substitute for proper medical care. These are essentially adjunctive therapies which can be helpful as part of an overall treatment protocol.

Migraines and Other Headaches

Migraines are a special class of headaches that are caused by the tightening of the veins leaving the head. As a result of this constriction, blood enters the brain more easily than it can leave it, creating an area of high blood pressure in the head. The basic treatment for migraines consists of relaxing and dilating these veins so that the blood is free to flow out, reducing pressure in the head.

Obviously the human body is quite capable of controlling itself in great detail and normally regulates the flow of blood quite successfully. In the case of a migraine, however, the internal monitoring and controlling devices have for some reason become slightly maladjusted.

In the normal course of events, the body eventually restores itself to a proper balance. The simplest treatment of migraines, lying down in a darkened room, is intended to minimize the distress while giving the body time to realize that it is hurting itself and needs to change.

Hypnosis allows you to take a much more aggressive approach, actively bringing the problem to your body's attention.

Cooling Your Head

By suggesting sensations of coolness in your head and warmth in your hands and feet, blood flows out, reducing the pressure in your head. Parenthetically, this technique can be useful for people who suffer from chronic cold fingers and toes and also for those who have to stand around outside on a cold day.

Enter a state of deep relaxation and concentration in hypnosis. Once you've become deeply hypnotized, feel yourself going off, traveling through time and space. Imagine it's a dark, chilly night and you're out of doors sitting by the campfire. It's cold out, but the fire is warm and toasty. You hold your hands and feet forward, and as you do, you feel the warmth of the fire warming your hands, warming your feet. Of course you're not going to be so foolish as to stick them into the fire and burn yourself, but you will put them as close as you comfortably can.

The chill that had previously got into them is going away. You feel them becoming very, very warm. They may become so warm that your hands and feet begin to sweat. You feel a tingle pulsing through your hands and your feet as they are warmed by this campfire. You just keep looking at the flames as they dance about. Watch the patterns of the flames as they flicker and dart; watch the embers glowing; watch them change shades as branches burn through, crackle, break, and turn to glowing coals. That's right. Listen to the fire. Smell the clean scent of the smoke.

As you do, however, you realize that it really is quite chilly. That's right. The temperature has dropped. While your hands and feet are very, very warm, so near to the fire, the parts of your body which are farther away from the fire are cooling, becoming cooler and cooler. In fact your head, which is farthest away from the fire, is feeling rather cold. In fact your head is feeling quite chilled. You feel the wind blowing across your head, cooling it, chilling it. Perhaps you've leaned back against a rock for comfort. As you do you feel the rock so cold, so cold against your head, draining the heat from your head, sucking the heat from your head. You feel your head becoming colder and colder while your hands and feet become warmer and warmer. It's really a rather interesting study in contrasts. When you arrived at the fire, your hands and feet had been cold, while your head was warm. Now it's reversed. Your hands and feet are warm, becoming warmer and warmer by the minute. Your head has become cold, colder and colder, colder and colder.

But it's a good feeling as you watch the fire, smell the smoke, watch the embers glow, watch the flames dance, and listen to the cool wind blowing through the woods. And as you do, you realize that you're becoming more and more comfortable, more and more comfortable, that it's nice to be at this campfire. And you're going to stay at this campfire for as long as you need. You're going to stay until you feel perfectly fit, completely ready to go on with business. There's no need to rush. You can stay by the campfire as long as you need. Stay by the campfire as your body heals. There's no rush, but you find that as you sit by the campfire, as your hands and feet warm and your head cools, you feel better and better, comfortable and at ease, comfortable and at ease.

The purpose of this exercise is to communicate to your body in a physical way what you would like it to do to correct the problem. Since you're not really sitting by a campfire but are imagining it in hypnosis, you are describing to your body how to create the necessary special effects. Anyone who has ever blushed knows that the rush of blood to the cheeks which produces the bright red mark of embarrassment also feels warm. Where there is more blood, there is a sense of warmth. If blood had gone to your hands and feet, the result would be that they would feel warm.

With hypnosis we are doing the same thing but reversing cause and effect. Instead of a flow of blood producing a sensation of warmth, the sensation of warmth is vividly imagined. As a result, the body tries successfully to create the sensation that is being imagined. Since there is no real campfire to produce the feeling of warmth, blood is shifted to the hands and feet, which makes them feel genuinely warm. The amount of blood in your body does not fluctuate from one moment to the next. If your hands and feet are more richly supplied with blood, if the arteries and capillaries supplying them have become dilated to allow a free flow, that means there must be less blood present in other parts of the body.

Suggesting the sensation of cold in the head works in the mirror image of the hands and feet. In order to feel colder, your head needs to get less blood. The warm blood in it needs to be allowed to escape easily. The veins need to dilate, allowing the easy flow of blood from the head to the extremities. What you have been doing has been explaining to your body what it is you want it to do. Once the process gets going, once your body starts to successfully reequilibrate, it will tend to stay properly balanced, just as it would have if a migraine had been allowed to run its complete course.

The Boiler

The sensation of a migraine has been likened by some sufferers to a boiler under such pressure it is in danger of exploding. You can persuade your body to reequilibrate by visualizing a reduction in the boiler's pressure reading.

As you settle back into a comfortable and relaxed state, you think about how the migraine is linked to a sensation of pressure in your head. As you think about this sensation of pressure, you imagine in your mind's eye a large boiler. Imagine not a realistic boiler but rather the kind drawn in a cartoon for a locomotive or a steamboat. And as you see this cartoonish boiler, you see how it is expanding and straining, threatening to explode. As you look at this boiler straining, with the pressure building and mounting, a link is made between the way your head feels and the way this boiler looks. The pressure on your head is throbbing outward. The boiler is pushing and expanding in the same fashion. As you look closely, you see two things in the front of the boiler. The first is a huge pressure gauge. The second is a large wheel. As you look at the pressure gauge, you see that the needle is pointing all the way over to the right, indicating a huge amount of pressure. And as you look at the wheel, you realize that that is the wheel that allows steam to escape from the boiler, reducing the pressure.

You realize the pressure is too great. The pressure is not what it should be. So you begin to turn this wheel, and as you do, you see how the pressure begins to reduce, slowly at first, but steadily becoming less severe. As you turn the wheel and the steam escapes from the boiler and flows through the system, as it is supposed to do, the needle on the dial begins to inch its way to the left. As it does, you see and can even feel that the boiler is no longer straining quite so much. It is still under pressure, perhaps too much pressure, but it's beginning to ease off, to lessen, bit by bit by bit. As you continue to stare at the dial, as you watch the needle move, the pressure becomes less and less, and you remember how you had made a connection between that boiler and your head. You remember how you had connected the image of that boiler to the feeling in your head. And as you do, you feel how as the pressure in the boiler decreases, so also the pressure in your head decreases. And as you twist the handle to let the steam flow into the system, so also your body is letting the blood flow out of your head. You feel the pressure lessening; you feel the pain subsiding.

You'll have to see how long it takes for the pressure to go down to where it should be. You're letting the excess steam out of the boiler as fast as you can. You're watching the needle move from right to left, from too much pressure to the proper pressure. But there was a lot of steam in that boiler, and there's a limit on how big an opening the valve has. You'll have to see how fast the steam can go. You'll have to see how much the valve can open. The pressure may be going out as fast as it can, but it may take a little while to accomplish the task. You're going to do it as quickly as you can, as fast as is possible, and you won't fall prey to discouragement if it takes time. As you stare at that dial, you move the needle, slowly, perhaps, but inexorably to the left. And as that needle moves, the pressure changes. And as the pressure changes, the pain subsides. Each bit of movement of the needle changes the sensation in your head, making it less and less pressured, less and less painful. And you continue to do this until the pain is completely controlled, until it is gone. And then the needle will be pointing exactly where it should be, and you can end this exercise feeling relaxed and pain-free.

Twisted Rope

Nonmigraine headaches caused by a feeling of tension are amenable to treatment by this last technique, which describes a relaxation of tension by relaxing a rope. It tends to work best on headaches where some feeling of pressure is involved and, if your sinuses are full, sometimes produces a draining of them. It begins by describing the pain in order to alter it.

As you settle into a relaxed state of attention, imagine a thick, heavy rope that has been looped and tied around two trees. A metal bar has been put into the loop and it has been turned so that the rope has become more and more tightly twisted. It's rather like a rubber band that powers a toy airplane propeller which has been twisted so that the rubber band is tightly coiled upon itself, ready to propel the airplane. But as you look at this heavy rope, you see that the metal bar has been twisted so often, so tightly, that this rope is under tremendous pressure. It has produced such pressure that the trees have been pulled toward each other.

You see how the rope has twisted and become so tight, and you can just feel how tense and painful that rope must be. It feels like the muscles in your head. You feel how the tension is just twisted and tightened across your temples. You experience the tension feeling as if it's pulling your head into itself, as though your skull would implode, just the way you can see how those trees look, as if they're about to be pulled in together, pulled up by the roots. And as you see and feel the tension of that rope and feel the tension on your head, you realize how good it would be to release the tension on the rope.

That's right. You slowly begin to reverse the spin, you slowly release the iron bar. You don't do it too fast. You don't want it twirling around, flying around and hitting someone, but slowly you allow it to untwist, and as you do, you see how the rope loses its tension, how it loses its pressure. And as you do, you see how the trees begin to relax, how they begin to straighten up. They're no longer threatened with being pulled up by the roots. They're able to relax. The rope is loosening its tension. It's no longer twisted and strained. It's starting to sag and relax. That's right. It's now dangling, hanging stretched out in a gentle arc between the trees, stretched out as a hammock would be, relaxed, inviting, comfortable, and peaceful. And you realize that your head is doing the same. Your head is no longer tense. Your head no longer aches. And you are going to be able to let your head stay relaxed.

If the tension should begin to creep back in unawares, you're going to become aware once again of the image of that rope, and as you become aware of it, you're going to recognize immediately that the rope is no longer relaxed like a hammock but is twisted and tensed, and you're going to do something about that. You're going to untwist that rope once again. You're going to relax it and feel the relaxation return once again to your head, because that tension in your head serves no purpose. It doesn't help you; it doesn't protect you. It serves no good. It's something to put aside.

When you are ready to end this exercise, bring yourself back to the usual waking state feeling relaxed and refreshed.

Warts

Warts are a fascinating example of how your mind can control symptoms that are purely physical in origin. Warts are caused by a virus. Because it hides inside a cell, the virus can evade the body's natural defenses for a long time. In a way, the germ behaves like a soldier dressed in the uniform of her or his enemy's army. Being dressed up like a compatriot, she or he is not immediately detectable as an enemy.

The body does have natural defenses, such as lymphocytes, that are capable of destroying the virus. The trick is to alert the body's immune system that an unwanted virus is present and needs to be destroyed.

A variety of techniques can be used to achieve this necessary attention. Many of them are dependent upon belief for efficacy. Folk remedies such as cutting a potato in half, rubbing it on the wart, and then burying it can cause the wart to disappear; so can tying a string around it. Liquid nitrogen, acid, or surgical removal are also treatments for warts. Sometimes these direct kinds of treatment work well, but other times new warts develop near the site of the original one. The surviving virus has merely moved. Speculation is that these medical techniques, while primarily physical, are not completely so. When they work well, it seems likely that a serendipitous effect of the treatment has been to bring the warts to the attention of the body's immune system. The alerted immune system then deals with the virus.

Hypnosis has been demonstrated in repeated studies to be extremely effective in getting the body to mobilize itself against the virus and so to cause the physical changes that destroy the wart. This following exercise should be repeated twice a day until your wart disappears. Although treatment with liquid nitrogen requires much less effort, hypnosis has the advantages of not hurting and of working even in places that are difficult to reach surgically, such as under your fingernails.

The Shriveling Wart

In this example the wart will be assumed to be on the back of your hand. (If it were in a place where it would be covered by clothing, imagine seeing it as if with X-ray vision. If it is in a place where you cannot see it, such as on your back, just imagine having a special perspective.)

As you're sitting here fully relaxed and settled in, you begin to think about the part of your body that has a wart: the back of your hand. As you begin to think about it, you begin to visualize the back of your hand, wart and all. In your mind's eye you see it more and more clearly. It might help to point your head in the appropriate direction, one that would allow you to be looking at that area if your eyes were open. As you stare at it, you pay particular attention to that wart which is growing there. You look at the entire back of your hand, but in particular you stare at that wart with your mind's eye. You let your mind's eye trace the outline of that part of your body, but keep returning to the wart, focusing on the wart, looking at the wart.

And as you do so, a visual image is going to develop before your very eyes. As you stare at the wart, it begins to shrivel, to shrink, to die. It does so slowly, but not too slowly. It's rather like time-lapse photography showing a flower opening. But instead of a beautiful flower opening, you are watching an ugly wart shrivel, dry up, and die. Just keep watching it. See how it shrivels and becomes a husk of dead skin. Watch how the edges shrivel up and begin to detach from the skin beneath. Watch how the blood supply is sealed off. See how the tiny capillaries are closing themselves off where they meet the wart. The wart has been deprived of its supply of blood and nutrients. It's drying up, shriveling, withering. It is turning into a bit of dead, dried skin.

And as you watch, that wart becomes so desiccated, so shriveled, so dry, that it falls right off. And when it does, underneath you see a round pink circle of fresh, clean, healthy skin.

That's right. No more wart. Just a bright pink spot of brand new skin. And you know that of course this skin will soon quickly blend in and look like the rest of your skin. But for the moment it's pleasant to look at its pink, bright newness, and to feel how much healthier, how much more attractive, how much more right this pink new circle is than that dry old wart which it's replaced.

━━━━●◆●◆●━━━━

Practice regularly and you should soon begin to see the changes which you have visualized occur in reality.

Psoriasis

Psoriasis is a skin disease characterized by red, itchy patches with white scales. The condition responds well to dry heat, so psoriasis sufferers often improve during the summer when they go to the beach and the sun's rays heat up their skin while drying it out as well. Tanning salons duplicate this effect as well. The combination of warmth and dryness can be produced quite nicely hypnotically even though the atmospheric conditions are not right. Also, hypnosis does not age the skin or cause skin cancer the way ultraviolet rays do.

Sunbathing

Imagining yourself sunbathing can in fact produce a significant measurable rise in skin temperature. This elevation occurs as the flow of blood to the skin increases, warming it. You should repeat the following exercise daily or, better yet, twice daily.

━━━━●◆●◆●━━━━

As you settle back so peacefully and comfortably, you feel yourself floating off, off to a peaceful, comfortable place. You find yourself floating off to a beach. It's a beautiful beach by the ocean. You look out at the waves as they come rolling in one after the next after the next. You watch their shapes change, you watch the foam form and be washed away. You watch the endless progression as wave follows wave follows wave all the way out to the horizon. You smell the fresh salt air. You can almost taste the salt upon your lips. You listen to the waves as they come rolling in with a soothing primal rhythm. Perhaps you can hear the cry of a sea bird. You look up at the cloudless blue sky, and most of all you feel the sun beating down upon your body. That's right. You feel the sun baking down, baking down.

The sun is so strong that you feel it warming your skin quite nicely. It's a very healthy warm feeling as the rays and the energy soak down upon your skin. You feel its healing, health-restoring waves washing down upon you. You feel your skin baking. You can almost feel the dried salt from the ocean upon your skin. The combination of the sun and the breeze keep your skin very dry, keeping your skin dry as it absorbs the healing energy of the sun's rays. Feel it baking down, baking down, warming, drying, healing, bringing healing to your skin, healing and peace, healing and dryness. And you just continue to do this. Continue to lie in the sun soaking up its healing rays for as long as you remain in this state.

And once you leave this hypnotic state, you're not going to leave this beach, this scene, totally behind. In fact, you will find that as you go about your daily activities, a part of your mind is going to hold on and remember this healing sunbath and the sensations it has produced. And you're not going to be surprised at all to find that your skin is daily becoming healthier, stronger, and healed.

The Dead Sea

Bathing in mineral-rich waters such as the Dead Sea or the Great Salt Lake leaves a salty crust on the skin if allowed to dry in the air. Many people with skin disorders such as psoriasis find that leaving this complicated mixture of salts on the skin promotes healing. Imagining such a coating on your skin can have the effect of telling your body to heal itself.

Picture yourself on the shores of the Dead Sea. You look out across the waters that are nearly saturated with all the salts and minerals that have washed down into the water for century after century. You think about how rivers have brought all these elements to this spot and how, as the water has evaporated, it's left behind this unique, rich, chemical soup. You think about the healing properties of this rich water. As you look at the shore and feel it beneath your feet, you feel the salts that have evaporated at the water's edge.

Now you go wading into the water. Deeper and deeper you go, feeling its wetness surrounding you. You feel the strangeness of the water. How buoyant you are as you go deeper and deeper. As you get deeper and deeper, you feel how easily you float on the surface, how much higher you float than in ordinary water. And you feel the salts soaking in, into your skin. Feel them going right in, into the very cells of your skin, bringing healing to your skin. You soak in these health-giving waters for as long as you wish, for as long as you wish. But then, when you are ready to leave the water, you paddle to the shore and sprawl out upon the beach. You don't shake the water off. You don't dry yourself on a towel. Instead you're going to lie there in the hot sun and feel its rays evaporate the water while leaving behind these curative salts. Some soak into your skin, others form a dry crust upon your skin. As you lie there, feeling the sun beating down upon you, feeling the salty crust form upon your skin, you feel how this mineral layer is drawing all the sickness out of your skin, leaching out any problem, pulling out anything wrong. Left behind is the healthy, recovering skin. You feel any red areas drying out, drying out and healing, and even after ending this exercise, as you go about the day, you're going to have a feeling, a pleasant feeling, of having this healing salt keeping your skin dry, healthy, and clear.

Herpes

Although herpes, including genital herpes, is caused by a virus, the outbreak of lesions is a more complicated phenomenon. People who have genital herpes do not have outbreaks all the time. Rather, stress seems to play a major role in the timing of outbreaks. This stress factor often leads to a circular dilemma as an outbreak or the fear of an outbreak can in itself be a major life stressor.

Because reduced stress is a key factor in reducing the occurrence of herpes, hypnosis, with its emphasis on relaxation, can be extremely effective in limiting the frequency and duration of outbreaks. You should spend twenty minutes twice a day hypnotized, practicing the "Pleasant Scene," even when there is no outbreak. The following extra idea might be included.

Healthy Skin at the Pleasant Scene

As you're lying there on the beach, peaceful relaxed and at ease, you're aware not only of the sound and sight of the ocean, of the smell of the fresh salt air, and the warmth of the sun upon your body, but also of how good your body feels. Your body is feeling healthy and intact. Your skin in particular is feeling intact and whole. You're aware of how good it feels not to have any lesions. You're aware of how healthy, soft, and supple your skin feels.

Imagining Healing

Practicing the "Pleasant Scene" can significantly reduce the likelihood of an outbreak. Once an outbreak has occurred, apply the following technique.

Settle back and get deeply, thoroughly, completely relaxed, and visualize in your mind's eye the part of your body where you're having the herpes outbreak. And as you do, you work first of all on visualizing it very, very clearly. You can see it through your clothing. If it is an internal lesion, you can visualize it perfectly even though you could not do so in reality. And as you look at this area and focus upon the lesion, the image in your mind's eye becomes clearer and clearer. You see the whole area and you see the lesion at the center of it.

And as you stare at that lesion, a strong, powerful sense of pity washes over you. You feel sorry for that poor area of the skin. You feel sorry that it has been hurt so. A sense of compassion floods over you.

And you want to help that poor, painful area. You want to bring soothing, healing peace and comfort. You want to take away the pain. You want to make it feel better. And as you do, you feel how your skin is responding. You feel a pleasant sensation of warmth as a strong, healthy blood supply suffuses the area around the lesion. It's bringing healing. It's bringing supplies necessary to repair the damage and antibodies to defeat the offending virus. And as you watch, you both see and feel how the wound begins to heal, how the skin closes up and repairs itself, how the blood supply brings in nutrients, oxygen, and the body's own defense mechanisms to heal and protect this area. You see the redness disappear, replaced by healthy new skin. You see how the remnants of the lesion are drying up, shriveling up, becoming a powder that crumbles and sloughs off. And you see how your skin has healed, and you feel very good and happy and pleased that this skin that you love is healthy again.

See and feel this set of events for twenty minutes. When you are ready to end this exercise, bring yourself back to the usual waking state.

High Blood Pressure

High blood pressure may be a response to stress in one's life. Sometimes it may have more to do with diet. Sometimes genetics are the most important factor. Medications or changes in diet are usually suggested to alleviate the problem.

Hypnosis, however, can in some cases be as effective as medication in controlling the disorder. A single application will not produce a permanent change. Instead, just as blood pressure medication needs to be taken daily to keep the problem from returning, so also does hypnosis have to be practiced daily to reduce pressure.

If you choose to use hypnosis, you should of course continue to be monitored by a physician, just as you would with any other treatment.

The basic hypnotic strategy for high blood pressure is to become physically very relaxed and then engage in some pleasant hypnotic task. You can use either the "Pleasant Scene" in Chapter 3, or the attention-focusing devices of "Floating on a Cloud" or "Keeping Your Mind Busy" used for insomnia in Chapter 6. It does not really matter which specific task you do provided the suggestions are simple, pleasant ones. The watchword is *calm*. You should practice whichever exercise you like twice a day, once in the morning and once in the late afternoon or early evening. Stay in the hypnotic state for twenty minutes each time. Following this regimen can lower your blood pressure not only during the time of hypnosis but in the hours between as well.

Colitis, Irritable Bowel, and Similar Disorders

There are a number of conditions varying somewhat in cause and severity that have as the main symptom frequent bowel movements or uncontrollable diarrhea. Since this symptom may be dangerous in itself or may mark some other underlying problem, it should be checked out by a physician. Once this has been done, hypnosis can be quite useful in controlling the symptom.

Calming Your Insides

As you settle into the hypnotic state, you feel yourself becoming more and more relaxed, more and more comfortable, more and more peaceful. And as you do, you focus your attention on one of your hands. It doesn't matter which one it is, right or left. In fact you may be surprised by which hand it is. Just focus your attention on your hand and the feelings in it, and as you do, you notice a sensation in the fingers of the hand. Perhaps it will be a tingling sensation, perhaps a sensation of microscopic movements in the fingers. Perhaps it will be a sensation that is hard to describe or impossible to name but one that you can feel. And when that feeling has become nice and strong, you allow your hand to move over and settle upon your lower abdomen.

And as it does, the sensation sinks in from your fingertips down through your abdomen into your bowels. As the sensation moves, it will probably change somewhat. The sensation feels different in your fingertips than it does deep inside your body. But you let this sensation sink in, settle in, and permeate your bowel.

And as it does, you become aware of a comfortable, vaguely pleasant, but most of all peaceful sensation there in your body. Your bowel is feeling soothed, comfortable, relaxed. Nothing is wrong. It's the way it should be. A soothing sensation is washing over it, telling it that everything is all right; everything is as it should be; nothing is wrong.

And as you feel this sensation of peace and of goodness, of soothed comfort, you realize that your body has gotten confused. Your body has been thinking that whenever there's something in your bowel, there is something wrong and it needs to be emptied. Your body has been acting as though anytime something gets into your bowel, it needs to be gotten out as quickly as possible. But in fact, that's not so. Your bowel is meant to be a place where your body's waste products can be gathered up and held until a convenient time. In a way, your bowel is like a wastebasket. Every time you have a piece of scrap paper, you don't want to have to run down to the local garbage dump to get rid of it. Instead, you toss it in the wastebasket and let it sit there. At an appropriate time, when the wastebasket has gathered a number of pieces of scrap paper, the trash is taken out. Just as you don't let the wastebasket go on being filled to overflowing and beyond, so you don't fail to empty your bowel at a reasonable interval. However, it doesn't need to be emptied immediately whenever anything gets into it.

There's nothing poisonous, nothing wrong; there's no need to evacuate your body too quickly. There's a pace for everything, a proper timing that you can follow. In fact there's an important job to be done by your bowel. When waste reaches your bowel, it arrives as a liquid. That's because this is the main place where your body absorbs water. When the waste reaches your bowel, it needs to be allowed to sit there for a while. Your body needs that water. Your body needs to get the opportunity to absorb that liquid to get its needed water. When the waste enters your bowel, it needs time to be processed. Only then is it ready to be eliminated.

But you have been emptying your bowels so quickly for so long that your body has gotten confused. You have gotten confused. You have learned that the sensation of something entering your bowel is a signal to empty it. But it's not. You need to learn that it is simply a sign that the next stage of digestion, the absorption of water and the collection of waste material, has begun.

And your body needs to learn, you need to learn, that these feelings that are going on are not indicating that something is wrong. Instead they simply indicate that this part of your body is doing its job. And you leave your hand on your abdomen to send the reassuring message that goes with the sensation. As the sensation reaches your bowel, you experience a feeling of calm, of peace, and of curiosity. You're going to get to see just what your body is supposed to be doing. You begin to recognize that these sensations are not urgent demands that you get to a bathroom to get something bad out of you. Instead you recognize that your body is simply proceeding as it is supposed to do. Your body is merely absorbing liquids and gathering waste.

It's kind of a strange new sensation because you had been getting it out so fast. But there's nothing wrong. It's all OK. Your body is doing what it's designed to do, doing what it's made to do. It's operating correctly. It's doing the right things. Just because it feels unusual doesn't mean that it is wrong. Just because it's not what you usually have felt doesn't mean that it isn't the right way to feel. In fact, you feel your body becoming healthier, stronger, gaining strength, not being weakened and sapped. You feel your body growing accustomed to this new way, that as you focus on the sensation that has reached your bowels from your fingertips, you feel what a sensation of health it is, and it quickly becomes a good sensation, a pleasant sensation, a healthy sensation.

And you realize that you do not have to be a slave of your bowels. Instead you allow them to do their job, to gather waste, and when you decide it's a convenient time, and when you feel that you have gathered a sufficient amount of waste to make it worthwhile, when you have absorbed enough water, then and only then do you choose to go to the bathroom, do you choose to empty your bowels.

When you are ready to end this exercise, do so, keeping its main ideas in the back of your mind.

14

Cancer

Although hypnosis can cure a number of physical ailments, such as warts and psoriasis, it is not, by itself, an effective treatment for cancer. The destructive powers of cancer are too powerful to be treated solely by any psychological technique. However, hypnosis is useful in a number of ways as a part of an overall treatment scheme. Anxiety accompanying cancer can be controlled (Chapter 4), as can the pain of a tumor or surgery (Chapter 15). Allowing use of the imagination as a powerful ally rather than a saboteur, hypnosis can provide a confident and hopeful sense that everything possible is being done.

Chemotherapy

One dreaded aspect of cancer is its treatment. Hypnosis can be extremely effective in dealing with the unpleasant side effects of chemotherapy.

———•◆•◆•◆•———

As you arrive at the hospital for your chemotherapy, you settle yourself down and enter a state of hypnosis. In that state you give yourself the following set of suggestions. You know that you have discussed this form of treatment with your doctor and thought about it already. You made the decision to do this, and it was a good decision. You don't need to think about it right now. You've decided to do this, and there is no reason to question that decision. Any thoughts or questions about it you can dismiss as not worth thinking about. You have a job to do: to heal your body. Right now your part of the job simply consists of bringing your body to these people whom you have chosen to do some work on it.

Your body needs a certain kind of medicine, a very powerful sort of medicine that the hospital workers are delivering to your body. This medicine is so powerful that it can kill the cancer cells. You really like this idea. You like the idea of this medicine that kills the cancer cells.

Those cancer cells have been strong, so the medicine needs to be strong also. But you don't mind. You know, for example, if terrorists had burst into your home and held you and your family hostage at gunpoint how you would hate them. That's how you feel about this cancer. You hate it. And you know that if the police were to come in and rescue you from these bad people, you would not greet them at the door saying, "Be sure to wipe your feet. I don't want any mud tracked in the house." You wouldn't say, "Please be careful not to knock over a chair as you are subduing that thug" any more than you would say, "Be careful not to bruise his poor wrist when you are putting his hand in handcuffs." You want the police to rescue you, and that's far more important than any trivial incidental damage.

Same thing with the medicine. This is powerful stuff, so powerful it can kill cancer. Your doctors have been very careful. They're giving you enough to kill the cancer, but it's not going to kill you. It might do the equivalent of tracking a little mud on the carpet, but you know that that doesn't matter. To give you the medicine, they have to put a needle in you, breaking your skin. You don't mind. This is what you need to do to get the medicine that can get your enemy, cancer. Perhaps you're getting the kind of medicine that will make you lose your hair. That's all right. That's like getting a chair knocked over. You don't mind losing your hair in order to get the cancer killed. Your hair will grow back, but the cancer won't. These side effects don't really matter. You just keep thinking about how the police are rescuing you from those murderous terrorists. You're glad that they are doing it. You don't mind a little incidental damage. You'll heal.

In fact, that's the point of all of this. You're giving yourself years of future health. If you lose your hair, for example, it doesn't really matter that much because you're giving yourself the possibility of years of life to grow the hairs back. If the chemotherapy is unpleasant, that's still not so bad. You're realizing that you're trading a few days or weeks or months of discomfort for years and years of happy and productive life. That's right. No matter how it feels in the short run, it doesn't matter. You're not in this for the short run. You're not just thinking about today. You're in it for the rest of your life. You're earning yourself years and years of the future.

Sometimes chemotherapy can play tricks on a body. For example, sometimes the medicine makes a part of the body feel warm or cold. Sometimes it makes it seem as though there is a taste in your mouth. Sometimes it gives a person an upset stomach or nausea. But there are things that you can do to help yourself when the medicine tricks your body this way.

If you were to eat something that had spoiled, your body would protect itself by getting it out of your body as fast as possible. The fastest way out of your body is by vomiting. Throwing up is a defense that your body has developed to get rid of poisons. When there is something bad in your stomach, it's a very useful defense. As you know, though, the medicines that are doing such a good job of killing the cancer sometimes have as a side effect the fact that they trick your body. Now, this tricking your body is not important in making the medicine work. If your body is not tricked, if you do not have nausea, the medicine will still work just as effectively. That's right. The medicine does not need that side effect to show that it's working.

Sometimes your stomach might be tricked into thinking that there was something bad in it. But you know better. You know you haven't eaten anything bad; you know there's nothing in your stomach that shouldn't be there. You know that there's nothing wrong, nothing that needs to be gotten out of you. Everything is as it should be. That means that you can relax. It's OK. Everything that's in your stomach belongs there. Your body was just being tricked. Your body was just being fooled. But since you know about this trick, you can do something about it. You can take control. You can take charge.

You're going to focus attention on your fingertips. That's right. Focus your attention on your fingertips, and as you do, you become aware of a sensation. Perhaps it will be a tingling sensation, perhaps a sensation of mild warmth or coolness. Perhaps it will be a sensation that is hard to describe in words, but that's all right. When you have that sensation, bring your hand and your fingertips over to your abdomen and begin to transfer the sensation inward. Transfer the sensation down into your stomach. Then gently bring your hand up your body and transfer the sensation through your esophagus into your throat. As it sinks in, it will probably change. The sensation will not feel the same inside your body as it did when it was in your fingertips. That's fine. And with this feeling comes a message, a message of peace, of calm, of tranquillity. As you feel the sensation, there is a feeling of calm, of peace, of tranquillity that enters your stomach, your esophagus, your throat. It's as though the entire lining is being coated by a soothing, comforting protective layer. It soothes and coats and protects. It brings peace. It brings comfort. It makes your stomach realize that all is OK.

Just as a parent can often calm and comfort a frightened child who has just had a nightmare by letting the child know that everything is all right, that there wasn't really a monster, so you, with your sensation, can let your stomach know that it's all right, that there really isn't anything wrong. You may well find that your stomach feels so peaceful, so comfortable and at ease, that it gives you no more trouble. If it should work incompletely and your stomach is fooled anyway, you'll say to yourself, "Oh, my stomach has been fooled by the medicine. Since it wants to empty itself, I'll just let it pour itself out." You won't have unpleasant vomiting. Instead it will be as though you were emptying a pitcher. You'll say to yourself, "OK, if my stomach really thinks it needs to do that, it will happen gently, peacefully, and easily."

If you can overcome this side effect and any others, that would be great. You know how one side effect can be that you get a funny taste in your mouth. Perhaps that doesn't seem like anything bad but like something curious. You may have a feeling of bemusement saying, "Isn't that funny," to yourself. But you may wish to try to do something different.

Imagine that you have just cut a lemon in half. And as you do, you begin to smell the fresh lemon scent. That's right. Imagine bringing it up and rubbing a little of the oil off the skin and onto your upper lip. Just smell that fresh lemon smell. And when you have smelled it, imagine taking a lick of the freshly cut surface of the lemon. It tastes so fresh, so clean, so healthy. It's so tart it almost puckers your lips. It tastes clean, fresh, and healthy.

If any other tricks should happen in some part of your body, you'll be able to handle them, too. How you do it depends on what the feeling is. For example, if a part of you should feel cold, you'll imagine yourself lying in the sun feeling its rays warming you. Or perhaps you'll imagine a nice hot water bottle on that area. If you should feel too warm, you can imagine a nice cooling, soothing breeze. You might imagine rubbing an ice cube or an icy glass across your skin. Whatever it is that bothers you, you just think about what would make it feel better and imagine that.

Now you know how to deal with any of the side effects which might interfere with your ability to settle back while you're having your medicine. Now you have these tools if you need them.

But when you don't need to do any of these things, you're going to think about the fact that while you're here, having your chemotherapy, what you've really done is to bring your body to the hospital so the doctors and nurses and technicians can work to heal and fix it. You don't really need to be here. If you could have stayed home and just mailed your body in without you, that would have been just fine. The doctors and nurses and technicians know their job. They know what they're doing. In fact, *you* don't know what they are supposed to be doing. For this part of it, all you can do is get in the way. There's no help that you can offer that will be helpful. There's nothing useful for you to do.

What you really need to do is to go off to your peaceful place. That's right. You know how to do it. Go off to your peaceful scene. You might want to go to the same one each time, or you might want to go to different places. You might want to be at home, resting comfortably in your own bed. You might want to go for a walk in the park, looking at the flowers, smelling the fresh air, feeling the sun shining upon you, listening to the birds chirping in the trees, seeing the beautiful blue of the sky and the green of the grass. You might want to go into the future and there see yourself healthy and strong, your disease a thing of the past.

Or you might want to go somewhere else. You might want to go inside your body, inside your body at a microscopic level. You might want to go along through your bloodstream with the medicine as it goes out hunting and killing the cancer cells that are hiding inside you. You hate those cancer cells, and you're channeling your anger into attacking them. The medicine is joined by your body's own natural immune system in hunting out, finding, and destroying those cancer cells, every last one of them. Feel yourself coursing through your body, leading the charge as you track down and destroy those cells.

Or you may wish to settle back and feel the healing taking place. You may do it by just feeling the healing coursing through your veins as your body fixes itself. You may feel as though healing rays are pouring down upon you like light, pouring down upon you like a blessing on your body, making it better, bringing healing, healing to body and mind. You know that you're doing the right things. You know that you are doing what you can to heal yourself, and as you do, you feel this healing cascading down, streaming down, down and through you to your innermost fiber.

Now you've learned a number of things that you can do to help yourself and to take care of yourself during chemotherapy. Each time you do chemotherapy, you might find yourself using some of these things more than others. Sometimes you might want to work with a side effect; sometimes you might not need to. Sometimes you might focus more on going off to a peaceful place; sometimes you might instead focus on coursing through your veins and arteries killing the cancer cells. Whatever you need at that specific time is OK.

At other times in your treatment, when you're not actively having chemotherapy, you will be able to use different techniques that you have learned. For example, while recovering from chemotherapy you might find it helpful to use hypnosis to give yourself sleep or rest. If you feel nausea, you might want to use the exercise for taking care of that. You might wish to go off to your nice scene. You might need to use the exercise for pain. You might want to bring some of the images of healing or fighting to your general use of hypnosis. That will be fine. You'll be able to stay in this state as long as is necessary. If one of the workers needs to ask you a question, you'll be able to answer appropriately and then go right back into this state if you wish. When you're ready, you'll be able to bring yourself out to your usual state of consciousness. The combined feeling of peace, because you are bringing yourself healing, coupled with the sense of aggression as you actively fight the cancer, will continue to stay with you and help you.

15

Pain

The experience of pain is a strange and complicated phenomenon. Sometimes an injury is very painful until you see that the damage is not great, at which point the pain seems almost to evaporate. Sometimes you might not be aware of anything hurting until you see that you have been injured. Once you notice the injury, you can't stop thinking about how much it hurts. Something might be very painful if another person did it to you, but not at all bad if you did it to yourself.

At its most basic level, pain is a signal to the brain that something is hurting the body. If you have carelessly dangled your hand in the fireplace, pain from the fire serves a very useful function. It tells you that your hand is in the fireplace, and that if you do not move it, it will burn off. The function of pain as a warning, as a danger signal, is a very important one.

A basketball player, for instance, once had an injury to his foot that caused so much pain whenever he ran on it that he was unable to play. As soon as it was determined that his injury, though extremely painful, would not be worsened by running on it, he was given a shot of Novocain and rejoined the action. Unfortunately, the first time he played on it, he broke a bone in the foot. Because the Novocain indiscriminately blocked all pain, he didn't realize something was wrong. He played the basketball game on a broken bone with the predictable severe damage as a result.

Similarly, though less drastically, when you go to the dentist and are given the shot of Novocain that allows for a thankfully painless procedure, you may sometimes later find that you have unknowingly bitten your cheek or tongue hard enough to make quite a gouge. Although not critical, an injury resulted from the absence of the normally felt pain.

Pain not only signals danger. It can as well be a sign to your mind that something desirable is happening, though your body may not understand. A stabbing sensation signals the entrance of a foreign object into your body, but it need not be a stiletto. The stabbing might indicate, for instance, that you are donating blood for another person, are giving a sample for a necessary blood test, or are having an injection to make you healthy. The soreness that frequently accompanies dental work is a sign that something helpful is being done even though our bodies may be in some ways too primitive to recognize this form of care.

There are times, however, when pain serves no good purpose. Bone cancer, for example, can be excruciating. Although the initial pain may be helpful in alerting a person to the presence of a problem and may lead to early diagnosis and treatment, once appropriate treatment has begun continued pain is simply needless. When the cancer patient is awakened in the middle of the night in agony or is unable to sit comfortably enough to watch television or read a book, the pain is not delivering any useful message. It is as though the nerves are saying, "By the way, you've got bone cancer."

"I know," you reply.

"Right," says the pain. "But you have bone cancer."

"This is no news," you answer.

"By the way," says the pain, "all's not well in your body. There's something wrong with your bones." After hearing this announcement twenty-four hours a day, for months on end, it gets a little repetitious and wearing. People with treated burns, arthritis, or amputations often similarly suffer from such needless, unrelenting messages.

A huge amount about the experience of pain has been learned relatively recently, and such knowledge is useful in controlling unnecessary discomfort. Pain is produced in a two-part manner, one being that the body sends a sensation to the brain, and the other being that the brain interprets and reacts to it. Accordingly, one way of dealing with pain is to intercept it before it gets to the brain. Nerve blocks such as Novocain work this way. The drug deadens a section of the nervous pathway and blocks sensations from continuing up to the brain. However, chemicals are not the only way of blocking sensations. As discussed in the chapter on memory, not all sensations experienced by your body necessarily make it to your brain. At various points along your nervous system, what might be thought of as mini-decision-making centers, called *gates*, choose what to pass along and what to block. What does not get through these filter stations never makes it to the brain. There are a number of these gates where sensations are either stopped or allowed through. Learning to control these gates and not let painful stimuli through is the basis of one set of hypnotic strategies.

The other part of the experience of pain takes place in the brain. When a sensation from the nervous system does reach the brain, it goes to a sensory area where it is recorded in a rather factual manner. The sensation may, however, also be sent to an emotional center of the brain, where the added element of fear transforms it from feeling into pain. For an easy example, think of how different it feels to pull out a splinter yourself rather than having someone else do it. The difference is even more extreme when you think that this someone else is intentionally trying to hurt you. In both cases the physical sensation may start out the same, but fear can transform it into pain.

Removing the emotional element attached to a sensation is the basis of the second kind of pain control strategy. Many painkillers—including the most powerful one, morphine—work on this principle. Typically, a patient on morphine will report an awareness of the sensation that causes pain, but somehow it doesn't really seem to matter very much. Patients become distant and detached from their own bodies and so are not bothered or are not frightened by bodily sensations.

A number of hypnotic strategies can produce a similar sort of effect. This similarity has led to much speculation that one way hypnosis controls pain is by inducing the brain to release large amounts of endorphins, the naturally occurring, morphine-like chemicals in the brain. Although there are strong data to support this notion, they are inconclusive.

Pain control is one of the oldest, and possibly most important, uses of hypnosis. It is thought that humankind's capacity for hypnosis evolved because it was so valuable as a survival mechanism. An injured cave dweller, for instance, who could ignore the pain of an injury until back at a place of safety would be more likely to survive than one who was so overcome with pain as to be disabled in the wild.

Much of scientists' early fascination with hypnosis had to do with learning to master and to use intentionally what they first saw as a spontaneously occurring ability to control pain. Just before the discovery of ether in the 1840s, great surgical strides were made by using hypnosis for pain management. Although not everyone was a suitable candidate, patients able to anesthetize themselves with hypnosis could let a surgeon operate in a way that allowed greater neatness and skill. Previously, the unbearable pain experienced during an operation marked the main parameter within which surgeons worked. The prime directive was to do surgery fast. With hypnotic anesthesia, doctors could begin to take more time and more care. You need only think of what kind of job a carpenter would do if required to make a chair in under five minutes to realize what effect pain control could have on the quality of operations performed.

Soon after the advent of hypnotic anesthesia, ether was discovered, and the chemical control of pain that has flowered in the modern science of anesthesiology revolutionized surgery. Chemical control works for almost everyone. Additionally, it is more predictable and requires less patient participation and patient responsibility than hypnosis. Chemical management has become the anesthesia of choice.

Hypnosis, however, still has a variety of uses in pain control. Some people who need major surgery are allergic to conventional anesthesia. If they are fortunate, they are among the group that is capable of using hypnosis for a suitable degree of pain control. Some people would simply rather not use avoidable chemical anesthesia. For them, the discomfort of dental work or getting stitches can be more adequately controlled with hypnosis. It is similarly useful to manage the discomfort of labor in childbirth.

Also possible to control with hypnosis are all kinds of chronic and recurrent pains. Some of these pains will eventually go away, but in the meantime they can last for months. Some may never improve. Others will come and go from time to time. Often these kinds of pain—the "phantom limb" pain from an amputation, the ache of arthritis, or the discomfort of a bad back, for instance—fall into a "difficult-to-treat" category. Relatively minor pain medications, such as acetaminophen or aspirin, aren't really strong enough to do the job. The pain medications like codeine, which are strong enough to effect the pain, are so powerful that they may leave the sufferer unable to function. In these sorts of situations, the ability to control pain without knocking oneself out is very useful.

People interested in chemical-free anesthesia often ask if hypnosis is related to acupuncture. Some authorities belief so, others don't. The best answer at this point seems to be "Who knows?" The two techniques developed in very different cultures, are based on very different sets of assumptions, and are not readily understandable within the other's frame of reference. What is common to both is that each is the subject of many groundless, though popular, notions.

It is an unfortunately common misconception that hypnosis works only with pain that is "all in your head." Many people, including a number of physicians, make the mistake of thinking that just because a technique takes place in your mind, it can change only the mental aspect of it. Not only does hypnosis work on genuine physically caused pain, but in most cases that's the only kind that it does affect. A man, for instance, whose disability-income check keeps coming in and allows him to avoid going back to a job he hates for as long as he can experience pain has a powerful, though not necessarily conscious, motivation to stay hurt. If he stops hurting, he has to go back to work. Hypnosis is useless in such a case, for while the hypnotist is saying, "We are going to control the pain," the person will be saying, at some level, "Oh no, we're not. I need this pain." There is no doubt who will win an argument of this sort.

Although a pain that's "all in the head" cannot be treated with hypnosis, a physically based pain can be. Tension speeds up nerve conduction and so increases pain. Relaxation, integral to hypnosis, slows down the speed with which nerves deliver messages of discomfort, lessening the intensity of the pain.

Hypnotic pain control has the added benefit of being selective, unlike other nerve blocks. The basketball player with the broken foot or the dental patient with the bitten cheek, while protected from the initial pain, couldn't recognize additional damage being done. Anyone using hypnosis to control pain would stay alert to other possible injuries.

An absolute precondition to using hypnosis for pain control is understanding the cause of the pain and knowing that it is safe to control it. In many cases, it's important to seek professional help to find out the nature of an injury. You need to know whether your pain is a warning of danger or if it's just a reminder that an injury has taken place. If you do not believe that it is safe to ignore a pain, there is no way that hypnosis will be effective. Once you know that it is safe to do so, you can feel free to use hypnosis for the residual symptom of pain.

Any of the following techniques, done while deeply hypnotized, can be very useful for acute, transient pains. These include, for example, the discomforts of a dental procedure or of a fall. In the case of chronic pain, a slightly different approach is needed. The goal is to be able to live life without awareness of pain, not to sit around in a trance. That goal means you need to be able to get the benefit of an hypnotic exercise without being deeply hypnotized.

If you have chronic pain, start by doing the short-term exercises as described, building up your confidence in your ability to control pain by using them. Once you feel confident, the techniques you have learned can begin to take on a life of their own.

When you began to read, for instance, you sounded out words, transforming letters on the page into thoughts in your mind. You still do that, but you don't have to think about it anymore. Just so, as you increase your capacity for these exercises, you will be able to allow one part of your mind to continue the suggestions even when you are not hypnotized. So while you're going about your daily business, a part of you might, for example, be constantly reminding yourself to stay relaxed. Or as you are doing different tasks, a part of you, knowing that it is safe to ignore the information from the pain, might be reminding you to focus very intently on what you are doing. Thus focused, you distract yourself from the pain as effectively as in the exercise "Concentration." Or once you have learned to establish a "filter" in your neck, it can continue to work even though you're not consciously attending to it.

Remember that the techniques you are about to learn are not placebos but in fact are very powerful methods of controlling pain.

Learning a Safe Pain

One problem that develops in any attempt to work with pain is a deep-seated sense that it cannot be changed. When you have been in pain, you know that you would like to be rid of it. You know that you haven't been holding onto it for some complicated reason. You are therefore likely to feel that if you could have done something about it, you would have done so already. The very fact that it hasn't changed makes you believe it cannot change.

This helplessness has also set up a fear of the pain. A person becomes afraid to experiment with the pain for fear of making it worse. It is as though it is bad enough already, and you are afraid of making it worse.

In order to combat this fear, you are going to be introduced to a new pain outside hypnosis. This new pain is one that you can inflict upon yourself whether hypnotized or not. When done, it will produce an intense pain. It is also a pain that will go away almost instantly when you stop it. Because you can choose to start and stop this pain at will, it is not a frightening pain. Because it is new, there is no belief that it can't be changed.

Look at your hands. Pay particular attention to one hand and look at the webbing between your thumb and index finger. With your other hand pinch that webbing near the edge very hard. Experiment with it. If it doesn't hurt a lot, you're not pinching it in the right spot or hard enough. It should be a sharp and intense pain. However, because it's just in a tiny spot, it should be contained and not excruciating. As soon as you feel that sharp pain, stop pinching and flex your hand. The pain should completely cease within seconds of letting go. Try it again. Learn to feel comfortable in your ability both to initiate and to stop this pain.

Now you have a new pain that has none of the psychological baggage of your old, chronic pain. You can stop it at any time. You can choose to let it happen or to let it not happen. You don't have to be afraid of it. You haven't spent a lot of time helplessly trying to change it.

These next exercises are going to be done, first of all, learning to control that pain. You're going to go into hypnosis and in hypnosis pinch to produce that pain. You are then going to learn techniques that you can use while pinching to reduce that pain. Once you know how to control that pain, you can apply the lessons you've learned to any other pain that might bother you.

The final task before you begin the hypnotic exercises is learning to objectify the level of pain. Pain hurts. Severe pain hurts a lot. One thing that happens when people try to control pain is that if they just ask themselves, "Does it still hurt?" the answer is likely to be "Yes." As a result real improvement in the amount of pain can go unappreciated.

Imagine a scale that runs from zero to 10. Zero represents the complete absence of pain, and 10 represents the most unbearable degree of pain imaginable. Go back and pinch the webbing of your hand once again. See how much it hurts. Decide where on the scale you would locate this pain. Assign a number to it. You now know that pinching that nerve bundle produces a pain of exactly that intensity when done in the usual state. As you practice learning to reduce that pain by various exercises, you will assign a number to the pain at different moments. That will allow you to see how much change is brought about by each method (e.g., from a 6 to a 2) even if the pain is not completely eliminated. When you have learned how to do these exercises, you will similarly assign a number to your chronic pain as it changes.

Also, on a day-to-day basis you can chart the extent of your pain. In fact, it is usually a good idea to keep a chart and to mark down the number that you would assign to your pain for that day. This should be the average amount of pain for that day, not the best or worst moment. This allows you to see how different strategies can be helpful to you.

Relaxation

When your muscles are tense, sensations, including pain, are carried to the brain much more swiftly and intensely than if you were relaxed. If, for example, you make a fist and tense your arm, painful sensations in your hand will feel much worse than they would if your arm were relaxed. However, your body generally perceives pain as an indication of threat. The natural response to threat is to prepare to fight or flee, that is, to increase muscle tension. The fact of pain, then, naturally provokes your body to a status that makes the pain hurt even more. In this exercise you're going to learn to relax as a way of reducing pain. Before you do, make sure you remember how you rated the pain from squeezing the nerves in your hand.

As you settle down, deeply and comfortably hypnotized, you focus in particular on relaxation. You feel yourself very relaxed. You focus on draining every bit of tension from your body. With each breath you exhale, you become more and more relaxed. There's no tension in your body, none at all. You feel your muscles, limp and relaxed. You feel your whole body sinking down into the chair, letting it hold and support you, peacefully settled in, comfortable and relaxed.

And when you feel yourself so totally, so completely, so deeply relaxed, while not disturbing the relaxation you allow your hands to come together lazily. The one bit of effort in your entire body is your thumb and finger pressing together on the nerves in the other hand. But while that thumb and finger pinch, the rest of your body stays so relaxed, so peaceful, calm, and at ease. You are totally relaxed. And now, take a second to evaluate the sensation from your hand. Assign a number to it, corresponding to how it feels: zero for no pain at all; 10 for the worst pain imaginable.

Now let go of your hand, move the hand about to make it comfortable, and as you're so relaxed, compare the score you just had with the original score. Perhaps your score went down to zero. That would be great. Perhaps your score went down only a little. At least you're moving it down. Perhaps your score went up. That's OK, too. At least you're changing it, and what you can make worse, you can make better. But almost certainly, if you did truly relax yourself, your score did lower. And so you see two things. First, relaxing your muscles reduces the sensation of pain. You also saw that being relaxed reduced your level of fear and perhaps made it just a sensation.

Above that, you learned something even more important: You can use your mind to effect changes in the way your body feels.

When you are ready, end this relaxed state of hypnosis.

Concentration

As with any of your senses, focusing your attention magnifies your awareness of the sensation. If, for example, some background noise occurred, you might hardly notice it or not notice it at all. Maybe you begin to listen to it, however, and it seems to become louder and louder. It's not that the volume of sound has actually changed, but that your focusing on it has made it a greater part of your awareness.

Pain naturally and instinctively commands a great deal of attention. Its basic function is to warn you of threats. Because a warning isn't of any use unless it's heeded, pain, unless you do something to change it, will command a great deal of attention, and when you are paying attention to it, pain, like background noise, will expand and seem to take up your entire consciousness.

————•◆•◆•————

As you settle in, peaceful and relaxed, you get your hands in position, ready to begin the pinch. You remind yourself that this pinch is not dangerous and that you will do yourself no damage by doing it. That allows you to realize that this is a warning which can be safely ignored.

Picture in your mind's eye a huge open expanse of smooth, flat space. And as you do, build in your mind's eye or create a huge solid, massive letter *A*. That's right. You're visualizing a large letter *A*, one that is solid and has substance. And when you have created in your mind's eye that very real *A*, it is joined by a letter *B*. That's right. You now have a huge *A* and *B*. And as you're doing this, you begin to pinch, but focus all your attention on the letter *C*. That's right. You have an *A* and a *B* and a *C* sitting there like monoliths. It's as though Stonehenge were created by alphabetarians. Now the *D*. Make it just as real and solid as the proceeding letters. And now the *E*.

If you were using this exercise to work with chronic pain, you would go all through the alphabet, first capitals and then lowercase letters. You could follow the alphabet with digits or a changed type face, forming your letters in italics or even in the Greek or Hebrew or Cyrillic alphabet. But right now you're just doing an exercise, so while continuing to concentrate, let one small corner of your mind rate the sensation in your hand on the scale. You may be surprised at how much it was lowered. You see that concentration works in two ways. First of all, it reduces the amount of attention being given to the sensation, making it less intense. Second, it again tells you that there's nothing to fear, that you are safe, which takes the hurt out of the sensation.

When you are ready to end this exercise, bring yourself back to the usual waking state.

Leaving Your Body Behind

Many powerful narcotics ease the sensation of pain not by blocking the sensation from getting to the brain, but by producing a sort of "who cares" mentality. This exercise will teach you how to mimic that effect without a prescription.

————————◆•◆•◆————————

As you settle in, so peaceful, comfortable, relaxed, and at ease, you are going to allow yourself to have a curious sort of experience. You are going to allow yourself to leave your body behind. Just imagine yourself seeing your body sitting there or lying there, comfortably hypnotized, and imagine seeing a sort of translucent image of yourself stepping out from your body. It looks kind of like a ghost in a movie. You see yourself stepping away from your own body, feeling safe and secure. You're not a ghost, but you are allowing your spirit, your mind, your psyche to become somewhat detached and removed from your body. You know that it's there. You know what's going on in it. It doesn't matter very much to you, however. Even though you're aware of your body, your awareness is rather distant, detached, and removed. Where you are, it's comfortable and safe. It's peaceful. It's relaxed.

Any sensations come to you only very slowly. In a way, it's as though you've moved about several times and it takes a while for your mail to catch up with you. You get news of your body. You get information about it, but only rather slowly and sort of after the fact.

You might wish to stay in the room with your body, feeling secure and comfortable knowing that your body is safe and protected. Or you may decide to leave your body behind, figuring that there are other people who are taking perfectly good care of your body, and there is no sense in your being there. Besides, if anything happens that's worth paying attention to, you'll find out about it quickly enough. In case of an emergency, in case of information you needed to know, you would find out about it instantly. But right now there's nothing you need to know. You can allow yourself to go off. Perhaps you'll go off to your peaceful scene. Or perhaps you'd like to take advantage of your bodiless state to float as an ethereal creature through a beautiful world of the spirit. As you're doing this, allow your hands to come together and pinch. You know that this is not dangerous, so you don't need to come rushing back to your body. Instead, simply allow your body to become aware of the sensation, and assign it a number. You may find it a little difficult to care enough to assign a number accurately, but that's all right. Just assign the one that seems most accurate.

Now, if you were dealing with your chronic pain, you would continue in this state of detachment. For this exercise, you bring your attention back, reuniting body and spirit, and see what number you assigned while detached. You may well find that this ability to detach produced a lack of fear, a degree of relaxation, and a lack of interest that resulted in a greatly reduced sensation of pain.

Bucket of Ice Water

Frequently the role of hypnosis is to get a message through to your body as to just what it is you would like to do. In this case, you direct it to numb an area. If you are more comfortable imagining getting a shot of Novocain rather than using a bucket of cold water, you can make the appropriate switch.

In hypnosis, imagine that sitting before you is a bucket of ice water, a bucket of ice water so cold that the water has almost turned to slush. The whole thing is almost ready to turn into a block of ice. It's so cold, so freezing cold, but you are going to plunge your hand into it. That's right. Plunge your hand up to above the wrist, deep into this bucket of freezing-cold ice water.

At first, the shock of the cold water is enough to take your breath away. But you keep it there, keep your hand in that ice water. It doesn't take long for your hand to change from feeling the painful cold of that ice water to becoming totally numb and for your fingers to lose sensation. They at first feel like sausages instead of fingers, but as they continue in that water they lose all feeling. Your hand is cold and frozen, cold and frozen. It is totally numb. It feels like a block of ice. That is, it has no feeling at all. Now reach over with your other hand and pinch that frozen block of ice. See if pinching can produce any sensation at all. Rate the sensation from zero to 10. Now relax the pinching and let warmth and life come back through that frozen hand. That's right. Thaw it out, and let it become comfortable and warm as it was before.

Changing the Number

Up to now, you have learned to assign a number to pain. In this exercise you learn to assign a degree of pain to a number. Because of the difficulty people have believing they can change pain for the better, we will begin by making it worse. For ease of presentation, it is assumed that pinching has produced a pain of 5 in the past.

As you settle into a state of deep hypnosis, you pinch the webbing and feel a pain. You rate it a 5.

Now, visualize in your mind's eye a large number 5. It may be rather like the letters of the alphabet you recently formed, or it may be different. It may look like a number on a scoreboard or perhaps like a neon sign. However you see it, it is the focus of your awareness. It not only rates the pain, but it is the pain.

The pain is the 5 and the 5 is the pain.

But now we are going to do something to change it.

In a minute you are going to change the 5 into a 6. Perhaps the neon tube will flex; perhaps the scoreboard lights will change. But however you can imagine it done, change the 5 to a 6 now. And as you do, you feel the pain intensify to a level of 6. The number is the pain and the pain is the number. The number is 6 and the pain is 6.

Now change it back to a 5, and as the number changes, so does the pain. The number is the pain, the pain is the number. Both are 5.

You see how you were able to change the pain for worse and for better. Now we are going to continue. Watch the 5 as it transforms itself into a 4, and as it changes, so does the pain. The pain and number are both now 4.

Continue to learn how to make lower and lower numbers and pain.

Getting Close to the Pain

The instinctive response to pain is flight. One naturally tries to distance oneself from pain. Paradoxically, the opposite response can be extremely effective. Some find this the best treatment for chronic pain.

As you settle into hypnosis, you think of how you have always tried to avoid pain by fleeing from it. That is one way, but there is another.

When a boxer is in trouble, if he backs up he gives his opponent the chance to really wind up and punch. Instead, he goes into a clinch. He wraps his arms around his opponent and draws him so close that the blows cannot hurt. The opponent can touch him but not really punch him.

As you pinch the webbing of your hand, do not try to escape. Instead, focus all of your attention on that spot. Get totally close to it. Move right into it. As you do, you get right down to the nerve level. It begins to lose meaning. You are so close that it has turned into a pure sensation. There is no meaning and no context, just a sensation.

It is rather like saying a word over and over again until it loses meaning and becomes just a sound. Say a word repeatedly until it no longer has a meaning. So it is with this sensation.

Or think of a person looking so closely at a single tree that she cannot see the forest. She is so close to the tree that it fills her field of vision and she sees nothing beyond it.

So you get so close to this sensation that it loses all of its hurt and pain, and only a dry husk remains.

The Filter

This final exercise, perhaps the most effective for daily use, works by teaching your central nervous system to shut a pain gate, so pain is blocked or altered as it approaches your brain.

As you settle into hypnosis, lift up your hand, either one, whichever you prefer. Focus on that hand and the feelings in it. As you do, you become aware of a sensation in it. Perhaps it will feel like a mild, pleasant tingle, perhaps a sensation of warmth, perhaps something hard to categorize. Let the sensation become strong and clear in your fingertips. When it is, lift your hand and touch the back of your neck. Feel the sensation transfer from your fingertips down into your neck, into your spine.

As it enters your neck, of course, it will alter. It will feel different because your neck is not the same as your fingers. But feel the sensation, strong and clear, in your neck. Perhaps it feels like a tingle, perhaps like a million points of light. As it settles in there, you realize that this sensation can act as a filter. As sensations come up your spinal column, they pass through this filter, and it is as if they hit a wad of cotton wool. Sensations are slowed and filtered.

Pinch the webbing of your hand, and this time feel how the sensation, which had been zooming through your nervous system, hits the area of softness in your neck and slows down. Its velocity is absorbed by this area. Instead of going straight through to your brain, it has to weave its way through the myriad pathways of a puff of cotton wool. It loses its intensity, loses its strength. Perhaps it will not make it through to your brain. Perhaps the gate in your neck will realize that this is old news, unimportant news, nothing you need to tell your brain.

Or perhaps some remnant does get through. It arrives in your brain stripped of its intensity, devoid of its impact. It is merely a bit of unimportant data that packs no emotional punch. It does not hurt.

As you work on this technique, you develop the ability to do it all of the time. It is as if a part of your mind learns to keep the filter in place without conscious attention on your part. Of course any new data, any truly important message, would be immediately and appropriately passed through, but the filter serves as an ongoing effective buffer between you and your body.

16

Pregnancy and Birth

Morning Sickness

Nausea during pregnancy, especially during the first three months, is such a common symptom that is simply known as *morning sickness*. This queasiness, which is certainly not limited to the morning hours, is a response to physical changes. A pregnant woman's hormones use up B vitamins at a very high rate, and morning sickness is the resulting symptom of that vitamin deficiency. Of course, any physical change during pregnancy should be diagnosed by one's obstetrician.

While morning sickness has a physical component, it often has a mental one as well. Not only does the initial degree of nausea vary, but so does the effect it has on a woman. Sometimes a woman, although aware at some level of a certain degree of upset, is able to put it out of her mind so that it essentially goes unnoticed. Sometimes, however, the thought of feeling nauseated becomes so much the focus of her attention that imagination adds to it, intensifying the feeling. The resulting nausea and vomiting can be so bad that the woman becomes dehydrated, loses weight, and even requires hospitalization.

The same kind of intense imagination that aggravated the

symptom of nausea in the first place can be used to alleviate it as well. The following simple exercise can be extremely effective in controlling nausea and vomiting, even in the most severe cases.

Calming Morning Sickness

As you settle back, comfortably and deeply relaxed, you focus on your body and the experiences and changes it has been undergoing. And as you think about it, you realize that these changes, while unusual, are healthy ones. Your body is doing something different. There's nothing wrong with it, just different. Your shape is changing. If you were not pregnant, this might be a problem. However, you are pregnant, so it's not. Perhaps you've been developing tastes for different foods. These cravings mean not that there's something wrong but that your body is adjusting to being pregnant. Perhaps you are feeling more tired than usual. Your tiredness does not mean that you're depressed, nor does it mean that you have gotten lazy. It means you're going to have a baby.

Now, sometimes a woman experiences some unpleasant sensations in her stomach during pregnancy. It sometimes feels as though there's something wrong with her stomach, perhaps as if she has eaten something bad. But that's not the case. She is simply pregnant. And these feelings indicate that and nothing more.

The human body developed nausea and vomiting as ways of getting things out of itself that don't belong there. If you eat some bad food, it's important that your body be able to get rid of it as quickly as possible. Vomiting, then, can be healthy. But you realize that there's nothing wrong with your body. There's nothing wrong with what's in it. You are not only not sick, but in fact you are extremely healthy. Your body is in wonderful shape. It's just doing something unusual, and sometimes it gets a little confused while adjusting.

Your body has been busy providing what's needed to build a whole new person. Of course that has made demands on your body. Of course your body has some adjusting to do. There's nothing wrong. It just needs to get used to it. And as your body has been doing this, it has made you feel rather strange at times. One of the ways that it's felt strange has been that sometimes you may have felt nauseated. Or rather, sometimes you may have felt a strange way and didn't really know how to interpret it. And it perhaps reminded you of nausea, and so it made you think you were nauseated. But you're realizing now that there's nothing wrong; there's nothing that needs to be gotten out of your body. Instead you're feeling a funny sensation associated with pregnancy. There's nothing bad; there's nothing wrong. You're healthy, the baby is healthy, and it feels different.

Now it may be that just reminding yourself that this feeling you're having is simply a funny sort of feeling may change it into something that is not uncomfortable. But to help you do that, you're going to learn some other techniques that will be useful to you. As you try them, you will learn which are more helpful to you because not everyone responds the same way.

First of all, imagine that you have just sliced open a fresh lemon. And as you do, you feel the air just being filled with the scent of lemon. It smells so healthy, so clean, so fresh. It's an interesting smell for you because you can't smell anything but the lemon. It eradicates all other scents, yet it is a very mild, gentle scent of lemon. It's not overpowering; it's not unpleasant. It is just a nice, gentle, peaceful smell of lemon. Perhaps you'd like to bring a bit of this imaginary lemon to your lips, to touch the freshly cut face of the lemon to your lips and taste upon your tongue the fresh clean taste of the lemon. It's such a clean, fresh taste. It cuts through everything else and leaves you feeling clean and fresh and healthy. It tastes good. It feels good. You feel good. You feel at peace, relaxed, clean, and healthy.

But now you can learn something else that you can do. Lift up your hand, either one, whichever feels more comfortable and natural. Lift up that hand and focus your attention on that hand, and in particular focus on the tips of your fingers, and as you do, you focus on the sensations of your fingertips, whether they are warm or cool, moist or dry, whether there is a tendency for the small muscles to twitch ever so slightly. And as you do, you become aware of a sensation in those fingertips. Perhaps it will be a tingling sensation; perhaps it will be a sensation which is difficult to describe. But whatever it is, you will recognize it, you will know it, and you can focus your attention on it.

And as you focus on this sensation, it grows stronger and stronger, more and more powerful, and when it is clear, you can take that hand and bring it over to your abdomen. And as you do, you feel the sensation settle in, through the abdominal wall into your stomach. Then gently and slowly begin to bring your hand up from your stomach along the midline of your chest, up to your throat. Now slowly bring it back down and bring it back up. As you do, you feel the sensation move from your fingertips down into your stomach, all the way up your esophagus, all the way up to your throat. Now, the sensation will change and become somewhat different as it moves from your fingertips to deeper into your body. Of course that's so because the nerves and the sensations inside your body are different from those closer to the surface. But that's fine. And as this sensation settles in, it brings a sensation of peace, calm, and tranquillity to your body. It makes your body feel good. It makes your stomach feel good. It makes your throat feel good. It makes your stomach and esophagus and throat feel very relaxed, peaceful, calm, tranquil. All is well. All is well.

If there are any sensations, they are the sensations that your fingertips have brought there. If there should be any other sensations, they will be peaceful ones, ones that you can recognize as simply being indicators of the fact of your pregnancy. Nothing is wrong. All is well. Your stomach is feeling calm. Your throat is feeling calm. You feel at peace, at ease; all is well, all is well. You feel a sensation inside your throat, inside your esophagus, inside your stomach, a sensation of being pleasantly and peacefully coated, soothed. Nothing bad can happen. Everything is as it should be.

Your digestion may seem a little funny because of all the other things that are going on inside your body. You have a baby growing inside you. Of course things feel a little different. It doesn't mean that there's anything wrong. It merely means that things seem a little different. But that's all right.

And you're going to find that you'll be able to practice this exercise as often as you need. You'll find that the more you practice, the more and more quickly and easily you'll be able to do it and to get its good effects. You'll also find that if you should begin to feel any unpleasant sensation, you will be able to take command of it by bringing your hand over to your abdomen and stroking from abdomen to throat, reminding your body of its sense of peace. You'll also find that the thought of the lemon will bring back the fresh, clean scent and taste of that refreshing fruit.

When you are ready to end this exercise, open your eyes and bring yourself back to the waking state, feeling refreshed and relaxed.

Labor and Delivery

People frequently ask if the Lamaze method of labor is hypnosis. It is not, but many women who are good hypnotic subjects may well be spontaneously hypnotizing themselves while using Lamaze and so end up taking advantage of both.

The following exercise takes for granted your familiarity with Lamaze or other similar breathing techniques, and the hypnotic suggestions are meant to be used in tandem with them, not as their replacement. All these methods are designed to make a woman as comfortable as possible during labor and delivery without medication. If at some point you should decide that you would be more comfortable using medication, there is no reason not to do so. This is a technique intended to help produce comfort, not provoke guilt.

Like Lamaze, this exercise should be practiced multiple times before actual labor and delivery. Do it daily at first. Then, when you have the hang of it, do it weekly. A week or two before your due date, once again practice it daily. As you practice, you'll learn how to use hypnosis intentionally during labor rather than accidentally.

Comfortable Labor and Delivery

As you settle back and become comfortably relaxed, you imagine yourself moving forward through time and space to the time when you go into labor. And when you first realize that you are beginning labor and have told the appropriate people what is going on, you immediately go through an induction to get your-self into a comfortable state of hypnosis. And having done that, you are going to remain at least partially hypnotized until the end of your labor. You're going to have the option of moving back and forth between two degrees of hypnosis, one very deep, the other quite mild. At times you may wish to be very deeply hypnotized as a way of dealing with the sensations of labor. At other times you may prefer to be hardly hypnotized at all. But you're never going to leave this state completely during your la-bor because you want to be able to get into it quickly and easily when you need to.

You might wish to imagine two different scenes, two differ-ent realities in practice. The first is what is actually going on around you. It might be driving in the car to the hospital; it might be being in the birthing room. That scene will be whatever reality you are in fact in as labor progresses. The other scene, the other reality, is a peaceful one that exists only in your mind. Per-haps you will visualize a lovely meadow on a clear day; perhaps you will imagine a happy event in the future or perhaps some-thing that you remember from your past. You may well choose to vary the pleasant scenes, but you will always have a little bit of your mind in each of these two separate realms to make it easy for a major part of your attention, of your consciousness, to flow swiftly from one to the other. So, for example, if you are comfort-ably chatting with your husband and a sudden contraction comes along, you are able swiftly and easily to move your atten-tion from the uncomfortable reality to a more comfortable hyp-notic scene.

In order to learn this process, you're going to practice going quickly into deep hypnosis as you would to deal with a sudden contraction. So, start by feeling yourself as only mildly hypno-tized. That's right. Come out of hypnosis part way to a state of only moderate or mild hypnosis. Now take a big deep breath and blow it out. And as that breath leaves your body, you feel your body plunge into relaxation, and you feel your mind dive down into deep hypnosis. This deep breath is the cleansing breath of

Lamaze. That's right. You recognized it. It's the cleansing breath. But now it's also the trigger for deep hypnosis. When you do the cleansing breath, you immediately, automatically push yourself down, down into hypnosis. If you wish to come quickly out of it again, you can, but you might well choose to remain deeply hypnotized for the duration of the contraction. That's right. As you exhale the cleansing breath, you feel yourself sinking down, and in fact as you continue to do your Lamaze breathing, you find that each breath you exhale blows out any tension that might be entering your body. That's right. Each breath you exhale also exhales the tension that might be in your body.

And it's very important that you keep your body relaxed. When you tense your muscles, it changes the way that your nervous system conducts messages. When your muscles are tense, information is carried along your nerves much more rapidly. Messages arrive at your brain more quickly and with more impact. Messages arrive at your brain and demand attention. But if your muscles are relaxed, then information arrives not with the punch of a news bulletin, but in a more gentle, more comfortable manner.

And you know that it's important to remember that once you know that labor has begun, there's no particularly important information that you need to send to your brain. In fact, your mind is rather like excess baggage on this trip. You want to be there for the labor; you want to be there for the birth of your child. It's good that you are, but you have to remember that your body knows what it's doing, and your mind is going to be merely a spectator. You know that you could not consciously choose to initiate labor any more than you could consciously choose to interrupt or stop it. You don't know how to dilate your cervix. Or rather, your conscious mind doesn't. Your body knows. Your body has instincts. Your body instinctively knows what to do.

If you had hired a skilled artisan to come and do a job for you, you would appreciate the need to stay out of the way and let him or her do the job without interference. You have a body that is skilled in how to have a baby. It's important that you stay out of your body's way and don't complicate matters. Your job is to stand back and to be a spectator. Sure it's tempting to get into the spirit of things by tightening all sorts of random muscles like your arms and shoulders and legs, just as spectators at an athletic event often tense their muscles in empathy with the players on the field. But you also realize that spectators in a stadium don't actually interfere with the team when they tighten these muscles. If you were to tighten your muscles, you would be interfering with your body as it goes about its work. You would be interfering with the natural process by creating unnecessary discomfort. Your job, then, is to keep your body so thoroughly, deeply, and totally relaxed that you do not get in the way of letting your body instinctively do the things necessary to deliver your baby.

So as you keep breathing, slowly, regularly, and comfortably, or in the short puffs and pants of later labor, you remember that with each breath you are blowing out tension and relaxing your body, relaxing your body as thoroughly and completely as possible.

Now, while most of your body is to be relaxed, a part of your body is going to be working very, very hard. That's right. A part of your body is working very hard to bring your baby to the light of day. And when you think about it, it becomes very clear to you that your body is doing some very hard work. That's why it's called *labor*. It is labor; it is work. It is hard, physical, muscular exertion. And you think back to times in the past when you have done hard physical labor. At the time you were doing it, in fact, your muscles might have been feeling a great deal of discomfort. They might have been working very hard, but you recognized that the sensations were not warnings that something was wrong. Rather the sensations told you that you were working hard.

Much of the way you experience physical sensations depends upon how you think of them. You might wish to try a little experiment to demonstrate the importance of how you think about a sensation. With your right hand, make a tight fist and feel the sensation of tightness spread through your wrist, forearm, and upper arm. Tighten the fist, tighten the arm muscles tighter and tighter and tighter, more and more, more and more, until they begin to cramp and hurt and feel painful. And as soon as they are feeling painful and you would like to stop this, you take your cleansing breath, and as you exhale and blow out the tension, you feel your arm relax.

But now let's try the same thing a different way. Once again make the fist and tighten your muscles, but as you do, this time you think about how strong your muscles feel. You think about how strong and powerful they are, and you feel the strength rippling through your arm; you're feeling very good, very strong, and it's a good feeling, a positive feeling, a feeling you like. You realize that the same physical sensation really feels very different now, and you take a cleansing breath and once again relax your arm and once again feel so very good and relaxed.

Just as with the feelings in your arm, if you were to give your imagination free rein to describe all sorts of horrible metaphors for labor, you could successfully make the experience of having a baby much more uncomfortable than need be. But that's not what you're going to do. Instead, you gently place your hand on your abdomen and take comfort in the knowledge that what you're doing is work, hard work but good work. It's work that has a unique reward. It won't be long now till you're holding your baby.

As you continue through labor, as you move toward delivery, you let your mind go forward through time. You know you should never practice actual pushing until the time when you are really ready to deliver your baby, but you can practice visualizing a future pleasant scene. So feel yourself moving into the future, not the distant future but the very immediate future. It won't be long now, not at all long, until you're holding your baby. Just let your mind go forward to that scene. There you are. There you are holding your baby. The baby's peacefully nestled in your arms; not asleep but relaxed, comfortable. It makes you feel so happy. It makes you feel so good. This new life, your baby, is there in your arms. This image is one you may wish to stay with all the way through labor as you realize that, sure, this is hard work, but there is such a wonderful payoff, such a unique reward. The work lasts for just a matter of hours, but the rewards and the joys of your baby will last forever.

As you go through the process of labor, you remember all the things you've learned in the classes you've taken. You recall how the contractions are like waves. They increase in intensity and then decrease. You remember each time you've passed the crest of a wave, that just as it gets steadily easier on the down side of the wave, so also soon the whole labor will be over. Soon you'll be here with your baby.

But perhaps you would like to do something else to help keep yourself comfortable through the work of labor. One thing you might choose to do is to set up a filter in your neck that limits sensations coming from your body to your brain. If you'd like to do this, just begin by focusing your attention on the back of your neck at the base of your skull. It might help to bring your hand up to the area to focus your attention on your spine at that point. And as you do, as you focus your attention, you begin to develop a sensation, a pleasant sensation or one perhaps better described as a sort of a funny sensation. It may almost be as much something you see in your mind's eye as something you feel. It may seem like thousands of tiny stars, flickering off and on. And as you focus on this, it has an effect upon how sensations pass through your upper spine to your brain. It's as though your spinal chord has been transformed from a tight, efficient wire carrying messages to a big, fluffy cotton ball. As sensations go through this ball of fluff, they are softened; they lose their impact. It may even be that they are totally filtered out. It may be so complete that you lose all contact with the sensations of your lower body. If so, that's fine. That part of your body knows what it's doing, and it will do fine without your help. Or perhaps sensations will come through, but fewer of them. And those that do come through are softened. Instead of arriving hard and fast with messages, they come in slowed down by the meandering, circuitous route that they had to take through the fluff. The sensations are softened. And as that happens, they become more and more distant. They matter less.

In fact, you realize that there are a variety of people involved whose job is to watch out for your body, to take care of it, to make sure that everything is all right. And it feels good just to let them do their jobs. Your body is hard ar work; there's nothing else you need to do. You deserve a break. Your awareness of your body is becoming rather dim, rather detached. You know that you'll be summoned back when the baby is born, but meanwhile there's a potentially uncomfortable situation and you would just as soon be somewhere else. So you go somewhere else. Perhaps you go to the beach, or perhaps to a few minutes into the future, to after the baby is born. But when you go there, it's as though your body has been left with the people who are taking care of it at the end of a long tunnel. You know about it. You're vaguely aware of it, but somehow it doesn't much matter. It's far away. It's removed, remote, and distant. And that's fine because your body knows its job and is doing fine without you. And the people who are there to take care of your body are doing their job, and it's OK to relax and let them.

While you're so relaxed, you remember that you are the star up here. Everyone else has the job of taking care of you. You're not there to take care of them. If your husband is bored and wants to talk, or if he's excited and wants to chat about the baby, you can if you want to, but if you don't want to, you don't have to. You just signal to him to leave you alone. You're busy. You're busy using your mind to control the experience. If the nurse or midwife or obstetrician comes in and wants to ask questions or talk with you, you can answer if you wish, but if you don't want to, you don't have to. The choice is yours. You are not there to please them, to make their lives easy, or to answer their questions. You're there to do some hard work and to be rewarded with a baby. There's nothing they need to say that's more important than what you think is important for you to be doing for yourself.

When it comes time to push, you will listen to the directions you are given enough to let yourself know what your coaches are advising, enough so that a part of your consciousness can cooperate. And you know you should never actually practice pushing at all until you are really ready to deliver your baby. Even as you push, you have the option of being more or less present mentally, more or less using any of your techniques, just as you have during any contractions.

And you remember that only you know what's going on inside you. Only you know what your experience is, and that even includes using hypnosis. As you use it during your labor, you see which parts of it work the best. You see which parts of it are right for you, which parts are really helpful. And as you do, you make use of what is good for you and discard what isn't. And if you find a way of using it that works that you haven't heard about before, then you use that. Whatever makes the experience best for you is what you should do. Whenever you are ready to end this state of hypnosis, do so however works best for you.

And congratulations!

17

The Gift

As you've used this book, you have learned to do many things. First of all, you've learned what hypnosis is and how you can get yourself into that state. You've also learned that the simple matter of entering a state of hypnosis by itself is usually not enough to do more than produce a sense of relaxation.

Once in an hypnotic state, though, you are allowed access to a special kind of ability to effect changes in your thinking, in your imagination, and in your physical state. Being hypnotized doesn't make psoriasis clear up. Being hypnotized and imagining yourself at the beach with the sun baking down does. Hypnosis enables you to use your mind to make positive changes.

The exercises in this book are compiled from hypnotic suggestions that different people have tried and found helpful. These collected exercises are not magical rituals, nor are they carved in stone and handed down from the ancients. Instead, they are ways of using hypnosis that people like you have discovered through imagination and experiment. In fact, the hypnotic induction procedures in this book are not the only nor necessarily the best ways for you to enter hypnosis. As you've practiced, you've probably learned ways of entering the state that are particularly good for you.

Self-hypnosis is something you can approach with a sense of adventure. You are learning about yourself, learning about what kinds of images work best for you, learning about what kinds of images help you best help yourself. Try viewing this book as a springboard, taking the techniques that you've learned and letting them be not the conclusion but the introduction to helping yourself in a personally customized way.

As you settle back, comfortable and relaxed, you think about what you've done. You realize that you have learned to use hypnosis to change your behavior, to change the way you live. You've learned how to get into the hypnotic state and how to select exercises designed to help you achieve your goals, to help you make changes in your life and in your behavior. And you've learned to make these exercises be just right for you.

Before you started, you may have thought that you were going to be doing something hard. You may have thought that you were going to be depriving yourself by taking away something you were used to having. You were afraid that it was going to hurt to take away your cigarettes, or your overeating, or your nervous habit, or even your tension. You were afraid that losing your fear would make you less.

But now you find that this is not the case at all. Now you know the last secret. What you have been learning to do is to give yourself a gift; a very precious and special gift. It is a gift that no one else can give you and a gift that no one else can take away from you.

You have learned to take care of yourself. You have learned how effectively you can be good to yourself. You've learned how to love yourself. You realize that your tension or your fears or your cigarettes or your overeating were things that you were used to, things that were familiar, but that hurt you. And you've learned that your new way of doing things is not a deprivation, not a loss, but a gain—a very special present, a priceless gift to yourself from the only person who has the power to give it.

And it feels very, very good indeed.

Selected Readings

This list is intended as an introduction to the literature behind the topics presented in this book. The serious reader can use it as a jumping off point for further research.

American Medical Association Council Report, Scientific status of refreshing recollection by the use of hypnosis. *International Journal of Clinical and Experimental Hypnosis, 34,* 1986.

Apfel, R.J., Kelly, S.F., and Frankel, F.H. The role of hypnotizability in the pathogenesis and treatment of nausea and vomiting of pregnancy. *Journal of Psychosomatic Obstetrics and Gynecology, 5,* 1986.

Barber, T.X., and Wilson, S.C. Hypnosis, suggestions and allied states of consciousness: Experimental evaluation of the new cognitive-behavioral theory and the traditional trance-state theory of hypnosis. *Annals of the New York Academy of Science, 296,* 1987.

Bauer, K.E., and McCanne, T.R. An hypnotic technique for treating insomnia. *International Journal of Clinical and Experimental Hypnosis, 28,* 1980.

Benson, H. *The Relaxation Response.* New York: Morrow, 1975.

Benson, H., Arns, P.A., and Hoffman, J.W. The relaxation response and hypnosis. *International Journal of Clinical and Experimental Hypnosis, 11,* 1963.

Bowers, K.S. *Hypnosis for the Seriously Curious.* Monteray, CA: Brooks/Cole, 1976.

Bowers, K.S. Imagination and dissociation in hypnotic responding. *International Journal of Clinical and Experimental Hypnosis, 40,* 1992.

Breuer, J., and Freud, S. Studies in hysteria. *The Standard Edition of the Complete Psychological Works of Sigmund Freud (Vol. 2).* London: Hogarth, 1955.

Case, D.B., Fogel, D.H., and Pollack, A. Self-hypnosis and mild hypertension: A study of acute and long-term effects of self-hypnosis and blood pressure. *International Journal of Clinical and Experimental Hypnosis, 28,* 1980.

Coe, W.C. Hypnosis: Wherefore art thou? *International Journal of Clinical and Experimental Hypnosis, 40,* 1992.

47 Conn, J.H. The myth of coercion through hypnosis. *International Journal of Clinical and Experimental Hypnosis, 29,* 1981.

Deckert, G.H., and West, L.J. The problem of hypnotizability: A review. *International Journal of Clinical and Experimental Hypnosis, 11,* 1963.

Edelstein, M.G. *Trauma, Trance, and Transformation: A Clinical Guide to Hypnotherapy.* New York: Brunner/Mazel, 1981.

Elliotson, J. *Harveian Oration.* London: Walton & Mitchell, 1846.

Eysenck, H.J., and Furneaux, W.D. Primary and secondary suggestibility: An experimental and statistical study. *Journal of Experimental Psychology, 35,* 1945.

Frankel, F.H. Trance capacity and the genesis of phobic behavior. *Archives of General Psychiatry, 31,* 1974.

Frankel, F.H. *Hypnosis: Trance as a Coping Mechanism.* New York: Plenum, 1976.

Frankel, F.H. Hypnosis and related clinical behavior. *American Journal of Psychiatry, 135,* 1978.

Frankel, F.H., Apfel, R.J., Kelly, S.F., Benson, H., Quinn, T., Newmark, J., and Malmaud, R. The use of hypnotizability scales in the clinic: A review after six years. *International Journal of Clinical and Experimental Hypnosis, 27,* 1979.

Frankel, F.H., and Misch, R.C. Hypnosis in a case of long-standing psoriasis in a person with character problems. *International Journal of Clinical and Experimental Hypnosis, 21,* 1973.

Frankel, F.H., and Orne, M.T. Hypnotizability and phobic behavior. *Archives of General Psychiatry, 33,* 1976.

Fromm, E., Brown, D.B., Hurt, W.S., Oberlander, J.Z., Boxer, A.M., and Pfiefer, G. The phenomenon and characteristics of self-hypnosis. *International Journal of Clinical and Experimental Hypnosis, 29,* 1981.

Fromm, E., and Shor, R. (Eds.). *Hypnosis: Developments in Research and New Perspectives.* New York: Aldine, 1979.

Fuchs, K., Paldi, E., Abramovici, H., and Peretz, B.A. Treatment of hyperemesis gravidarum by hypnosis. *International Journal of Clinical and Experimental Hypnosis, 28,* 1980.

Grossbart, T. A., and Sherman, C. *Skin Deep.* New York: Morrow, 1986.

Haley, J. (Ed.). *Advanced Techniques of Hypnosis and Therapy: Selected Papers of Milton H. Erickson, M.D.* New York: Grune & Stratton, 1967.

Hilgard, E.R. *Hypnotic Susceptibility.* New York: Harcourt, Brace & World, 1965.

Hilgard, E.R., and Hilgard, J.R. *Hypnosis in the Relief of Pain.* Los Altos, CA: Kaufmann, 1975.

Hilgard, E.R., and Loftus, E.F. Effective interrogation of the eyewitness. *International Journal of Clinical and Experimental Hypnosis, 27,* 1979.

Hilgard, J.R. *Personality and Hypnotizability.* Chicago: University of Chicago Press, 1970.

Hilgard, J.R. Imaginative involvement: Some characteristics of the highly hypnotizable and non-hypnotizable. *International Journal of Clinical and Experimental Hypnosis, 22,* 1974.

Kelly, S.F. Hypnotizability and the inadvertent experience of pain. *International Journal of Clinical and Experimental Hypnosis, 28,* 1980.

Kelly, S.F. Measured hypnotic response and phobic behavior. *International Journal of Clinical and Experimental Hypnosis, 32,* 1984.

Kelly, S.F. The use of music as a hypnotic suggestion. *American Journal of Clinical Hypnosis, 36,* 1993.

Kelly, S.F., and Kelly, R.J. *Hypnosis: Understanding How It Can Work for You.* Reading, MA: Addison Wesley, 1985.

Kroger, W.S., and Fezler, W.D. *Hypnosis and Behavior Modification: Imagery Conditioning.* Philadelphia: Lippincott, 1976.

Nemiah, J.C. *Foundations of Psychopathology.* New York: Oxford University Press, 1961.

Orne, M.T. The nature of hypnosis: Artifact and essence. *Journal of Abnormal and Social Psychology, 58,* 1959.

Orne, M.T., Dinges, D., and Orne, E.C. Rock v. Arkansas: Hypnosis, the defendant's privilege. *International Journal of Clinical and Experimental Hypnosis, 38,* 1990.

Putnam, W.H. Hypnosis and distortions in eyewitness memory. *International Journal of Clinical and Experimental Hypnosis, 27,* 1979.

Shor, R.E. Hypnosis and the concept of the generalized reality orientation. *American Journal of Psychiatry, 13,* 1959.

Shor, R.E., and Orne, M.T. *The Nature of Hypnosis.* New York: Holt, Rinehart & Winston.

Spiegel, H. A single-treatment method to stop smoking using ancillary self-hypnosis. *International Journal of Clinical and Experimental Hypnosis, 28,* 1980.

Spiegel, H., and Spiegel, D. *Trance and Treatment: Clinical Uses of Hypnosis.* New York: Basic Books, 1978.

Wolpe, J. *Psychotherapy by Reciprocal Inhibition.* Stanford, CA: Stanford University Press, 1958.

Index